Copyright and Reproduction Rights

Copyright © 2012 James Coomer
E-mail: mail@diycatamaran.com
Website: www.diycatamaran.com

A cataloguing-in-Publication record is available
at the National Library of Australia
www.librariesaustralia.nla.gov.au

ISBN: 978-0-9874060-2-6

Preface

This writing is intended to provide a practical and informative tool to amateur boat builders.

Here we have jotted how and why we tackled certain challenges with pointers that may assist others jumping into this maze.

These notes are not intended to replace any building methods, rather supplement the decision making process of those currently in use.

Our thoughts from the beginning were that this is our yacht and we need to keep this in mind throughout the build. When it comes to how many beds we should have - we planned this on our family, when it came to electrical, and water requirements - again it came back to what we wanted.

We soon found that 'what is thought to be the domain of the rich and famous' is well within reach of those with time and a very strong drive to achieve, which is very important especially toward the latter part of the build. While we do not discuss any budgets here, it can roughly be deduced by searching the local yacht brokers for your vessel type, then reducing that purchase cost by half to two thirds.

One soon learns too that kidding yourself with this budget figure puts you in hot water, as we discuss in Electrical.

With regard to the design, we chose an EASY series yacht as it more closely met our specific needs and budget. Structural design was key, not only for safety reasons, but when it comes time to sell, it is a good feeling if the Designer is on your side and gives his 'tick-of-approval' so to speak. This does ultimately affect the sale price.

We carefully compared 'apples with apples' and discuss our views, choices, and solutions. One soon finds that for the average budget conscious sailboat owner/builder, design choice is confined to either 'performance' or 'cruising'. Finding a design that carries 'all mod-cons' and sails at 20kts, is totally unrealistic.

We hope you find this book useful and look forward to meeting you somewhere on the water.

James Coomer
www.diycatamaran.com

Acknowledgements

Peter and Anne Snell, designer - EASY Catamarans (www.easycatamarans.com), always available at the end of the phone and communicating in layman's terms, finding us the cheaper items and always being available.

James's father, Charles Coomer, for his electrical know-how and perseverance in ensuring compliance. Many an evening was spent mulling over numbers trying to extract every last bit of energy and use it as efficiently as possible.

Michael De Marinis (Welder and our Fitter-and-Turner), for all the stainless steel welding and assistance in the steering system. Also his Mum Pat for her assistance in naming.

Sean Hartley, for keeping me on my toes and always questioning 'why'. John and Andy, your help, patience and enthusiasm was very welcome, thank you.

----- : -----

My wonderful family,
wife Mary-Ann and the two kids.

Thank you for holding the ship together,
jump in, hang on and
enjoy the ride.

----- : -----

Table of Contents

A Sailing Catamaran Building Project

DIY Desalinator or Watermaking

Chapter One:
Insubordination is no laughing matter

Navigating our way through 'bommies' and shallow water even with electronics on our side, is a huge challenge.

It's not until one-steps into the water world that you appreciate the feats of early explorers. Bartolomeu Dias was a hero, rounding Cape of Good Hope in 1480's.

Vasco Da Garma helped grow the spice routes to India from Europe. His travels took in the islands of Pemba and Zanzibar, conjuring thoughts of tropical get-a-ways. Yet it was their spice trade from this early period that put them on the map.

The food challenges, freshwater issues, and historical notes on scurvy from these early adventures are well documented. Nowadays we get frustrated and complain about mosquito bite or the price of petrol, even a weevil in the flour. Weevils were very common back then and still around today.

Captain William Bligh of HMS Bounty fame in the 1790's (Australasia and Pacific region), faced huge challenges on their mostly uncharted adventures.

It was this military belief, discipline, reward, and pride that drove those early explorers and it came at a high cost.

Bligh was a staunch officer of British graduation, everything was very serious...maybe too serious.

"The Royal Navy is not a humorous institution, sir, and insubordination is no laughing matter."

It is however from these early explorers that we learn navigation and food preservation, two key pieces in the puzzle we now enjoy.

----- : -----

Paging magazines and surfing the Internet almost certainly triggers an adventurous nerve somewhere in our thought processes, the envy of 'what if...' or 'I wish...'

...an impact on our Great
Barrier Reef that many
choose to ignore...

It's this mind set that commercial companies tap into offering well-calculated and rehearsed sales gimmicks that entice you and I into action.

Entangled in this excitement and a leaf out of Bligh's travels, we chose to take a trip to view southern creatures migrating past our front door.

------ : -----

The humpback whales were on their annual migration up the east coast of Australia. A truly spectacular sight, first north (and a few months later) south.

These animals are huge and their majestic wild appeal draws the curious to taste a piece of their wild world.

Escaping the freezing waters of the

Antarctic, some choose to adventure thousands of kilometres our way and to calve in the shallower bays of the warmer Australian east coast. Then, a few months later to mate and head south back to the rich plankton feeding grounds of the Antarctic.

You can't help but be drawn within metres as they stare 'at these strange onlookers peeking into their world'. Their pupils alone are the size of a grown mans hand, their eyes - larger than our heads and their brains, 10% larger than ours.

Returning home after this sightseeing trip, everyone was smiling and richer for the experience.

Episodes of the Sea Shepherds' 'Steve Erwin' and their Japanese counterparts, entangled in their southern whale harvesting feuds touches a different and slightly more sensitive nerve now.

----- : -----

Further north and on a much more sombre note, shark fins are still being harvested at an unbelievable rate in a very barbaric procedure practiced by many of our third world neighbours.

Then releasing these de-finned animals back into the water alive to die a very slow and painful death, if not mauled by their fellow sharks as they drop to the sea floor.

Talk of 'coral bleaching' is all the rage and associated effects of the earth warming even half a degree has an impact on our Great Barrier Reef that many choose to ignore.

Whether it be man-made or otherwise, a topple in this delicate eco system will destabilise this carefully balanced food chain.

It's this snapshot view of the water-world where few choose to venture, that we chase. It's right at our front door and there to enjoy.

Finding a way that is cheap in travel cost, has the ability to venture off the beaten track and supported by a few 'home' creature comforts was our challenge.

Welcome to our adventure, building a family friendly yacht with a few *lurks-and-perks*, that is safe, single-handed and can be built with limited experience.

----- : -----

Chapter Two:
Cornerstones of the building puzzle

To be able to progress, one needs direction and while direction for many is difficult to grasp, a few gamble by taking a punt and become our leaders in their specific fields. This does have many detractors though, as it's easier to criticise than to present direction.

It takes a thick skin and perseverance to win. This is not a win in the sense of 'I can beat you', rather the physiological advantage you get with providing direction that 'maps your ideas' and in the long term, everyone wins.

Key in this is being positive, practical and accepting criticism (with no caveats), learning from these experiences, which we treat as 'lessons', and it's these lessons that provide a solid framework for a good yacht building experience.

The average hours to build a large 40 foot (12 metre) yacht varies from 3000 hours to 8000 hours (or more), this is to build the complete vessel, not just a hull to drop in the water with bare essentials.

As we were told, the yacht should only see water when *'the cutlery is in the drawers and the sheets are turned down'*.

...Making the project 4 years in duration...

Depending on the finish you require, the build time will vary. If it's a glass professional finish - then it will be at the top of the building-hour bracket.

If it's a good finish with a few blemishes (that you know and others have no idea), it will be at the bottom end of the building-time range.

Having said this, we have seen some fantastic finishes done in 3000 hours.

Using an example of 3500 hours and with a fulltime job (and two days off per week), that would give 16 hours per week (2 x 8 hours).

Fifty-two weeks in a year (being realistic - say 40 weeks a year), that's 640 hours per year available to build (16 x 40).

This project would then take 5 1/2 years (3500 / 640).

*...Plywood
builds are the cheaper
way to build...*

Any annual leave you get will give the project a huge boost, maybe 52 weeks is then achievable. Making the project 4 1/4 years in duration (3500 / 830).

----- : -----

Moving on to find a designer who can reduce the build time will be your next challenge. All we can say here is that they are all much the same in build time for their size.

*'If it sounds too good to be true,
it more than likely is'.*

Don't get drawn into the theory of completing a vessel once it's launched, it won't happen.

So many half built vessels sit on the water and builders all of a sudden struggle to find the motivation and time to complete their dreams.

Doing it part-time is how many tackle their projects and this then lends itself to a 4-6 year building project. We gave ourselves four years and added one more year for all unforeseen challenges. As it worked out, we were boating after four and a half years.

This is the first corner piece in the puzzle and as you can see, can be modified to suit. One needs to be frank in calculating a build time.

----- : -----

We set ourselves a budget and came in 30% above what we had planned. We were very honest here and kept a log of every component bought on a spreadsheet (our choice).

What we did not account for were all the little bits that we wanted - our wish list.

Our budget included tools to do the job, the building shed, and sails, absolutely everything in fact. We could have got away with cheaper options or less equipment, but chose the alternative and in 98% of the cases, are very glad we did.

One that immediately comes to mind here is self-tailing winches, another being the Desalinator.

Not having a starting point can make the budget phase very difficult.

Start by talking to the designers, not those on chat forums. The chat forums tend to weigh their arguments to justify their particular builds which does not give you a true unbiased opinion.

The designers will normally give

you an idea of all up cost. Don't push them as they cannot and will not provide you an exact figure.

You are literally asking them 'how long is a piece of string' and we discuss this later. Remember to compare apples with apples, plywood builds with plywood builds, composite builds with composite builds.

Plywood builds are the cheaper way to build, where composite builds can be at the other end of the spectrum.

Start by looking at a 'bare-bones' vessel complete on the water. By that we mean one that can be sailed (if a sailing yacht) or motored (if non sailing). The lurks-and-perks can be considered later.

...Insurers are also chaffing
at the bit when it comes
to paying-out...

Resale should be considered here too. Have a look at yacht types for sale that you are considering, jot down their prices and take the average. Be very honest, it will definitely help you with your decision process.

Don't make a decision on designer just yet, take notes and make comparisons. It's here too that contacts come in handy. A rough idea of costings can be gauged.

This 'rough idea' of budget is the second corner piece in the puzzle. From this figure, add at least 25% to get a more accurate building figure

----- : ----

Make an appointment to see as many Designers as you can and see if you 'click', they can normally put you onto a yacht (for a look), but don't lead them on - tell them if you are 'fair-dinkum' about building or just sniffing around.

This is key in achieving your goal and when times get tough (which they will), they are the backbone to helping you and keeping you motivated.

If unable to meet with the Designer, try and build a rapport via e-mail or mail. It is so important because once your mind is set, it's all go and should be no looking back.

Just a word of caution, many Designers know each other. The industry is very small and word travels very fast about those who abuse or even copy.

Not an issue you may think, until it comes to resale or when you meet up on the water with other sailors. You will get to know the quirks of your design and even a novice builder can spot similar designs to their own.

Insurers are also chaffing at the bit when it comes to paying-out and the first person they call when in doubt, is the Designer. Don't put yourself in that position in the first place...very simple.

Get on a local Forum and chat up some of the members to show you their masterpieces. Many will be only too happy to brag about their design choices.

Choosing a Designer is the third corner piece in the rectangular puzzle. Make sure you 'click' with them and stay on their good side. You will need their help.

----- : -----

The last puzzle corner piece is 'available resources' and products.

The Designer should be the first port-of-call. But keep in mind that the Designer is there to sell their product. Having said this, many will go out of their way to source items for you at 'discounted rates' plus a bit for themselves.

It's win-win as they get the latest hardware for a group of builders and you get a good rate.

If you intend changing the design in any structural form, or building outside that stated in the plans, you are on your own.

Don't expect the Designer to oblige with changes that you have made. If in doubt - ask them first. This is very important to remember, especially if you need boating Insurance later or are selling and the new buyer calls the Designer.

...don't get tied up trying to re-invent the wheel...

Worse still is if the Insurance Company calls the Designer asking on feedback about your vessel that has had some damage.

One soon learns too that starting a conversation with the Designer with "but he said this" or "why haven't you" or "she said that" soon drives the Designer around the bend and the discussion will be frosty.

There are a few books we can strongly recommend and that we still use today with our day-to-day yachting challenges. They include:

- The Gougeon Brothers on Boat Construction,

- Nigel Calder's' Boat Books (2 key ones),

- The 12 Volt Bible, and

- Devlin's Boatbuilding

Check our websites as we have located some much cheaper outlets with these and similar volumes that deliver to your door.

----- : -----

If you only get two books, we would suggest Calder's books. They are a real treat in the fit-out planning and boating stages, where Gougeon is more helpful in the initial building phase.

The Internet is where we managed to pick up many tips and great ideas. If you are computer illiterate, don't discount this extremely valuable resource. Get a young 'guru' (normally the kids) to point you in the right direction.

Your local Library has this for free too, give it a shot - at least to have a look at some building websites such as www.puremajek.com (our building website).

This provides a great resource for an overview of each section of a build.

Search for inspirational videos on YouTube too, try www.youtube.com/diycatamaran.

Lastly, don't get tied up trying to re-invent the wheel. Thousands have been there and done that and it wastes your very valuable building time.

Don't get bogged down, losing sight of your planned goal and objectives. We did this on so many occasions only to do the full circle.

Cheaper is not always the better way to go either, as we discuss in our Electrical.

----- : -----

Now having the four corner pieces, decisions can be made given a more balanced approach.

Get a white-board (900mm x 900mm - you will need it later) and list your goals and objectives. Sleep on it over a few nights then return and see how they fit.

This is a great visual cue and easy to redo or remark. Later in the building phase, this board will come in very handy.

----- : -----

A Sailing Catamaran Building Project

Pointers:

1. Have a planned 'timeline'

2. Make an honest budget.

3. Choose a design that you like.

4. Use all resources available.

5. Think 'Resale', it could save you longer term.

Traps:

1. Going full circle by 're-inventing the wheel'.

2. Planning large goals that are hard to achieve.

3. Losing sight of your final goal.

4. Getting bogged down in minor issues that have little to no effect in the bigger picture.

Chapter Three:
Why be a Lemming?

Finally it was happening. What was thought to be unachievable was now in sight and while many said it's just the beginning, we are on our way to having our first Multihull.

Having a family of four (two under the age of ten) and very little sailing experience, we took the plunge to fulfil what many only dream. It was time for a change and a move to Brisbane as well as a new job gave us this opportunity.

Having lead a team of competent pilots of a large regional airline for three years did take its toll. The stress and smell of the hectic Sydney management lifestyle was soon far behind. It was a lifestyle that we were after and this gamble had no guarantees.

The kids were reaching an age where if any move was to occur, it needed to be soon and the last thing we wanted was to again upset the applecart finding new schools, and with that, new friends.

They needed a firm foundation and stability back in their lives as soon as possible.

It was the year that Ansett Airlines finally accepted defeat. They had struggled for their last few years. Seen as a saviour and much to everyone's delight, an International Airline then stepped in, however, they only added to their woes and they soon departed leaving Ansett gutted and in more debt.

Added to this, Ansett then chose to purchase a fifty-year-old regional airline called Hazelton Airlines. Qantas also made hay during this financial unstable period, bidding for the same regional, driving the share price well above its worth.

The outcome saw Ansett take control of an overpriced regional airline in the hope of forming an extensive regional feeder network to their domestic operation.

Being easier said than done and the Australian dollar being at an all time low, finally drove the last nails into the coffin for Ansett.

...therefore be stable,
as our young family had
never sailed before...

Having worked for Hazelton Airlines for fifteen years, it was very sad and added to this was our remuneration that was now outstanding.

The legal process as it existed then, saw Ansett employees being paid 95% of their outstanding monies, while the recently purchased subsidiary (Hazelton Airlines) received nothing. We soon kissed AUD 38,000 (being outstanding annual leave and long service leave) goodbye.

The Managed Fund market had also taken its toll that year after a few years of negative returns. We unfortunately entered the market at the beginning of this downward trend and after considerable loss around AUD 54,000, we decided to sell out and take the loss putting it down as a learning experience.

Feeling rather demoralised after seeing this hard-worked-for money disappear overnight, we tried to find the positive, learn from our mistakes and reassess our goals.

----- : -----

Browsing magazine after magazine and surfing the Internet for months on all articles containing the words 'multihull' or 'catamaran', it became clear that walking in off the street and saying "We'll have that one" was definitely out of the question.

The prices then (2003), varied from AUD 220,000 to AUD 600,000 and we did not have that type of capital to spend on a yacht, of all things. It was soon realized that it was either build your own or go without.

This brought us back to a book on Investment Property written by Jan Somers where she spoke of little creatures called 'Lemmings'.

This small rodent type animal had the uncanny sense of copying what the other was doing, one ran - they all ran, one jumped - they all jumped.

Jan said that many people sit and say it's too hard and follow the general trend of the day and this definitely stands true with many things in life with us, as with Lemmings.

Few take the bull by the horns in fear of failure, the gamble being too much or the job being perceived as too hard.

Having said that, the idea of a large Catamaran was lightly bounced

Full Spinnaker in 5hts of breeze

off some friends and work colleagues who all joined the *'Lemming Squad'*.

The thought of sailing out at dawn to Morton Island, off the coast of Queensland-Australia, and mooring in the quiet tranquil afternoon sunset has been driving the incentive of someday, being able to do this.

While James had been afforded the opportunity as a child to fish, dive and sail, the rest of the family were not so lucky.

> *...gifted sales pitch that would attract even someone who do not sail or like water...*

The boat had to therefore be stable, as our young family had never sailed before.

Contending with a possible constant lean of a monohull was therefore out of the question, this pointing us to the type of hull required and having a hot shower and toilet dictated the size and comfort:

- Was it to have sails?
- With outboards or inboards?
- Be a motor-cruiser?

Many a night was spent mulling over these challenges.

If the building of this type of yacht was to ever go ahead, we would have to closely assess the budget required to complete the project and as with every budget, ours was very tight.

This in turn forced us to narrow the building material to plywood/fibreglass and it's here that the first seed was planted toward the direction that we finally

took.

----- : -----

Australasia appears to have very good ship/boat building standards and appears to lead the world market in Multihull design, from internal design and development to speed and hull shape. Per capita, Australia also appears to be at the top end of the respected sailing market.

There are a dozen or so multihull yacht designers in this area who are all keen for our business, many not knowing that we had nothing to spend.

They all had gifted sales pitches that would attract even someone who does not sail or like water. After countless hours on the Internet and scanning of newspapers for seven months, we finally fell onto our feet.

Two stood out for their honesty and straightforward approach toward the complete novice. One even spoke at our level with no fancy sailing jargon. When we muttered the words "planks that hold the main entry door between the hulls", we got a kind answer and were not laughed at. (We should have said 'Bulkhead Frame').

After months of deliberation we opted for something that we were told the average person with a little common sense and hand co-ordination could accomplish with commitment and time. In pursuit of this new goal, a change in our retirement strategy was needed.

Up till 2003 we had been dabbling in the property market making hay on the Sydney and Brisbane property price spikes of the 1999 - 2003 period.

This had allowed us to pay off our own home, which in turn provided equity to invest in two other investment properties.

Having two kids and choosing to have a single income also played heavily in the about face which occurred. It was this second property, which was to be the building block for a large sailing Catamaran.

----- : -----

One afternoon our son (7 at that time) and James bundled into the 94 Ford Laser and set course to Landsborough in Queensland, some 45 minutes from north Brisbane.

...the average person with a little common sense and hand co-ordination could accomplish...

Met by a tall skinny man and his wife, we were directed to a rear shed and allowed to tramp over their newly completed pride and joy, an 11.6m sailing Catamaran.

With his blessing and movie camera in hand, we quickly filmed as much as we could, making the most of this valuable time trying to document ideas. This was then followed by a chat and coffee.

Thus began the 'love-affair' with the 11.6m EASY Catamaran. The couple were none-other than Peter and Anne Snell. Peter, being the proud Designer of all the Easy range of Catamarans, and Anne his

wife definitely in the know on everything about the vessel, right down to the recommended battery charging rates of the solar panels.

This was their first 11.6m series catamaran, which was to be put through its testing paces later that week.

The seed had been sown and some serious questions had to be answered about the budget. Would we attempt the first yacht-building phase and bury our heads in the sand when it came to the budget?

But then 'Investment opportunity' came to mind. Build the yacht; sell it for double, and wallah got the money back.

But that was not the reason for wanting to build it in the first place.

There had to be another way.

----- : -----

We decided that the building of the vessel had to be done within 15 minutes of our current residence or not at all.

This would reduce the travel time or in effect increase the build time over the five-year period, keeping in mind that our planned completion date was set for October 2009.

We did not want to move, so elected to purchase an investment property where a tenant could assist in the repayments and sufficient space was left to erect a temporary shed where we could make this dream come true.

This property search took nearly four months. And out of the blue we were shown a block that fulfilled all our tenancy/shed requirements.

Well, almost anyway - it was 20 minutes from home. While in a residential area, all the other houses around this property had huge sheds of their own.

Excitedly a deposit was paid and plans for a shed drawn up and lodged to the local Shire Council.

It was to be a 'Barn' style shed with two open sides, colour-bond roof and panels and measuring in at 12m x 8m x 4.5m, rather large in anyone's language. Over the counter and to my surprise the plans were approved.

We thought we would do the right thing here and set out to talk to the new neighbours, tell them what our intentions were and be off to a good start.

We took all the plans, colour charts and even drawings showing various facades of the property from the neighbours point-of-view.

We wanted them to choose the colours and style of the shed to make them feel part of the decision process. This neighbourly reception was extremely chilly.

My father passed on some kind words of wisdom during this time suggesting that we locate or get someone to complete the hulls at least, which would give a huge kick-start to the whole process.

These words of wisdom come from someone who has been there and done that. Armed with this, we tracked down a pair of 10.5m Easy

hulls on the Sunshine Coast, but for many reasons chose to go with a larger beamed yacht.

Things were moving well, so we went out and had another chat to Peter and Anne. If we wanted to be sailing within five years, we were going to need assistance during the building process and we needed to move fast.

We put our hull suggestion to them and our offer was made to build the hull shells and lower bridge deck floor for us. It came at a cost of course and these three components would be ready within two months.

...no shed, no money, no tools and at the moment, no idea...

"Two months" I muttered quietly.

"No shed, no money, no tools and at the moment, no idea".

However, we did part with a cheque that day. This was perfect, the building shed/ house would be settled soon, the shed erected and the hulls could be moved in soon after. Things were going very well, too well in fact.

Late one warm evening, three days before the property was to go 'unconditional', one (investment property) neighbour called with regards the proposed boatshed.

He sternly and in no uncertain terms told us that he and other adjacent neighbours where in the process of lodging a petition to Council against the erection of the shed as "they had enough sheds in the area".

Well, after climbing back up off the floor and quietly gathering our wits, my wife and I decided that it would be in the best interests that we pulled out of this Investment Property purchase completely, even though the shed had been council approved.

The animosity that would have been generated would have been hard to diffuse. To add insult to injury, the ringleader of the neighbourly rebellion works as an Officer with one of the waterway authorities where we had ideas of finally mooring the boat.

Added to this, the new neighbour did not want "another tenant moving into his patch". "I already have one there, one there and another over there", he told us.

So, it was back to house hunting.

----- : -----

While James is one to always find the positive of any situation, this time it was Mary-Ann, as she could see how this decision had just shattered our plans. With her positive re-assurance, he was back on the Internet that night searching the real estate pages.

A week later and by chance too, a little known real estate agent in the northern outskirts of Brisbane took us to see an 'old 3 bedroom home with character on a huge block of land'.

In fact, it had white ants and electrical cables loose below the bathroom area, which was leaking too. However, it was within 11 - 15 minutes from home, not 20 minutes like the other house that had just fallen through.

The home was sixty years old and positioned on the forward section of a 1600 square metre rectangular block of land.

The building was so old that the rafters in the roof were originally built 900mm apart. We found out that the current regulations require a minimum of 600mm apart.

The home had been added onto and instead of removing the old roof; they simply put a whole new roof over the top of the old one, very confusing when you first pop your head up into the attic.

The current owners had not mowed the rear yard for at least six months as the grass and large fruit trees had taken over, the grass being up to two metres in new growth.

Armed with a tape measure, we carefully measured out how and where we could section off an area to build our dream. Our biggest fear was snakes, and for Mary-Ann it was those little creepy-crawlies that tend to appear from places least expected.

We drew diagrams and tried to picture where we could spend the next five years working on our project, being a bit on the greenie side, we wanted to leave the large mango and guava fruit trees in tact.

Leaning on one of the 200mm timber creosoted fence posts, we soon found what we were in for as it collapsed at the base and a myriad of white ants came streaming out. In the end, it all did plot well from our basic drawings and this part was finally given the tick of approval.

The property purchase package

came in what we believed to be 10% below current market prices for the area. It was a buy with the understanding that it needed a lot of work and AUD 30,000 later; we had the home Gyprocked and painted with new electrical wiring and lighting in place and even new carpet.

We hastily learnt how to erect an eight-foot fence and after a hand full of cuts and barbed wire scratches, a plot was sectioned off at the rear of the property for the yacht.

Next was a three by four metre zincalume shed at the rear of the fenced plot to provide some form of security for the tools. At the same that the electrician was working on the house we got him to lay a separate power line and metre box to the shed for our use.

This allowed us to be billed separately to the tenants for electricity, negating any future arguments.

At the same time we put a tap to the rear shed as well. To our horror, although it should have been expected, the original pest inspection found active white ants and a treatment was sought to rid the little critters of their home.

Armed with this and the expense of removal, we chased a further price drop on the purchase and came out AUD1000 better off.

AUD3800 later, little holes were sighted in the concrete around the perimeter of the house where chemicals were laid and the chemicals proved very effective. We removed all traces of plants close to the house finding four new snake skins having been shed and as we found out later, a precursor of things to come.

...words of wisdom come from someone who has been there and done that...

While bragging about our find to one of the Gyprockers working on the internal fit-out at that time, he pointed into one of the huge trees in the front yard and yes...there was another shed snake skin, except this one was just over two metres long.

----- : -----

A Sailing Catamaran Building Project

Pointers:

1. If you are relying on the *financial market trends* to fund your build, have a Plan B.

2. Spending $100,000 on a build WILL NOT return $500,000. Planning to double your money is a good target.

3. Don't be ashamed to lower your design expectation. Better to have a successful completed vessel, than be trying to sell a half completed one that will be costly to complete for the buyer.

Traps:

1. Financially investing too much, or too little in the build, much the same as a house. Except, Marine Surveyors are savvy to traps at resale.

2. Kidding yourself with 'cheap being the best'.

Chapter Four:
The Building Shed

We thought we would give Peter a call and see how the first hull was progressing.

He was already up to the glassing stage of the first hull and he invited us out to have a look. Not that we needed that as we had an open invitation to visit whenever we wanted.

Well, there it was and it was HUGE, and that was just the one hull. A few days later we called Peter offering assistance for the morning, having commitments that afternoon, and James spent his first lesson in 'fairing'.

The fibreglass had been completed the day before and early that morning it was given a general sand.

James was handed the plastic stick cut from an ice-cream container with increments marked on it.

"Four parts of resin, one part of hardener and one and half cups of Q-cells, mix it well until it thickens" he was told.

Q-cells were this light white fluffy powder that added body to the resin mixture and that then dictates the consistency, however, depending on the section being completed, the less the Q-cell content, the harder it was to sand.

A fine line was being tread as the thicker the consistency, the more brittle/weaker the mixture, but easier to sand. Three hours later the first hull was 'faired' and left to dry.

This was our introduction to resin. It was to be the glue, it was used with the fibreglass, it was the filler and it was the 'fairing compound' (or bogging compound) for the whole project.

To this end, it is ultimately what holds the boat together with a few screws. Resin on its own will not set or dry and needs a 'reactor' to chemically react with the resin to make it set.

This 'reactor' is called Hardener and together, forms an extremely strong and waterproof bond. While gloves should be worn when dealing with this newly mixed unstable glue, the vapour that it exudes is toxic to the lungs and can be smelt but not seen, making ventilation mandatory.

...cheap alternative ,
right up our alley...

Using bulk packs of the very cheap latex gloves proved their worth. While they often holed from small burrs of timber, they could be quickly changed and it was back on the job at hand.

We used the very 'slow' brand of hardener, which again worked well. The time of year and hardener was what really dictated the time to set and this was between 30 minutes to four hours. Sanding was left till two days later but no more than eight days, as it tends to get too hard to sand.

The resin mixture tends to get onto everything too (in our case anyway) and for its removal, a shareholding in a white vinegar factory would have been an advantage.

There is much written about using white vinegar and resin and compared to its alternatives, it was right up our alley.

We did have a hospital picked out and the chemical contents of the resins written down in the event that we got any in our eyes, thankfully this never occurred. The two-dollar spatulas that we used were also cleaned straight away with the vinegar, reducing the amount of spatulas needed for the yacht.

----- : -----

A few months earlier, we had been advised to call a friend of Peter's to arrange a viewing of his shelter where he was also building an Easy 37. His first hull was up to the glassing stage and it gave us our first look at the challenge that lay ahead.

His shelter for building the hulls was so simple yet effective and was made up of seven steel tubular frames covered with an industrial tarpaulin, the plastic type. It was open on both ends and shaped in a dome standing five metres high, eight metres wide and twelve metres long.

With his blessing, we quickly scribbled down sizes, lengths and took pictures (of what we nicknamed The Studio), as we could see this structure in our backyard.

We finally chose a company in Toowoomba (Queensland) to make the tarpaulin, as we were after an unusually large single sheet ten by thirteen metres, made of Canvacon. Two weeks and seven hundred dollars later this huge green package arrived at our front door via courier.

The plan now was to have the Building Shed erected at the rear of the property in such a way that one open end faced the newly erected Zincalume shed and the other faced toward the front of the property.

After devouring copious amounts of Easter chocolate that year (2004), we had a call from Peter who now had the second hull ready to go. It was now that the realisation of what was occurring finally sank in.

----- : -----

We frantically drew up plans for our 'Building Shed' and started the process of sourcing quotes for the steel poles, clamps and screws needed for the construction of the dome.

...we were going to take the 'stealth approach'...

There was only one neighbour that may raise an eyebrow and we decided that this time we were going to take the 'stealth approach'. 'Once bitten, twice shy' was so true.

Between the planned 'Building Shed' and this neighbour we had huge pine trees and his shed to the rear as well as two huge mango trees.

The other two sides faced vacant scrub and trees, and could not be seen from the street. A rather busy one, at that, too.

This time, the plans were also designed to work around the local government building policies and avoid the 'council approval process'.

To do this, we had to avoid using foundations at the foot of each upright and make sure that the 'dome' was easily removable. Without solid footings the poles tended to sink into the soil with time. We discuss this later.

It was actually a friend who located the steel for us, some 20% less in price than my best price. He has now booked a place on the boat for that find. This had unfortunately coincided with a steel price rise of 20% some two months previous.

Credit for some of the Building Shed data and associated specifications come from friends of ours, who have asked to remain anonymous. They too were midway through an Easy build.

It should be made very clear that any council or engineer has not approved this shelter.

We did take the drawings of our intentions to Council to gauge their thoughts and while the Council would not approve such a thing, they did state that as long as it remained a 'temporary & demountable' frame with a tarp over the top, one should not have a problem.

Additionally, it must not have permanent foundations (one of his first questions the Council asked). The fact was that the grass needed to be mowed around the poles within a week of construction with a whipper-snipper.

A chat with the neighbours was all we did, their concerns soon swayed over a beer. He unfortunately was a shift worker and was worried about the noise the tools would make. If you are thinking of a similar setup, choose your tarpaulin colour carefully, externally and internally, as some colours are very hot.

The tarpaulin cost around AUD750 delivered. The steel about AUD 1,200 delivered and other bits about AUD200, all up a covered work area for AUD 2,200.

Eighteen months on, what did we think of the tarp? It was working well and was worth every cent as a cheap alternative however, does get very hot in summer, even with the sides open.

...sun did take
its toll on the Canvacon...

If we did it again, we would re-enforce the apex (of each steel frame) with carpet. Don't use carpet underlay as we did. With the heat, the soft carpet underlay hardens then starts to crumble, leaving little brown bits and dust all over the place.

We would also consider paying a bit more to get the tarpaulin re-enforced along the full apex area. Because we did not do this, the tarp will need replacing. The sun did take its toll on the Canvacon and ours lasted 40 months.

Construction of each of the 8 frames was from 2 x 6m lengths of pipe (75mm diameter). We chose to go galvanised in the hope of a resale once the boat was complete.

Make sure that all the piping is reasonably smooth as this does touch the tarp.

The frames are then held in place with 5 x 13m (25mm diameter) lengths of pipe, coach-screwed on the horizontal (10mm above each frame bend, and on the inside of the frames), using galvanised electrical clamps.

We used 10 x 6.5m joined lengths to achieve this. The joints are then wound with carpet to prevent scuffing in the wind.

Templates were made for the 30-degree and 60 degree bends and then we hired a pipe bender for a day. The build was all up over in two days and work was very hastily commenced after a beer or three.

The apex of the frames was joined with suitable pipe (that slips either inside or outside the frame pipes (inside fitting pipe being cheaper and easier to find). This was bent and secured as shown in the following drawings.

The apex joint frame was then covered in carpet and secured with plastic tape of some sort. It was important here to ensure that the carpet overlapped 300mm each side of the apex joint and it did pay dividends in the long term saving on wear and tear of the tarp.

Tarpaulin Dimensions

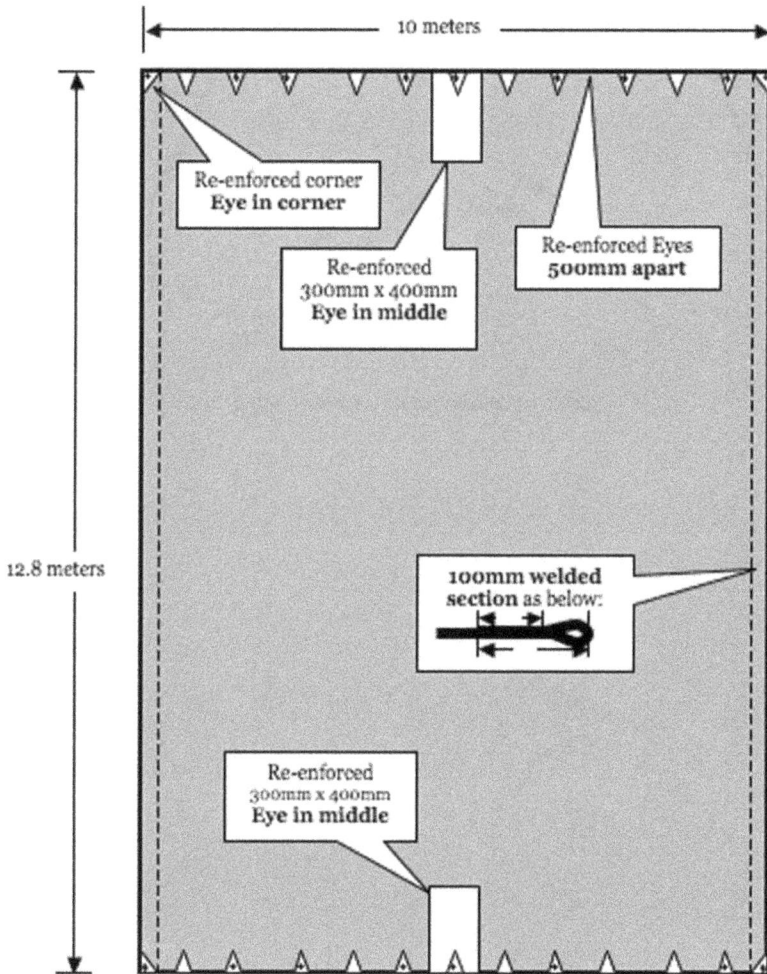

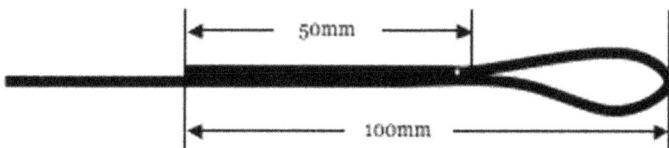

10 meters

12.8 meters

Re-enforced corner
Eye in corner

Re-enforced
300mm x 400mm
Eye in middle

Re-enforced Eyes
500mm apart

**100mm welded
section** as below:

Re-enforced
300mm x 400mm
Eye in middle

50mm

100mm

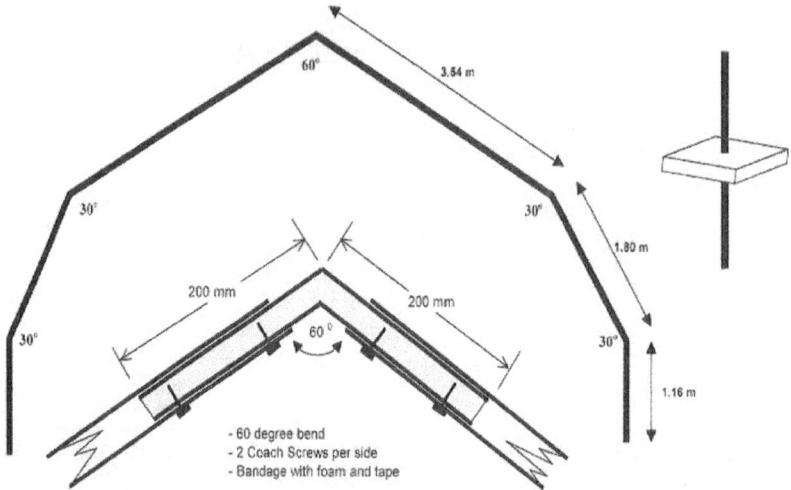

Guide to dimensions and angles of piping

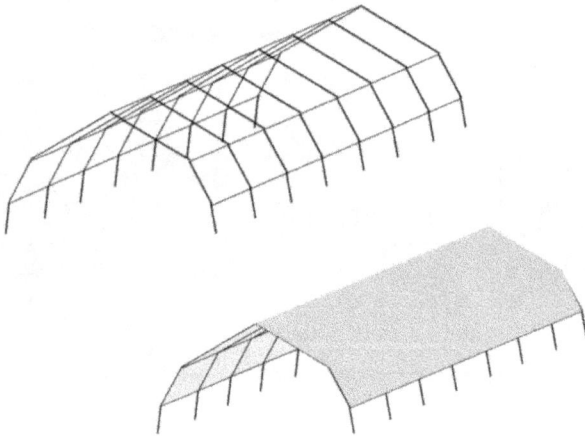

Our design plan of frames and cross beams

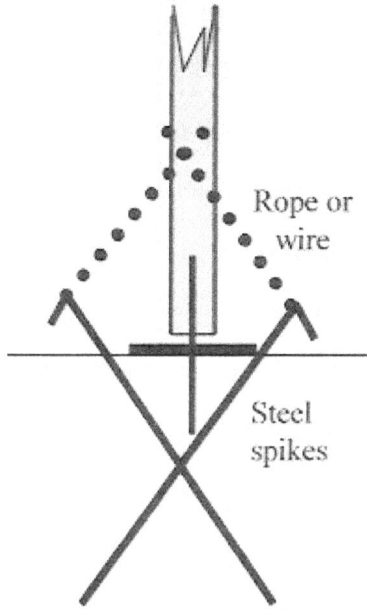

'Pole Spike' and tie down of steel frame poles.

Tie down of tarp to the crossbeam. Electrical pipe inserted in the lower fold and then
tied to the crossbeam with rope. Note 1.5m-security fence around perimeter.

At the base of each frame, we have placed a stake made out of (200mm x 200mm) 5mm flat steel plate with a spike welded through the middle.

This was fairly important, as the frame pole on its own tended to settle in the wind and slowly creep into the soil. This too helped stop the poles from sliding outwards.

The poles were then secured to the ground as in the **Shed Details** (this chapter). Two additional steel spikes hammered in at 60 degrees to each other, held the pole spike in place.

...The 'dome' withstood a huge hailstorm that wrote-off our car parked...

Before we draped the tarp over the frame, plastic electrical conduit was inserted along the sides of the tarp (within the 100mm welded section). The tarp was then draped over the top.

We started the tarp securing from the front apex all the way down the first frame. We used nylon 10mm rope here weaving around the pole, through the tarp eye etc. all the way down the frame. The rear frame was then completed in the same way.

The tarp bottoms were secured with light 7mm nylon rope to the lower horizontal crossbeam, making a small hole through the Canvacon around the inserted electrical conduit and secured adjacent to each frame.

The 7mm nylon was very important here as it acted as a weak point for breakage, which is a good thing on those extremely windy days.

The plastic electrical conduit also flexed at the base of the tarp preventing breakage. It is preferred that the rope break happen here (which occurred on a dozen or so occasions) than the tarp tear and the hulls get wet on a bad day.

The tarp was not pulled very tight, as it would have reduced the 'flexing' and may have even torn as the tarp aged.

The ends of the structure and lower sections of the tarp sides were not covered, as this would have caused the dome to collapse in strong winds. This did have its disadvantages, as dust was a continual problem.

We'd rather the cheap construction and frequent cleaning/vacuuming of the boat building than replacing the collapsed dome and trying to empty water from a newly sanded hull.

We did tie sections of weed mat by four points onto the upper part of the front frame to reduce wind flow, however, the mat moved freely in the wind.

The frame width opening was gently stretched to provide an 8m x 13m ground floor working area. And the hulls firmly planted at 100mm above ground level. Through the project, work was accomplished up each side and atop with no problems.

Should additional height be required later in the build, the plan was to raise the frames by sliding an additional section of pipe within the original frame pipe and then screw at the height required.

We had already tried this on one side. The simple insert with tightly fitting pipe and coach-screws worked a treat.

The 'dome' withstood a huge hailstorm that wrote-off our car parked out the front and severely damaged a steel roofed house adjacent to the 'dome'.

The only damage to the 'dome' was to the apex points around the frame where the 25mm hail stones cut against the carpet/steel.

----- : -----

A Sailing Catamaran Building Project

Pointers:

1. Try and locate your own premises.

2. A very secure lock-up area on-site is a must. Better with a 1.5m fence.

3. Bargain with a farmer (i.e. I'll leave you a new steel shed for free rental). The cost may work in your favour.

4. Must have power and water on site.

Traps:

1. Building a shed that fails in conditions out of the ordinary.

2. 9 out of 10 renters overstay their planned rental period and don't account for the resultant rental increases.

Building Pantry:

1. Cheap 100-pack thin latex gloves, about 20 packs.

2. Spatulas - stirrers, from the cheap store (about 200 or more).

3. Paint brushes - 20-25mm (around 300). Better the ones that don't lose too much hair. Chinese distributors sell them for 12 cents each, but in packs of 5000 (delivered).

4. Mixing containers - 300ml - 400ml tins are best. Ensure they are clean and don't have sharp edges (200 - 300 of them).

Chapter Five:
A HUGE Pair with Frames

After the two-day 'Building Shed' erection, all was ready for transportation of the hulls.

Three weeks later the first hull was positioned upright in its new home and a barbeque organised for the arrival of the second hull. The trick here was to supply beer and a sausage for brawn. We needed this brawn to manoeuvre the hulls into position and at half a tonne each, they are a little heavy on your own.

It was at this stage, too, that temporary frames were erected, only held together with timber and clamps, enough to be self-standing on the keels alone.

A lot of effort and time was spent here getting the hulls exactly plumb, kindly lead by the Designer . Having him on hand made the job

that much faster and by lunchtime, all was done. This would be their position for the next three and a half years.

The plan was then to tackle the main frames, gluing and screwing until complete. The yacht plans carry all the detail on this area and will not be discussed here.

...Already, the boatbuilding camaraderie of information was at work...

The key frames we have named and mention here are:
1. Bow Locker Frame - fore frame between the two hulls,

2. Main Room Frame,

3. Main Door Frame - at the

main entry area, and

4. The Aft Frame - toward the aft of the yacht.

Having never attempted such a large building project and having zero experience with resins, presented a very challenging initial experience.

*   Where do you start?

*   How much glue mix do you use per resin mix?

*   How many and what size screws do you use?

*   How do you screw the screws in and how far in?

*   Do you pre-drill holes and when dry, do you take them out again?

*   What spacing is required for the screws and is that spacing the same on all joins?

The list of questions went on and on. It was time for one of the hundred odd calls to the Designer.

We found ourselves starting the conversation by apologising for our ignorance until we found out that we were not alone.

In a calming tone and very patient manner, all was easily explained and we were directed back to various sections of the Designers documents. In our haste, we just glanced at many of these important titbits of information. Within a few minutes we were in business.

As the weeks passed, the phone calls got less and less, eventually one every six months (building related).

The other great help here was the contacts that the Designer had. He kept us in the loop whenever he could get items on special and this did save a tonne of cash, better still, our valuable time searching the Internet.

----- : -----

At this same time, the process of finalising where we would be moored was raised.

...the closer it is to home, the more frequently and enjoyable...

To this end, a proposed completion date (with all things running well) was needed and October 2009 picked as 'D-Day/Month'.

We needed some idea as applications for new moorings can take between eight months to four years (if there was a waiting list) and if it were to be a berth, well they are few and far between and very costly at that.

The priorities that drove our mooring position were price and proximity to home and we did not want our boat to be two hours drive away.

While it does not sound like much, the closer it is to home, the more frequent and enjoyable would be the use. This limited our selection to the northern areas of Brisbane, the Caboolture River being our pick.

It was now onto the Internet to find out how one goes about getting a mooring, who does one apply too and how much does it cost.

We were fortunate in that the Designer had just laid a mooring in a similar position on the Caboolture River and quickly pointed us in the right direction, with the application paperwork arriving from the Waterway Authorities a week later.

Already, the boatbuilding camaraderie of information was at work .One of the questions on the mooring application was 'the name of the vessel'.

Well, they reckon its bad karma to name a boat before it's complete, but how do you get around this issue if you don't?

...There was no way that anyone could have thought of this name...

Other application challenges included the motor engine numbers, gas appliance certificates and the list went on. So we used the motor engine numbers of units we already owned which could easily power the yacht and chose not to lodge the 'gas application' until a later stage.

Trying to involve the whole family, a 'naming suggestion sheet' was placed on the back of the pantry door where we encouraged the kids to participate and scribble down the names they really liked.

Suggestions from 'Show me the Money', Easy As, Life's Easy, Santorini and every conceivable name with 'easy' was touted, but we could not agree on one name, unanimously.

Later that month, Mary-Ann's Mum arrived for her annual pilgrimage to Brisbane and yes; we got her involved in the naming game too. It took a few days until MAJEK was invented (Mary-Ann, James, Elizabeth and Keegan) and this went down very well as the kids had started to lose interest.

Together with a shortlist of a few others and a silent vote, it was decided. MAJEK it's going to be. There was no way that anyone could have thought of this name...so we thought. After placing a search over the Internet, a monohull was found and it carried our name.

So, it was back to the drawing board and the word Pure was added, hence Pure Majek.

----- : -----

The 'Frames' form a huge role in the overall strength of the boat and certain frames are classed as 'Structural'. Most are cambered and will later form the base for the upper bridge deck.

..the implications on resale - where the Designer is key...

Insurers are very interested in the structural integrity component of the vessel and for this reason alone, this should be done perfectly and without modification. The last thing we wanted was a failure in a frame because we had moved an access port, or something similar.

We discuss this a little later too, the implications on resale - where the Designer is the key. Was the yacht built to spec? Is it worth this much? Etc.

----- : -----

Our start point was the *Main Room Frame*. It was on this frame that we learnt the assembly basics. The beauty with plywood is that if the cut is wrong, just grab another piece and try again.

Basically, sheets of plywood were roughly screwed in position and the upper part of the frame assembled. This upper frame had a camber, which needed careful planning.

Over 5m wide, we chose to cut and glue this cambered part of the 'upper frame' on the ground. Once dry and lifted into place, other beams were then cut and glued.

...the physiological power of this achievement definitely provided an incentive...

As there were spaces in between the panels, we heavily resined the surfaces providing a sealed shell both inside and outside of the frame and reducing possible moisture absorption while the rest of the yacht was being built.

The small 15mm - 20mm stainless steel screws took some getting used to as they were fidgety, especially if some resin remained on the gloves.

----- : -----

While the construction of the *Main Room Frame* was complete, the hulls were still a little unstable. For this reason we chose to go to the rear and assemble the *Aft Frame*. This time we completed the cambered top part on the actual frame on the structure, as opposed to on the ground.

Three days later, we were on to the *Bow Locker Frame*. This soon dried and it came time to remove all uprights that were providing the initial stability of the hulls.

----- : -----

The lower bridge deck floor was next to be installed. Already completed at floor level, it was brought into place and secured. A suggestion was made to paint the lower bridge deck bottom prior to screwing in place. This would have saved much backache later in the piece, while trying to paint upside down.

Peter's EASY Plans have many more photos with the required dimensions and structural specifications that we found easy to follow.

----- : -----

With the lower bridge deck in place, a platform was available to complete another key frame, the *Main Door Frame*. The *Main Door Frame* (being the bridge deck back-door/window frame) was the biggest frame on the vessel.

This part of the 'yacht shell' proved to be very sturdy and an obvious relief that just maybe, we had got the gluing right.

----- : -----

Port Hull complete

Internal View – all plumb

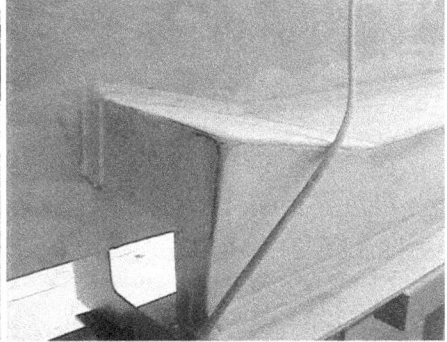

Engine Pod Areas

With the lower bridge deck in place, we were, for the first time, working off the ground on a yacht deck.

This does not sound too exciting, but the psycological power of this achievement definitely provided an incentive as we could now picture ourselves on the water.

All of sudden we now had something that looked like a yacht.

Prior to the construction of the *Main Door Frame*, we thought it prudent to investigate the options of steering and eventually cabling positions, prior to commencing the framework.

This would prove invaluable as changes were now required to the rear rudder shafts and seeds sown for bringing our thoughts to fruition with how we were to steer the vessel.

...Half the door can be easily latched in bad weather or cold windy days...

Our yacht plans incorporated hand held tillers at the rear of each hull and our preference was to move away from this with the use of a wheel and options for use of the hand tiller in the event of a failure of the main steering system.

Hand tillers are great for racing and are also geared to the amateur builder as they are easier (and faster) to build.

Once again we were on the phone to Peter who now pointed us in the direction of another friend of his, Alan who was also in the process of building an Easy.

In fairness to the designer, his plans did not come with a wheel, so in hindsight, it was a little rude asking for help.

----- : -----

In line with all other builders at this stage of their build, we were faced with the quandary of where to start with regard to steering.

...background investigating revealed that leaky windows, squeaky/poor-fitting doors, bug and mosquito access...

Trying to find a point to work back from on the rear of the Main Door Frame raised more questions than answers:

- What did we want this section to look like?

- Where does one place the steering?

- How big a steering wheel? This then dictates the height of the window sill and therefore the lower section of the actual window,

- What type of window - sliding, removable, tinted, glass, or even

- Fly screens? And so it went on.

----- : -----

After jotting down the requirements from a *'practical non-nautical point-of-view'* (Mary-Ann's area) and *'minimum nautical requirement point-of-view'*, we came up with a wish list.

Items here included:
- A large cockpit door - prefer bi-fold

- The largest possible windows
- The ability for maximum opening of doors and windows at the same time,
- Steering station to starboard, and
- A steering station seat (that would include a lower enclosed area for a gas hot water unit).

While these may appear to be common sense items as you read, it is another story plotting them out, remembering that the complexity of the idea/build directly influences the cost.

Some background investigating revealed that leaky windows, squeaky/poor-fitting doors, bug and mosquito access, non-glass windows were common problems for the average cruiser type yacht.

...removable windows are all fine and well, until its time to store the window internally...

Armed with this and some other thoughts, we took the bold step again to seek more guidance. While additional cost was to be incurred, we chose to get our windows made by a professional.

Given that we had kids who were going to be a large part of our sailing team, we tried to weigh up the pros and cons of:

>Timber vs. aluminium,

>Acrylic vs. polycarbonate vs. glass,

>Tinted vs. laminated.

Finally settled on clear toughened safety glass in aluminium frames.

With this decision came weight and our calculations together with that of the manufacturer came in the vicinity of an additional 8kgs for the glass windows and frames.

Having had feedback from others with tinted rear windows, we chose to go clear however; they were delivered tinted (we bit our tongues, maybe we should have forced the issue - time will tell).

Our aft turret roof was extended well aft to the rear of the yacht. While this is not common, it resolved our sun challenge. This also provided clear vision forward from the steering station.

The window on the port side of the cockpit doorframe is sliding with good all-weather seals and a reasonably large drainage gutter at the base. On the starboard side, the whole window can be quickly removed, providing full airflow when required for those hot days.

We had previously been alerted to the fact that removable windows are all fine and well, until its time to store the window internally. Once removed, it is rather large and cumbersome.

We chose to make a sleeve-type storage area along the *Main Door Frame* specifically for its storage when removed. It happens to be a perfect place now too for the storage of fly-screens .

We mandated that the window frame be a single piece with a clean welded join and both windows must have flyscreens. Additionally, we wanted an internal lip, as part of the window frame, that overhung inside by 20mm.

This would prove an asset providing a clean finish internally and making installation extremely fast.

The main saloon door is a bi-fold type for two main reasons. Half the door can be easily latched in bad weather or cold windy days and still allow easy access to the helm station.

The second reason allows the door to be easily stowed when fully open.

The door tucks away behind the frame centre pillar allowing for easy access to all the large windows internally.

The only other challenge to face was the sealing of the door once closed.

----- : -----

Pointers:

1. Get Insurance - especially for fire.

2. Find a reliable timber supplier that delivers.

3. Select your resin supplier - 20 litre container supplies as a minimum. We tested and steered away from brands that required heating.

Traps:

1. Build 'not set plumb'. Small issue now - but HUGE performance issue later. Talk to your Designer.

2. Find you have an allergy to resin, we all do to fibreglass.

3. Doubting yourself.

Building Pantry:

1. Coveralls - disposable overalls with hood (30 pairs).

2. Good comfortable shoes that you can stand in for long periods and will be thrown away after build.

3. Face masks - disposable types, and at least one good quality with filters on the respirator.

4. Face Mask - A good quality unit required for two-pack painting (Hunter type respirators with external filter housing - or similar). This is not required initially but can be sourced over 6-12 months from Ebay.

The vast, clear sky stretched before me, coupled with the occasional bird fluttering past.

As I sat on the sand, high above all others, surrounded by bush and long dead, decrepit trees, I spotted a yacht; sailing past the dune I sat above.
The white sails fell into stark contrast with the crystal blue water, like a star in the night sky.

The shade provided by the trees gave a welcome respite to the beating sun and cooled the sand at my feet, while the smell of a beautiful summers day, gave light to the wonderful aroma of eucalypt and other trees, however none surpassing the invigorating salt air, crawling its way into my very consciousness.

Nudging some sand, I watched it cascade down the high dune, eventually stopped by the lapping, tranquil shores and bare feet of content 'yachters', strolling past way below.

The occasional sound of laughing children and the hum of a distant tinny wafted on the wind, but it all contrasted perfectly with the blue backdrops of sky and water, the soft coloured sand mingled with green bush and white sails, gently rolling by.

(Scribed by one of the kids;
Southern Stradbroke Island,
Queensland, Australia

Chapter Six:
Steering Considerations - Part 1 of 2

We chose to diverge from the plans here and add a single steering station with no hand-tillers.

This in turn has presented many a sleepless night as little documented data is freely available and it's a bit rude asking the Designer for information that was not on the plans in the first place. It needs to be remembered that all these little extra bits do add to additional costs and time. So where does one start?

We wanted to keep all our external 'walking surfaces' (on the deck) as free from clutter as much as possible so as to protect our family or friends accidentally testing the waters without our knowledge (a lot easier said than done).

While we cannot watch them one hundred percent of the time,

reducing deck clutter would only assist in preventing a slip or trip.

Additionally, we wanted the rudder connection arm internal, to prevent kids playing Tarzan and using this as a balancing bar or swinging beam before falling into the water.

...A yacht of this weight could easily utilise a simple system...

While this thinking process was underway, the Designer put us in contact with friends of his who happened to be onto their second Easy catamaran build.

Well, talk about an interesting bloke, Alan is a Scotsman and while a 'jack of all trades', he is a Cabinet Maker by trade and is

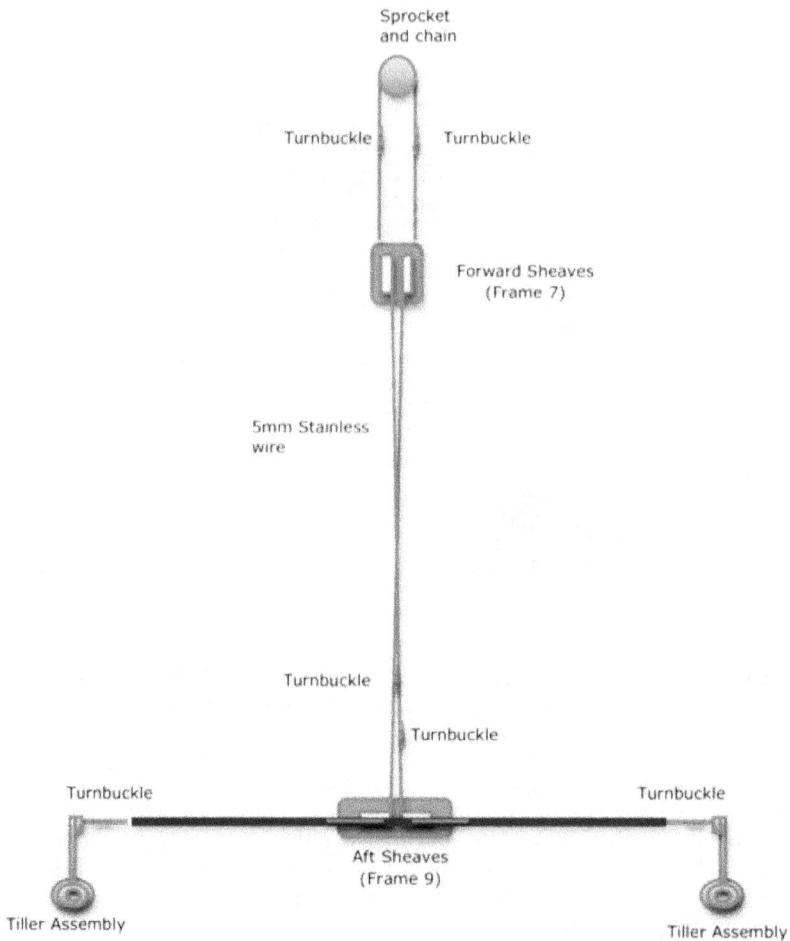

Sprocket
and chain

Turnbuckle   Turnbuckle

Forward Sheaves
(Frame 7)

5mm Stainless
wire

Turnbuckle

Turnbuckle

Turnbuckle   Turnbuckle

Aft Sheaves
(Frame 9)

Tiller Assembly

Tiller Assembly

Brake Limit Specifications:

Tiller Assembly	BL 3000kg+
Turnbuckles SS 8mm Full Body	BL 2500kg
Sprocket & Chain	BL 2000kg+
Tiller Connecting Bar SS 25mm	BL 2000kg+
Fitting – Inner lower (Frame 7)	BL 1500kg
Fitting – Outer lower (Frame 9)	BL 1500kg
Stainless Wire- 5mm	BL 1490kg

Steering Control Mechanics Diagram

fastidiously perfect in what he does.

He is embarrassingly clean in the way he builds his boats down to the last degree (literally) and a credit to him, something we couldn't do.

We trampled all over his yacht trying hard to absorb all we could, picturing this and that on our boat. It was here that we recognised the importance of getting feedback from others, those little tricks and small changes that definitely helped.

...Less parts - less problems. ..

Self trained in stainless steel welding, he happens to be extremely good at this too and it's here that he has helped us with some stainless work - at 'Scotsman mates rates'.

Within a few days, Alan had ideas streaming with myriads of suggestions. The final steering system he suggested was simple, fitting in with the major requirement of ours of keeping it simple, easy to access and easy to maintain.

We had also managed to stay away from a hydraulic system, something James had experience with and was trying to avoid. A yacht of this weight could easily utilise a simple system with less moving parts. Less parts - less problems.

We mulled over Alan's ideas for the steering and next thing we knew, he had made the stainless parts for the top of the rudder shaft. This was the start of our single helm station, while still keeping the advantage of hand tillers on either hull if required for emergencies.

It was important that this be considered in the early stages of the build, as access holes need to be cut during the early construction phase of the boat and cleared with the designer.

----- : -----

Following on the **'Steering Control Mechanics Diagram'** (this chapter), will help explain these next paragraphs a lot easier.

...be easily adjusted or changed if need be from an internal position...

The internal *rudder connector arm* (the single linkage between the two 'tiller assemblies') had to have its own enclosed area at the rear of the boat outside of the *Aft Frame* and the last thing we wanted was the possibility of any type of jamming around that arm in bad weather, for whatever reason.

We wanted it to have its own enclosed operating space that could be accessible for maintenance purposes, however sealed securely against the elements.

All components for the remainder of the Steering are made of Stainless Steel, which do carry weight and cost penalties.

Basically, the rudders are connected via *rudder arms* (part of the 'Tiller Assembly'), to the *rudder connector arm*, then via pulleys (commonly called 'sheaves') using 4mm stainless steel cable to the steering station via more sheaves and finally, via a chain and cog to the wheel.

Back to the *rudder arm* (right), this sits on top of the rudder pole. The arm had to be very easily removable in the event of a mishap, which may require the rudder to be removed for repair.

We all know Murphy's theory here and we have been told that there are those who have had repair here and those who are going to have repair here.

This arm is held in place by a central bolt with locknut and the whole assembly secured to the rudder pole by one or two external bolts with locknuts.

*...Get spare grub screws
and keys cut too...*

Both *rudder arms* (each 435mm in length) are connected to the stainless steel *rudder connector arm* running the full length of the boat to the rear of the *Aft Frame*.

The method of attachment to the *rudder connector arm* is via Turnbuckles, which are cheap and can again be easily adjusted or changed, if need be, from an internal position.

This would also help in the event that one rudder needs to be disconnected during a trip for whatever reason.

During the planning stage, we sought the manufacturers specifications for all the 'Break-Limits' (BL) of the various components and bought appropriately making our weakest point the stainless steel cable, which at 1490kg, will need one and a half metric tonnes of steering force to cause a breakage.

The sheaves we used were off the shelf from Ronstan and available from our local chandlery. We chose the largest diameter sheaves, in this case 58mm, which we hoped would place less working strain on the parts due to this larger size.

Not too sure how true this is, but we were told that they are being discontinued which is unlucky for us, but great news for those who specialise in making money from such discontinued lines. Apparently, the 58mm size sheave was never a good seller.

Mary-Ann's brother, a fitter and turner by trade, kindly stepped in and welded two sheaves onto some 4mm plate and this provided a solid bracket for the turning point of the stainless steel cable from the back of the boat (near the Rudder Connector Arm) to the front.

Continuing from the back of the boat to the steering station, a second bracket was inserted with two sheaves turning the rope up toward the steering pinion.

Another two stainless steel turnbuckles connected the rope to each end of the 600mm piece of motorbike chain.

This is then fed around the sprocket (another easily available component from any motorbike shop) and that closed the steering loop.

Working out the size of the sprocket did take a little time.

It was strongly suggested that one needed at least 80 degrees rudder travel in the water from the port extreme point to the starboard

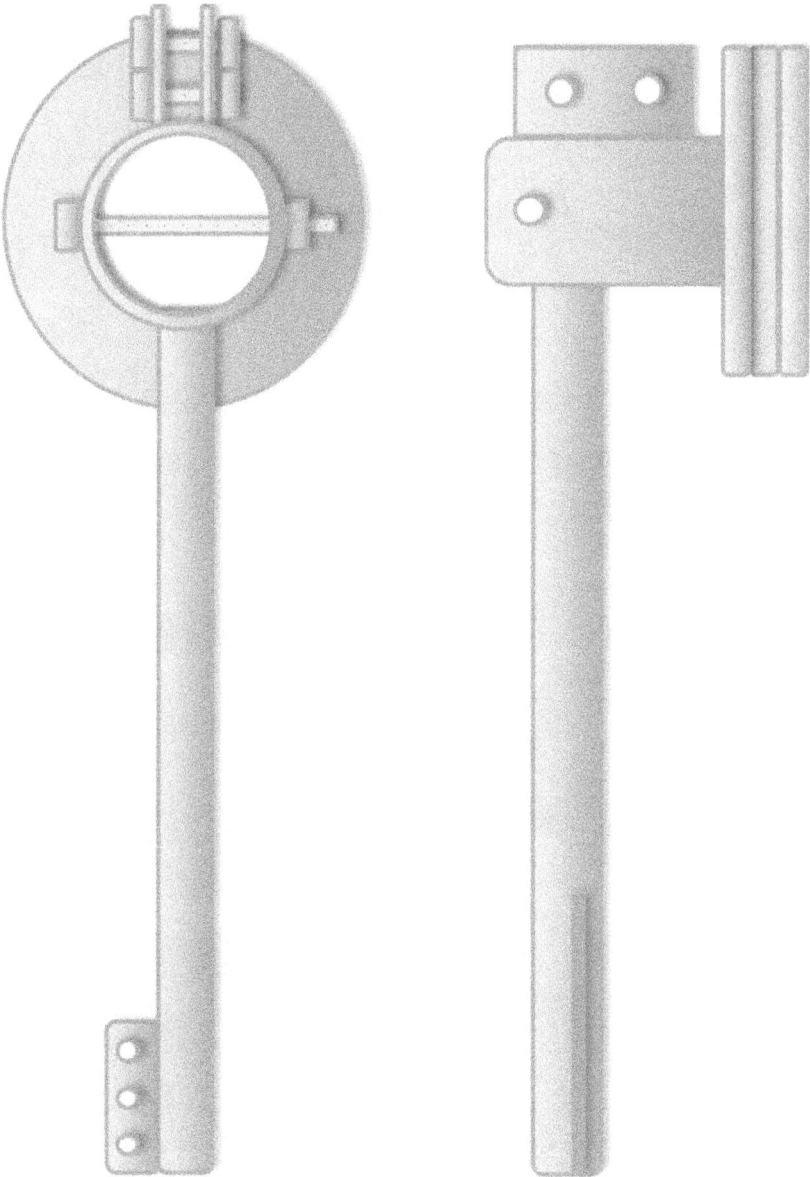

Rudder Arm

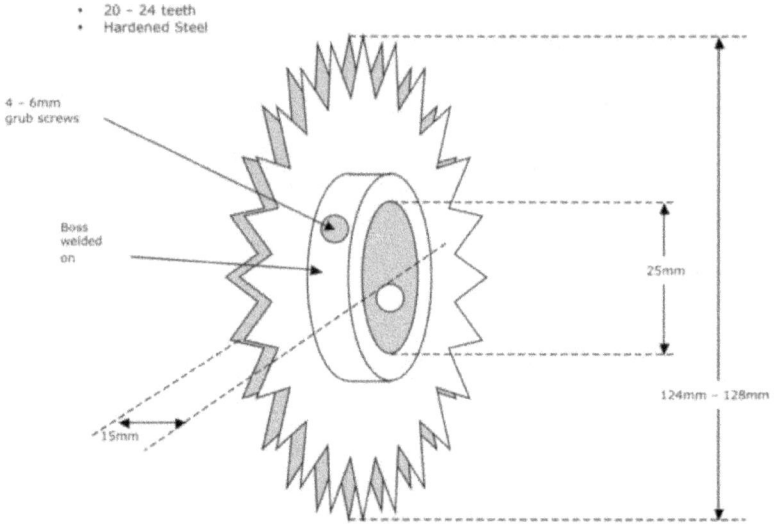

- 20 – 24 teeth
- Hardened Steel

4 – 6mm grub screws

Boss welded on

25mm

124mm – 128mm

15mm

Sprocket

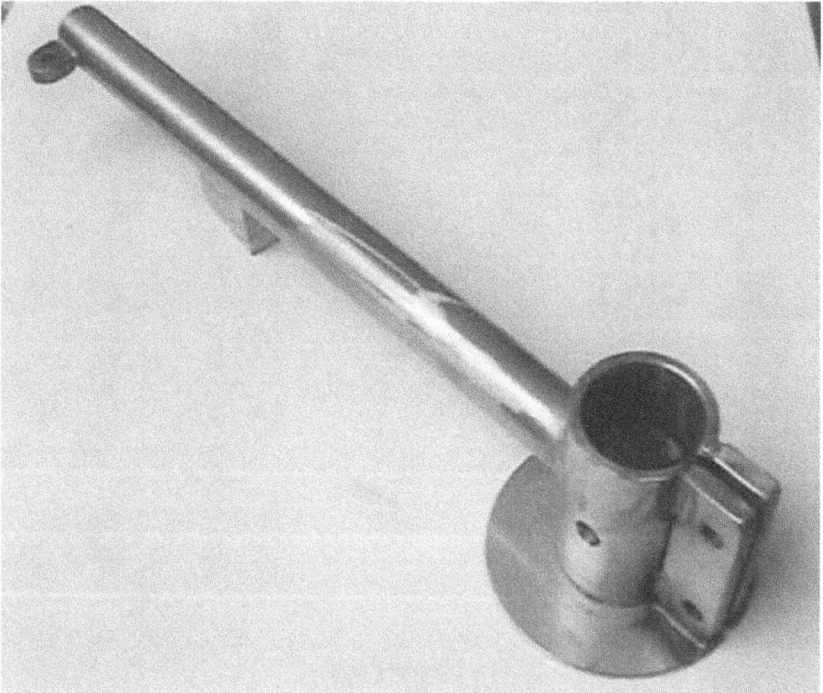

Tiller Arm Completed

extreme point and this was later confirmed with Peter.

They say, any more than this becomes ineffective and in some cases detrimental causing drag and slowing the yacht down.

Somehow, the turns on the steering wheel also had not to exceed 1 1/4 - 1 1/2 turns from one extreme to the other. This was very important, as the autopilot system we intended to use would not be effective outside this range.

The steering planning and design has worked extremely well and is very easy to use. Since launching, the adjustment areas have worked a real treat.

Calculating the sprocket size is not that difficult. The rudders should move no more than 40 degrees either side of centre (80 degrees in total).

Anything more is ineffective in a sailing vessel and will actually cause the water to 'stall' around the rudder slowing the vessel down.

The number of teeth depends on how many steering wheel turns one wants. The Raymarine autopilot dictated this for us. 11/4 was their recommendation.

Our calculations were based on the length of our *Rudder Arm* (435mm from centre of the *Rudder Shaft*). We connected the *Rudder Arm* to the *Rudder Shaft*.

The *Rudder Connection Arm* was then connected and we physically measured the distance of travel from lock-to-lock. That is, from the most left to the most right positions.

..undo two grub screws and slide the wheel off, simple...

This gives us the amount of travel needed and it had to be done in 11/4 wheel-turns. We then cut various circles from scrap ply to simulate the sprocket and then rolled this 1 1/4 turns down this 'lock-to-lock distance'.

We eventually came up with sprocket 120mm in diameter (128mm with teeth).

The above size sprocket has worked famously. The grub screws and 'key' in the sprocket (not shown) are critical. Get spare grub screws and keys cut too.

The diameter of the centre was based on the Steering Wheel we bought (standard one *off-the-shelf* from our local Chandler).

----- : -----

A Sailing Catamaran Building Project

Pointers:

1. Consider the simplest system.

2. Talk to the Designer.

3. There is nothing wrong with tillers, autopilots are engaged most of the time .

Traps:

1. Trying to re-invent the wheel.

2. Being 'hell-bent' on a particular system.

Chapter Seven:
Construction - Mid Stage

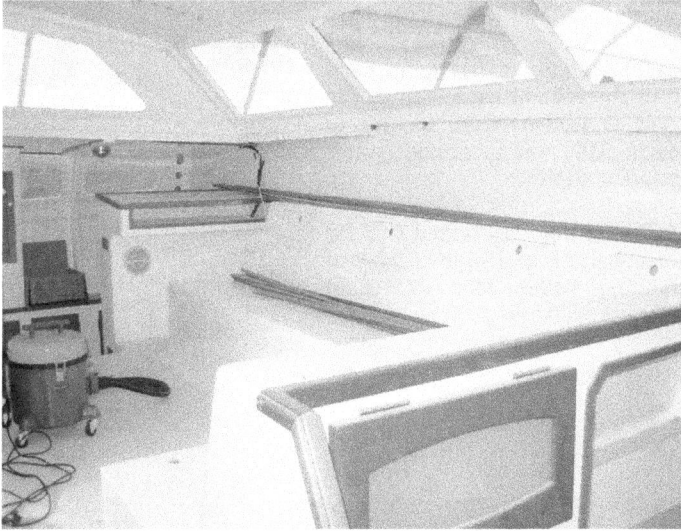

One of the things that stood out about a Catamaran was the easy access onto the boat. Both sides had a set of stairs that raised you on top of the world before you had even unlocked the doors.

We had chosen to add a couple of things here, which would add a little to the building time, however, pay dividends later.

After carefully cutting into the hull, the initial rear step construction started to take shape with the plans calling for two steps.

Construction was planned at two days per side and soon it was time for a trial before gluing. Keegan ran up and down a few times and it was obvious at this stage that the step height (for our boat), had to be smaller.

Given Mary-Ann's stature and thoughts of food, water and fuel being carried aboard, we found the excuses to consider an additional step. We are still very pleased we did this.

Because of this addition, the lower step was now reduced to 400mm x 600mm.

To provide a psychological appearance of size on our lower step platform, all steps were designed narrower in width on the inside than the outside giving this neat slight swirling effect.

On the lower step of the starboard hull we took the idea from Peter's boat and installed a fold out set of three stainless steel steps, which stowed flat when not in use.

When unfolded, they drop over the rear hull and into the water. This again would prove to be a treasure providing easier access for everyone in and out the water after swimming.

We also chose to put 5mm drop from the rear of each step to the front as well as from outside to inside. This was to provide water runoff at all times.

The last thing we wanted was for someone to take a slide because of standing water that we could reduce.

Below the port stairs, is where we have located our autopilot connection. Two access panels provide very easy access to this area for adjustment or removal, for whatever reason.

...here one sees the hard work really starting to take shape...literally...

As a follow up on these stairs and to improve boarding, we have now a portable unit that has some small handles and is wider than the commercial fold-up types.

While there was nothing wrong with the original, we want ease of access on our side.

Aft Steps Construction

When unfolded, they drop over the rear hull and into the water. This again would prove to be a treasure providing easier access for everyone in and out the water after swimming.

We also chose to put 5mm drop from the rear of each step to the front as well as from outside to inside. This was to provide water runoff at all times. The last thing we wanted was for someone to take a slide because of standing water that we could reduce.

Below the port stairs, is where we have located our autopilot connection. Two access panels provide very easy access to this area for adjustment or removal, for whatever reason.

...here one sees the hard work really starting to take shape...literally...

As a follow up on these stairs and to improve boarding, we have now a portable unit that has some small handles and is wider than the commercial fold-up types. While there was nothing wrong with the original, we want ease of access on our side.

----- : -----

Cabin sides were next on the list. Its here one sees the hard work really starting to take shape.

The cabin sides were an item we had delayed and we have no idea why as they form a pivotal foundation for the gradual walkway fall from 'cockpit area' to the bow.

Additionally the Turret is reliant on its construction.

This construction includes the rear deck steps that allow access to the top deck. There was a marked change in appearance once this was completed.

The panels seemed easy to cut and install however turned out a little trickier than first thought. The angles of the step drop and rear cabin sides proved a challenge, but finally worked well. The other side went up in a flash.

...The five 'bow lockers' are quite large...

The cabin side windows are cut from sheets, that when following the plans, are reasonably easy to complete.

Our challenges arose when after cutting the window holes; we decided to add the internal cupboard against one of the pre-cut window holes.

Re-enforced sections are also cut and glued at this stage to be utilised later for bolting the stays that assist in holding the mast.

By far the trickiest component to cut here was in the rear section and involved a vertical 'step panel' for both sides. The angles/drop were a challenge that took a few hours to design.

There are two ways that the cabins side window cut-outs can be constructed and of course, we chose the harder of the two.

The first involves 2 x 9mm panels, forming the cabin side (not shown here), with the second panel being glued from the inside once the first is in place and dry.

Cabin Window Frames

Starting the Bow Locker build

Frames follow the line of the yacht

Bow Locker partitions in place

Bow Locker fronts in place

Bow Locker Hatch drains

The windows are then marked and cut.

The second way is similar to the first except that instead of a second 9mm panel being inserted, rather a trim, made from 9mm ply and about 30mm wide made to fit the window cut-out from the inside.

This provides a reinforced window edge.

At the end of the day, the extra work doing the latter worked out to about 20 hours. On top of this was the additional bogging sanding that was required in all the tight curves, very testing.

While the finish looks great, the average 'Joe Bloggs' would not pick this up and it was purely aesthetic with which we are very pleased.

----- : -----

There are seven Bow Lockers on our boat, five forward of the bridge deck on the leading edge between the front hulls (bow lockers 1-5) and additional ones further forward again in each hull (hull bow lockers 6-7). Only two are accessible from within the boat and they form part of the 'bow locker' assembly.

The 'bow locker' build is a little different than normal as the under face uses ply that is bent (roughly 750 up) to form the rounded front of the boat between the hulls.

Vertical frames were installed fairly quickly, dividing the mid bow area into five equal compartments. The plan here called for two layers of 6mm plywood rounded and glued onto preinstalled vertical frames to complete the front of the lockers. With the designers blessing, we used 3 layers of 4mm plywood that took a little longer to build, however much easier to handle.

Again, being a one-person builder on the day, a tricky/sticky few weeks were had here.

The five 'bow lockers' are quite large (700mm x 700mm x 600mm) with the middle three fibre glassed, as they are prone to the external elements. The middle locker will be our chain/anchor locker with electric winch and for this reason we chose to use three layers of glass here.

The intention was to layer the floor with a removable thick rubber lining, to assist in dampening the fall of heavier steel objects like chain and anchors etc.

The two outer lockers will only be accessible from the forward bedrooms and used for general storage.

On an earlier visit from one of Peter Snell's friends, a suggestion was made that the lockers with access hatches need to be fully accessible i.e. that one can climb in with a squeeze.

There words were "....it makes life a lot easier later, believe me".

While this meant extra work and timber framing, we took up this suggestion hoping it would pay dividends. We can now testify to that change and are pleased we made the change.

To save costs it was decided to build the hatch door assemblies, rather than purchase the hatches.

The challenge faced here was obviously the 'sealing from the elements', even though these lockers were classed as 'wet lockers'.

It was decided to build a 'U' shaped edge below the hatch edges to capture any excess water and vent it overboard.

...not much information regarding the use of treated pine..

This sounded simple in theory; however, the build took a lot longer than planned. Reasons here included the timber used which was treated pine, the general fiddling around and then finishing in a few coats of resin.

The other two 'Hull Bow Lockers' (lockers 6-7) are a lot larger and will be used for gas bottle storage (starboard hull), with 'bollard storage' (port hull).

Their hatch assemblies are built the same as the mid bow lockers. To finish the lockers, two-pack paint was used in single layers, more for aesthetic appeal than anything else.

There is not much information regarding the use of treated pine however, we can only recommend kiln dried treated timber that has worked very well for us. Our timbers were selected on how dry they appeared.

We have heard of others that have had trouble with their treated pine and our thoughts are that the timber may still be raw or may not have been dried thoroughly.

Additionally, there are chemicals used in the 'treating process' that may react unduly with your resin. Tread carefully and ask your resin supplier about compatibility. Our supplier gave us the nod *'as long as the timber was very dry'.*

As a follow-up four years on, we are still very happy with this decision.

----- : -----

We chose to build an additional locker in the forward area (locker 8), which we called the *Main Forward Locker.*

We chose to include this external locker to provide space for the 'Odd Items' that normally clog the internal spaces, which could be left outside if space permitted.

...This inclusion has been worth its weight in gold...

Such items include:
- The watermaker - suitable for 1.5 metre membranes (5 feet),

- Hose pipes and all connections including external taps and plumbing,

- Crab Pots ,

- Fishing Rods to 1.5 metres (5 feet),

- Spare Anchor (chain is aft due to its weight),

- Deck Chairs,

- Two roll-up canoes,

- Spare 200 litre water tank, &

- Even space for the dingy outboard motor.

This space was drawn from the two rooms either side. Our design has a huge beam with two over-king-size beds side by side.

*...another item we are
very glad we installed...*

It's this space that we have utilised to build a 1m x 2.2m x 1m (high) locker.

The beds now became queen-sized and still have 200mm to spare in the room cavities.

----- : -----

The locker has been glassed with a re-enforced aft slanting floor.

There is a 20mm drop aft with two water outlets that vent below the bridge deck. It is designed to take a fair bit of weight (spare battery in mind). The locker is a 'wet locker' and any rain or spilt water simply drains overboard.

Another great use for this locker is the vents that we have installed.

When it's raining, we can open this external locker door, and then the internal sidewall 'ventilation ports'. This allows air to flow through the whole yacht while venting rainwater overboard via the drains.

This inclusion has been worth its weight in gold.

----- : -----

The fore-beam construction took about five days. It utilised some solid blocks of timber, which we constructed from off cuts of ply, glued and screwed to form solid sections.

Together with a solid middle section they formed the backbone of the build.

Onto this we glued the other sections finally forming a very strong 6m fore-beam.

We took up the option of rounding the forward part of the beam and decided to place an internal electrical pipe for later use with spotlights. Final sanding and glassing were left to closer to the completion date.

----- : -----

Bow Locker access through
to winch section

Bow Lockers covered and
painted internally

Main Forward Locker

Forward Locker hatch and drain channel

Bow Locker covered. This is taken later during the build and
shows a better perspective.

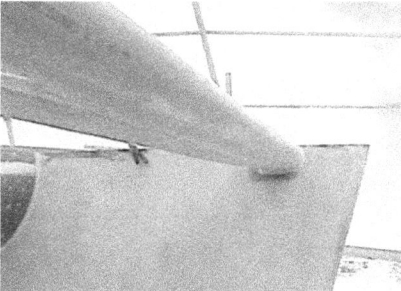

Fore Beam from below.
There are alternatives with
the use of aluminium, which
saves a lot of time and will
be lighter.

Fore Beam was a clever use of
the plywood off-cuts,
extremely strong and rock
solid. This section really turns
up a treat after painting.

Pointers:

1. Clever use of space can be very effective.

2. Have a plan of where you intend to stow large items (i.e. Crab pots)

3. Thought of where your batteries are going to go yet? They are very heavy.

4. Start planning access ports for electrical cables.

5. Start to watch your centre-of-gravity. Not sure about this? Talk to your Designer.

Traps:

1. Re-inventing the wheel.

2. Not ensuring ALL components are resined inside and out.

3. Planning using space effectively without considering centre-of-gravity.

Chapter Eight:
Saloon and Hull Make-up

In our case both hulls are basically divided into three internal areas:

- Forward section (being forward of the Main Room Frame - the frame that divides our main bedrooms from the saloon area).
- Middle section (being between Main Room Frame and Main Door Frame).
- Aft section (being rear of Main Door Frame).

Given the internal space of the Easy 11.6, a decision was made to include a separate vanity area adjoining the shower and toilet .

The middle section carried stairs from the port hull to the saloon and 'electrical panel' area.

These next paragraphs can be followed on a **Layout Drawing** (in this chapter).

The port forward section contains a full queen size bed, running fore/aft. The inner side of the bed has an adjacent two level coffee/book table. The lower part of this table contains a small locker.

This bed area in most vessels is prone to much mildew due to the warm humid environment and lack of circulation.

To try and reduce this we have chosen to install timber slats providing ventilation below the mattress at all times.

Additionally there is an overhead opening hatch and an access hole to one of the front Bow Lockers and the Main Forward Locker.

These access holes have been carefully planned to provide

airflow during wet weather conditions. Slightly opening the *Main Forward Locker Door* and/or the *Bow Locker Doors*, allows airflow while any rain or moisture will be drained forward, venting overboard.

At the forward section of the port hull walkway is a full-length single bed.

There are very large lockers below the forward part of this bed, the rear part being removable for extra space when required. This single bed also provides access to one of the bow lockers, providing copious amounts of storage up forward.

...Easy access equates to an easy life...

Down the walkway below hip-height are additional storage lockers along both sides.

The port middle section is broken into cupboard/locker and set of stairs on the inner wall of the hull and a tall yet shallow cabinet on the starboard side of the hull.

The latter being the backside of the keyboard in the main saloon area and also one of our electrical cupboards. One of the storage spaces here too is capable of storing any items long and thin (i.e. brooms, pipes, tubing etc.).

The port aft section allows for a vanity area giving a little extra privacy for our soon to be teenagers as well as friends.

This will also serve as an area to hang towels to dry when not in use, something seldom thought of until it's too late.

The rear of the vanity unit extends into the saloon. It is here that we have continued the vanity wall (while a little lower) into the saloon area to form a cupboard where our stand-up fridge is stationed.

Conveniently, on top of the fridge is a chart table and chart stowage area.

Moving further aft of the vanity area is a shower and an electric toilet with waste system out of sight behind the toilet.

Many have told us of their experiences with electric shower bilge units and 'hair'. As our daughter has very long hair and James' continues to moult at an excessively high rate, it was thought more prudent to nip this in the bud at this early stage and plan for repair.

This sees all our water pumping units (fresh and salt-water) plus filters, stationed here below the vanity sink. Easy access equates to an easy life.

----- : -----

With the toilet, where does one start? The thoughts of smell, sewerage and blockages soon come to mind and no matter how many excuses you come up with, to stop you from maintaining The-Loo, the fact is that you are going to get your hands dirty some day.

Having got our heads around that fact, getting the least dirty became one of the major priorities during planning.

This meant some forethought in:
- Access-to-components, and
- Simple components that can be replaced.

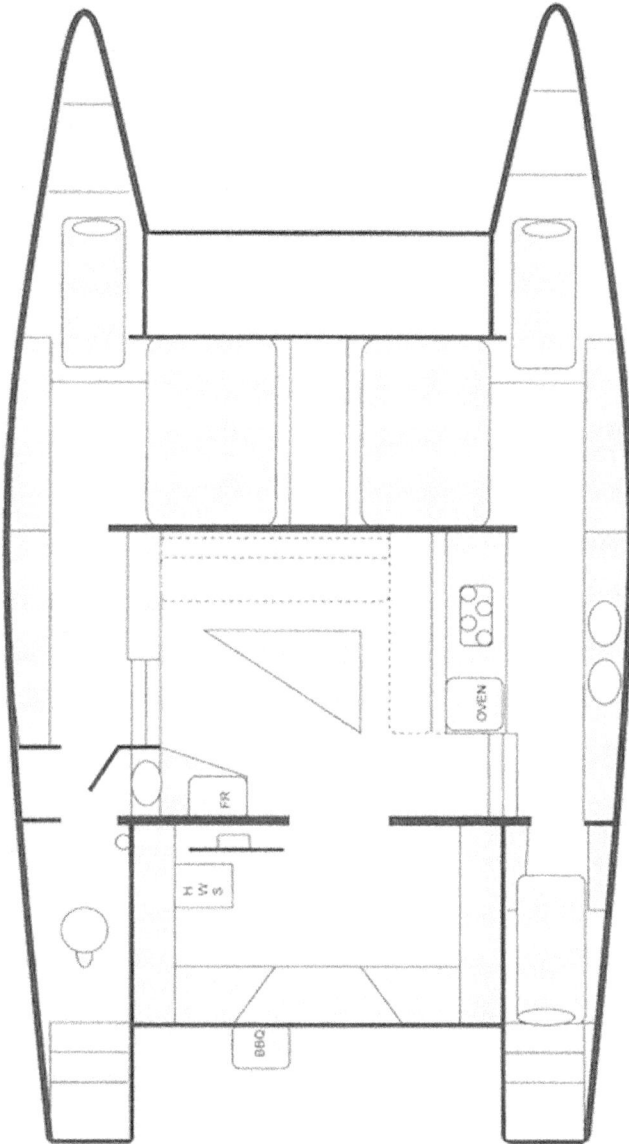

Layout Diagram
(Used as a starting point and made with 'Word ' - Draw)

Having lost the trusty Laser some months back in a hailstorm, it was into our new Camry (11 year old actually) for a drive to Peter and Anne Snell's house for a smelly chat on the toilet installation.

It was decided after some discussion that we order the top of the line toilet with electric flush and wide flared base with built-in macerator.

The thoughts here were simple, get the widest base. In the long run it will prove more secure when compared to the smaller base units and some of the stories floating around about them.

...thoughts of smell, sewerage and blockages soon come to mind...

Secondly, get it automated. In today's world, these systems have been well designed and improved and are now very reliable. For the extra few dollars, this also provides that little bit of extra padding.

The waste system consists of a 'Y' valve, a single ball valve, collapsible 50 litre holding tank and a 13mm breather hose.

We have chosen all plastic components, with the exception of the bronze 'below-waterline' skin fittings.

From the toilet, the waste piping is teed via the 'Y' valve. While not shown on the drawing a few pages on, piping is looped 600mm vertically up and down:
- Before entering the toilet inlet, and
- After the 'Y' valve to:
- The top of the holding tank, or
- Overboard.

Another pipe takes the waste from the lower part of the holding tank, via the ball valve, to the overboard outlet. This outlet sits just below the water line in the 'Antifouling area' making it less conspicuous and hiding staining.

We have chosen to place a single saltwater inlet for the toilet under the shower floor, where access is easy and other 'wet area' components are stationed.

The valve has been strategically positioned so that when closed, the handle faces up, forcing the 'Shower Drain Cover' to be dislodged.

While this may look unusual, it is a great reminder when returning to the yacht after an extended period, that the toilet has no inlet water flow.

From there, the saltwater goes through a valve. We have had tremendous trouble here, as no one seems to make a 'skin-fitting and 900 elbow' in bronze.

Many make them in plastic but not bronze. For this reason we went to stainless steel.

The inlet then splits two ways:
1. To the toilet, and
2. To the Deck Wash system.

The single inlet is our choice as we wished to reduce the openings through the hull. The piping here is 25mm to the toilet, increasing in size to 38mm from the toilet to the waste-tank/exit

In Port Hull - Aft looking forward

In Starboard Hull - Main forward room, looking aft past galley

We have chosen to use PVC pipe below the fixed floor area as we can't afford to pull this up in the event of a plastic pipe failure.

The only access here will be via the 'shower access door', a simple piece of resined ply.

Being below waterline, this section of the hull has been glassed as it's going to get wet from the shower waste and saltwater inlet maintenance.

It is also easy to keep clean and provides easy access for shower pump replacement.

-----:-----

...easy access for
shower pump replacement...

The starboard forward section is an exact duplicate of the port side with the exception of the following. This too can be followed on the previous **Layout Drawing**.

The starboard middle section contains our galley. Behind the saloon bench is the three-burner gas cook top, just far enough away from the forward bedroom to reduce cooking odours.

A gas oven is also in place here.

Adjacent to these on the outer hull wall are two galley sinks. We have chosen not to have hot water here, the theory being that this can be either heated via a kettle or obtained from the vanity, saving on an extra item that could present potential problems especially considering that the plumbing would have to be routed under a sealed floor area.

Instead, we use the Mixer Tap (Hot and Cold) for fresh water (filtered or unfiltered), available to both sinks.

This area is also heavily covered with cupboard space and today we still struggle to fill.

The starboard aft section has another wide single bed. Below the bed are two very large lockers and up one side is additional storage space. We have never used this space since launching.

There are copious amounts of locker space everywhere.

----- : -----

...with cupboard space
and today we still struggle
to fill...

The saloon area is huge. Given the musical prowess of the kids and our music interests, we have built in a keyboard.

The cabinet is stationed on the port side of the saloon seating. This has also been made to be used as a computer area if needed, with 12vDC power positioned here.

The keyboard sits atop the electrical cabinet.

Saloon seating then complements this area in an 'L-shape'. The backs of the seating have more locker space, while underneath we have re-enforced to take the weight of batteries (130 kilograms) and water bladders (350 litres).

The forward turret windows are large and open out and up, so to catch air and vent into the saloon. With the rear door and windows open, this ventilates the area extremely well.

As previously mentioned, we have the map table and fridge stationed in the saloon area too, above part of the vanity from the port hull.

The saloon table we have made removable, so that this space can be used for additional sleeping space. In hindsight, we would prefer a fixed unit as we have only used the area once for sleeping.

Our navigation and electronics (wiring and controllers) for sailing are stationed near the rear door. This space was chosen as it is away from the elements and prying eyes and is very easily accessible.

----- : -----

The hull floors are normally sealed in the Easy series yachts, however we have chosen to make access here for many reasons, one of which is to keep the wine cold.

...many reasons, one
of which is to keep
the wine cold...

The make-up is with well resined frames spaced to provide reasonably hard floor stomping without movement, The lower sections of the hulls were then glassed and lightly painted with any excess paint we had left over.

It is also at this stage that thought needs to be given to skin-fittings for any additional components, such as a Desalinator or securing point for the Depth transducer.

In our case, the transducer installation point is on the lower forward section of the port hull.

Here we chose to re-enforce the area, making sure that it was extremely well resined and that electrical cabling access was available right to the back where the instruments were to be attached.

Sounds easy until you realise that the thought of a depth gauge was not on the 'to-do' list just yet.

Remember, too, that these gauge electrical plugs have a large diameter, so access holes need to be made to suit.

We also chose to include 12vDC power points in various spots throughout the yacht. The cabling for these also runs through the floor area.

The 12vDC outlets are used for Emergency Bilge Pump use and Freezer (when required). There is more detail on this in the Electrical Section.

----- : -----

A Sailing Catamaran Building Project

Pointers:

1. Easy access required to water pumps.

2. Self drain gradients to bilge pump.

3. Install sewerage holding tank early.

4. Excess space in rooms is a waste.

5. Carefully balance storage/weight forward of centre-of-gravity, talk to Designer.

6. Insert 12vDC plugs throughout build.

7. Gas plumbing in some States cannot pass through a sleeping area.

Traps:

1. Lack of planning of pre-install electrical.

2. Getting hung up and piping water everywhere - be practical.

3. Installing more than the vessel is planned to carry.

4. Filling the vessel with AC outlets.

Chapter Nine:
Mooring or 'in a Pen'

While the excitement grew with each stage coming together, one thing still presented a challenge. Having this beautiful yacht presented a new set of challenges.

Were we to moor the yacht or keep it on a berth?

Historically, up the west coast of Australia, the building of large vessels that required berthing was outstripping the growth of the marina berth market. Fewer and fewer berths were being approved by the authorities and along with that was the increased regulation governing the requirements of owning a berth.

Large developers such as the group who developed the 'Raby Bay Marina Precinct' south of Brisbane or the Mackay Marina (west north coast of Australia) got wind of this looming struggle 10 years earlier, broke into this market and have never looked back.

...it HAD to be within 30 minutes of our place of residence...

In January 2003, we sought to purchase five such berths as an investment, mainly for supposed capital growth.

At that time an 11m berth was retailing at AUD $34,000 and returning a net income of AUD $3,600 per annum. Not brilliant however also not too shabby considering the share market at that time was delivering similar returns

As is happened, our funds did not mature earlier enough to go ahead with the purchase.

Added to this was the consideration that if a loan was taken to support the purchase, lending institutions were not going to allow one to borrow against this 'marina berth investment' for future investments, say in property or shares.

This did present a dilemma for us.

In May 2005 (some 16 months later), we again revisited the marina berth investment strategy and were astounded to find that while the net return had only gained a few points, the same berths were now retailing at AUD $51,000.

This only strengthened our concerns that the market would soon be out of our reach if we were to go this way.

...again, the EASY connections came in very handy...

In earnest, we had to look at all other avenues and weigh up the pros and cons.

Three options came to mind. Some of the reasons behind the marina berth option were that fresh water was always available, making a Desalinator not necessary (saving AUD $14,000) and even reducing boat weight by having to carry less water, say back to 200 litres as opposed to the 500lts, which we were considering.

Electricity was also readily available saving the batteries and therefore power generation for those batteries.

Lastly, was security of the boat itself. While this could not be guaranteed in a Marina, it would definitely be much better than on a mooring in a river.

A second choice was a 'hard stand option' where the yacht would be towed out of the water after each use and towed to a hardstand area.

With a vessel of this size, we were very limited to where this could be done. Additional costs would be for the hardstand area itself and then for each movement in and out of the water.

One could argue that the hardstand costs weighed against the annual antifouling costs could end up being cost neutral. Three or four days forward planning would also be required to give notice to the hard-stand operator.

This presented certain limitations on use and the idea of just 'popping out for a night or two' at short notice, made it impractical.

The last option was our own mooring which is the avenue we chose initially.

This would allow us the freedom of coming and going when we wished and be a cheap alternative.

Our plan of attack included:
1. That it HAD to be within 30 minutes of our place of residence. Any further away it was thought that it would became a grind to pop on the water for a few hours.

2. That it needed to be in the vicinity of other moored boats of similar size.

This meant that access to the

mooring at low tide would normally be fine and that others with similar interests would unconsciously 'keep an eye on our boat' when not in use, as we would do for them if we were there. Caboolture River (close to the small town of Beachmere, north Brisbane) became our target area.

...other cats to the right with mangroves in the background, a beautiful spot as the sun goes down...

It took us 15-20 minutes to drive there, had a fuel station within the Beachmere Township as well as grocery store for all the little bits that one forgets. There is a very good public ramp with easy vehicle access where one could park their car whilst away.

With this attack in mind, it was into the car again and up to the Designers place for advice on our thoughts (the importance of a good rapport and relationship again reaps reward).

He had just recently set his own mooring in this area which gave us comfort knowing that if an experienced yachty had his own 12m yacht there, we may be onto a good thing.

----- : -----

Again, Peter and Anne gave us all the information, plus more, and the decision was made.

Added to this mooring position was the advantage of another 'private jetty/launching ramp' in close proximity to the public ramp.

For a small fee, the owner provided a courtesy tinnie to get to and from one's yacht, allowed use of the facilities (which included a Barbeque area, drinks etc.), vehicle security on those nights away and fresh water from his small jetty.

We could not go wrong. The only thing standing in our way now was mooring approval.

...it's the chain together with the concrete weight that provides the security of the mooring...

The local Maritime Authority was contacted and within two weeks all the paperwork was being assessed. One of the questions was the exact location (GPS coordinates) of the proposed mooring site.

We left this to the authority and to our amazement, we were charted a position 100m from the private ramp.

In fact, sitting at the very small but quaint rustic looking 'Fishermen's Club house' (appropriately located within the private ramp area) you look directly at Pure Majek to the left and other cats to the right with mangroves in the background, a beautiful spot as the sun goes down.

The approval took four months and in that period a second approval had to be sought from the Marine and Wildlife Authority before any mooring could be placed.

To our amazement, all paperwork was approved by March 2006 and we were given 30 days within which to 'stake our claim', with a buoy of some sort, or lose it.

This fired up the kids as at long last they could do something different relating to the yacht. Their time helping at the yacht had understandably waned as in their eyes, there was no visual progress.

Having never set a mooring before, the challenge was definitely different.

James' father, being a master with numbers, was canvassed for his thoughts on the mooring set-up with regards to the block required to secure the mooring.

While he charted specific gravity of concrete and fiddled with cubic feet, we nodded. The outcome was 3 blocks of concrete (570 x 570 x 570cm each) providing roughly one tonne of weight at the base.

As the yacht's weight was 4.7 tonne, this together with the chain set-up was planned to be sufficient.

To this were fastened 7m of 8mm short link chain.

For the uninitiated, it's the chain together with the concrete weight that provides the security of the mooring. As the maximum water depth at high tide in this area only provided 3m in height above the sea floor, the remainder of the short link chain would lie flat on the bottom, increasing the drag and improving the 'holding force' of the mooring.

The issue we had was at low tide where the water depth could get down to 0.1m, in other words there would be occasions where our yacht would 'ground'.

While we have no issue with the yacht grounding here because of the very soft mud, we do have a challenge with the yacht accidentally grounding on our three mooring concrete blocks.

Thoughts of arriving to see the yacht 'holed', made sure of that.

The base of the mooring had to be changed and an idea of using a truck or grader tyre filled with concrete had merit. It is almost impossible for a truck tyre to disintegrate in salt water while providing a cushioning around the concrete base.

As we were going to so much trouble to build this base, ease of changing the attachments and chain drove the casting design.

----- : -----

On the Internet while searching through a hurricane site, we located a section that discussed the issues of moorings verses hurricanes.

While this would be highly unlikely in our area, the statistics and make-up of their mooring systems were interesting.

It involved a 2 metre length of 30mm galvanised round steel, with an eye at one end and a horizontal spade at the other (allowing the unit to be screwed into the ground when turned).

This was then screwed into the ground and attached with very

heavy chain. It was tested by a ships tug for strength and at 20,000lb force, the chain gave way, the spike did not move and this was good enough for us, although on a much smaller scale.

...at no time of the tide is the vessel allowed to bottom...

We took a ride out to our mooring position at low tide to assess the length of steel that we would need.

The ground was reasonably soft, but hardened at around one metre.

While passing a scrap metal yard, we popped in and located all the goodies to produce our own spike (in stainless steel too) all for AUD $85.

The spike was 25mm stainless steel with a horizontal spade diameter of 280mm. This was welded to the pole, 250mm from the lower end. With the remaining spike steel, my brother-in-law welded an eyepiece and 2 hours later, the spike was ready to go.

Late 2008 (around launch time), we found a quirky little paragraph inserted on the mooring renewal form, which read "...at no time of the tide is the vessel allowed to bottom...".

This now presented a real challenge as we had planned for our yacht to bottom. After a few phone calls it was decided to let sleeping dogs lie.

We were caught between a 'rock and a hard place'. If we squealed, we would raise a red flag at this mooring area and other catamarans would be affected too.

To add to this, in late February

2009, the Maritime Authority approached us seeking our interest in a trial of a new mooring system.

The trial would be with a screw type anchor, very similar to the one we had already made. This trial was free and after two years would be available to us, if we chose to keep it.

While we took up the offer, it did not eventuate.

----- : -----

In 2010, the Authorities pointed us to a change in policy, where *'no vessel was allowed to bottom'*. This threw a spanner in the works and in the process of deciding what to do, finally succumbing to a Marina.

The convenience and more importantly, our commitments to employment, have made this option a must.

We now park the yacht, clean and top-up fuel and water, then leave in 50 minutes.

When we next go away, it takes fifteen minutes and we are underway.

----- : -----

Chapter Ten:
Steering and Cockpit Build - Part 2 of 2

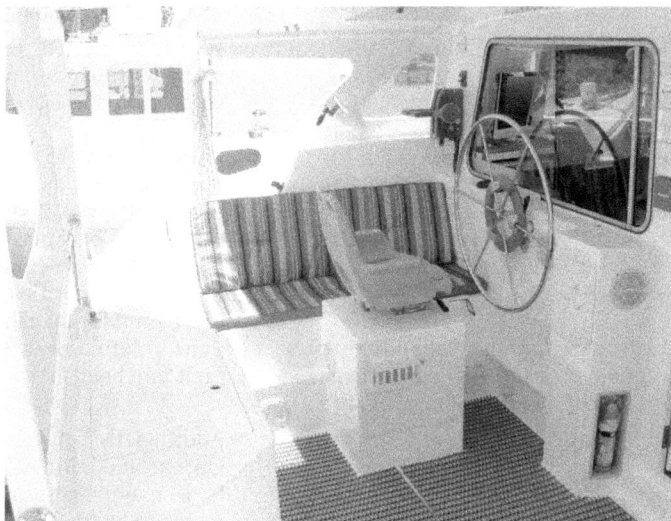

At the same time as building the Steering, we also had intentions of modifying the rear bench seat slightly, so as to include a larger less intrusive step used to step down to the cockpit area.

This was a result from feedback of our family asking for this larger step for stepping into the cockpit.

This also had to be cleared with Peter as the rear bench seat on the plans forms part of the structure preventing a twisting movement of the frame.

Access had to be simple with large stairs that were slip resistant when wet.

Against The Aft Frame, the seating/bench area has been modified to include large step-

down stairs to the cockpit (one either side) and a raised table area in the middle.

The table was a new idea for us, which was included as a result of feedback from two yachters.

Understanding that storage space is normally at a premium on boats, we had plenty and a small loss in this area for improved lifestyle additions, was worth it.

The table was to have large doors and has been designed to take a large esky, with some spare space. Got to get the priorities right.

As the yacht has outboard motors as opposed to inbuilt diesel engines, provision had to be made at this stage of building for their inclusion.

They are located both port and starboard under the seats.

Our intentions were to place an outdoor barbeque/oven behind and to one side of the table (bolted to the aft of the Aft Frame).

A dream at a later stage is to include a generator, which would be placed under the table with the esky. When needed, a rear flap door could be opened, the generator started and front doors closed, providing easy access and ease of use.

This was on the wish list and never eventuated and has since been moved to the Main Forward Locker.

...harder to get gas units approved internally due to the ventilation factor...

Late in December 2005, we made contact with a gas plumber who came and cast his eyes over our 'belle'.

We had already given him a heads up on our thoughts of what we wanted and where and diplomatically chose our words in asking him for his ideas (little did he know that we already had the appliances and they were going in).

We were very keen to get the gas (in particular) all 'ridgy-didge' as the sign-off of approved appliances and installation was required at some stage prior to launch for Insurance and Registration purposes.

We did not want to be running around undoing all our hard work at the last minute.

What has this to do with the cockpit? Well our gas hot water unit will be placed in the cockpit area under the helm seat.

We have chosen to do this for many reasons, the main one being ventilation of the appliance.

It is becoming increasingly harder to get gas units approved internally due to the ventilation factor and this then becomes an 'internal placement problem' as they (the local Gas Authorities) are clamping down on internal exhausting of the units, often not approving units built into boat shower/toilet areas.

Additionally, given our very hot Queensland climate, temperature is a major factor and the unit stores 12 litres of hot water.

While the unit is insulated, it still releases warm air into the surrounding area, thus reheating an already warm boat, something we are planning hard against during the build stage.

Other reasons include very easy access for maintenance and gas leaks remain external.

The gas plumber had promised to do the initial piping installation this month (January 2006), which meant that the helm seat needed to be built and glued in place before he arrived, thus the haste and change in build direction.

Before this could be done, the engine pods needed completing to the pre-glassing stage and fuel storage areas completed.

Cockpit table and storage

Cockpit table completed

Helm station build

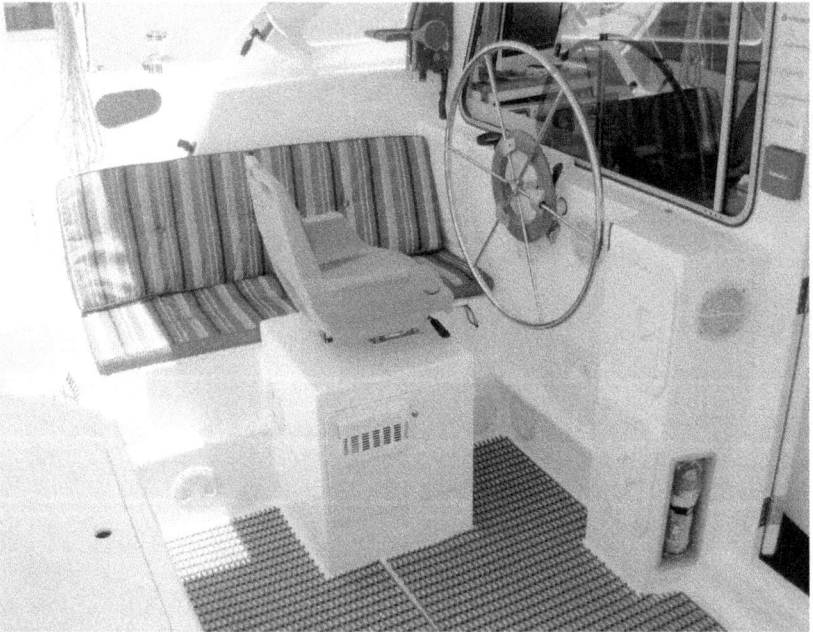

Helm and Gas Hot Water

The plumber needed to see this to guarantee the required 300-500mm clearance between gas and liquefied fuels and ensure separate ventilation ports, part of the Gas Installation requirements. Gas, being heavier than air, sinks. This brings it into conflict with any fuel spills.

At 06:30 one Tuesday morning (extremely early for yours truly by the way), this project began.

We had earlier discussed the issues of an extended roof going to the full aft of the boat, which was now going to happen.

...make decisions that we knew we later had to live with..

This presented yet another 'challenge' as the stair entry to the cockpit had to be modified as everyone would be belting their heads on the way in.

Without this change being built now, we could not attempt the rest of the engine pod and fuel storage area.

As the helm station is not part of the plan, much time has been wasted in advanced planning the helm set-up.

We have also managed to get a pair of 1" heavy-duty stainless steel kitchen conveyor bearings for the steering wheel.

The plan is to have an easily accessible steering system in the event of component failure. To do this, we have chosen parts that are readily available and can be changed with ease, even in rough seas.

A 250mm x 80mm casing runs along the floor/engine pod walls. Within the casing are a gas pipe (for the hot water heater and external BBQ) and steering cables.

All of these items, especially the steering cables have been installed with a few things in mind, safe, simple and dry changeover and/or repair access. Access to the Hot Water System will be from the side.

One build challenge lead into the next and we did 'bite the bullet', and make decisions that we knew we later had to live with, thankfully it all worked well.

----- : -----

A Sailing Catamaran Building Project

Pointers:

1. Hot Water system is fully external.

2. Helm wheel can be steered through the roof as well as inside the cockpit.

3. Engine controls are at hand when standing or sitting. Most important coming into a pen.

4. *'Standing steering position'* built for the shortest crewmember.

5. Second anchor winch switch situated at helm.

6. Chart plotter can be viewed from any position in the cockpit.

7. Sail instruments are large and can be viewed from any cockpit or step position.

8. Turret has a hatch.

9. Fast self-draining cockpit floor.

Traps:

1. Lack of solid sun cover externally.

Chapter Eleven:
Painting – Interior

This topic has been well mulled over by the Pure Majek's builders.

Having had the unfortunate task of painting all our homes we have lived in, some of them twice, we put a lot of thought into how we would tackle this task.

On speaking with the designer, it was suggested to use a 'high-build' marine undercoat.

Cutting to the chase, this paint assists in hiding some of those imperfections that one tends to make in the process of building.

If it can't hide the imperfection, the last option is 'fairing', then repeat the process.

Being part-time builders, much of the timber is left to age well in our humid environment prior to painting. This presents another issue with raw timber in that timber discolouring occurs around areas where there is no resin.

While much of this discolouration can be sanded off prior to painting, some resort to using bleach to bring up better colour and kill any organisms that may be promoting the discolouration.

Our belief is that if there are any remaining organisms after sanding, they will get the same chemical treatment that human lungs/skin get from the same paint.

The 'high-build' undercoat is sprayed on with a large nozzle (around 2.5mm - 3mm), anything smaller tends to be further thinned prior to spraying.

They (the Wattyl paint technical advisors) are fairly particular with the thinners used too, as a stronger type is required with the resin based paints, a small blow as this now has doubled the thinners cost.

The spray gun we used was a 'gravity-feed' unit. The reason here was twofold (again the tip coming from Peter):

> The less working parts make cleaning a lot easier, and

> There is very little paint waste, as the paint self drains to the lowest point.

For those who don't mind the heavy duty 'thinners' all over their hands, disregard the above.

----- : -----

Our next challenge lay with the compressor. We chose a 24Lt - 2.25hp AUD100.00 unit at initial start-up of the build and it has proved very helpful. However, this unit does not have the grunt for the continual use of the spray gun.

The resolve was:

1. To purchase a 50Lt unit 15CFM+ for around AUD600.00, or

2. Find a separate cylinder that could be added to the current unit to provide additional capacity, or lastly

3. To purchase a second AUD100.00 compressor and join the two in parallel (this is the road we chose).

This provided us a 50Lt capacity with 5hp engines for AUD240.00, including AUD40.00 for all the joining bits and a water separator, saving around AUD360.00.

Well, we managed to get all the protective clothing reasonably cheaply, but the mask was an issue.

...remaining organisms after sanding, they will get the same chemical treatment that human lungs/skin get ...

All the paint companies we spoke to recommended 'positive pressure face masks', and the dollars ticked away (about AUD1500.00 for the set-up including connections to the compressor). This brought this idea initially to a quick stop and we resorted to the dual filter chemical respirator.

The initial undercoat took four full days to apply, which completed 95% of the internal fittings and what a magical difference.

All of a sudden the small imperfections had mysteriously gone and the white undercoat had done two things:

- Made the boat look larger internally, and
- Definitely lightened up the darker areas.

The undercoat was laid on thickly too (using the 2.8mm spray nozzle). The advantage with this was that all the blemishes were covered and small timber indentations / marks would be covered and when sanded back should come out reasonably smooth, which it did.

The disadvantage is the cost due to

the increased amount of undercoat. We have chosen to sand this initial coat back to a smooth surface (using 120 grit paper) even if it meant coming back to the timber in places. This did take a very long time, in fact four days longer than planned and we are not after a car gloss finish either.

The loss of these four days did highlight a few things if and when there is another boat build.

We will certainly use BB grade pine plywood (as recommended by the Designer) as opposed to meranti plywood (used in some spots on this boat as a cheaper fill-in plywood).

...you had to turn your head onto a side, which he forgot in his haste...

The meranti (for us anyway) required more work to fill little surface cracks during the undercoat stage, which took half to one day's work, plus all the additional painting and sanding.

All in all, a negative for us as we wanted everything done yesterday and only once too.

----- : -----

The internal cupboard faces were sanded back soon after painting and any touch-ups were re-undercoated. The final coat was then sprayed on prior to final assembly. Once dry, all bits were joined and the cupboards fully installed and glued.

One lesson we have learnt is to ensure that any excess resin / glue is very carefully removed and not 'finger-wiped' into the corners.

We thought this would add to the cupboard strength (which it does), but once dry leaves a rough corner finish over one's newly painted surfaces.

This then became a haven for the odd large spider, so a decision was made to cover all cupboard access holes with paper to reduce the dust and bug infestation.

A spider (4" in diameter) was found one morning by yours truly who had poked his head into one of the cupboard access holes to admire his handy-work, only to be met by this monster.

The only snag was that to get ones head out of the cupboard access hole you had to turn your head onto a side, which he forgot in his haste.

This resulted in an embarrassing bleeding forehead, chin and ear, fast heart rate and a rush for the 'Bug Spray'.

Cleaning the little red drip marks all the way out to the shed and back came second to finding the spray.

Next thought was 'bug spray on the newly painted surface....

"What chemical reaction could there be? "

"Do I or don't I?"........I didn't'.

----- : -----

Does not look like much...but a huge morale booster at this stage.

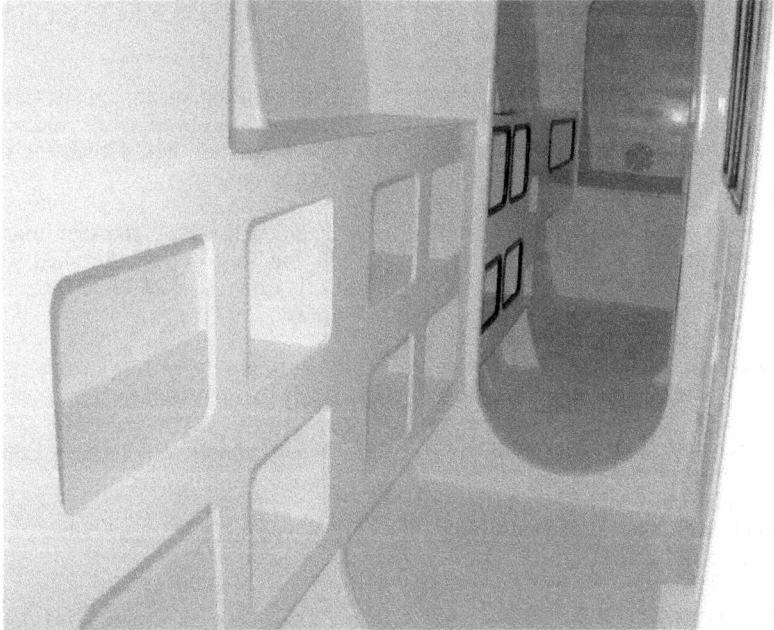

Testing 'trim' on the newly painted surfaces

After a few minutes, the spider came out from sheer fright we think and made a dash for it only to be met by my shoe.

Anyway, covering the access holes did work well and resulted in less vacuuming and sore heads.

It was some time after the completion of the cupboards that we returned to the painting scene. The reasons were many, starting with little items not being completed (i.e. access hatches, underfloor plumbing, vanity cupboard etc.).

Added to this was the requirement for the gas plumber to do his bit. They tend to make a mess and repainting unnecessarily is not our intention.

We also had to start making decisions on equipment that we were going to use internally and purchase those items to ensure they fit(remembering that this was our first boat and lack of experience shone through, compared to those who have 'been there and done that').

This included the fridge, gas oven, stove and hot water system.

As the Main Door Frame window cut-outs had to be ready for painting too, the frames were cut to size and bogged.

The type of window we bought was purchased with an internal aluminium frame as well as the external fitting frame. This did make less work in the long run and allowed for very quick installation when that time came. See the section 'Turret Windows' if you want more information on our windows.

The last two days were spent trying to ensure that little holes had been bogged and all the cupboard access holes covered to prevent any over-spray did not damage the completed cupboard interiors.

This, too, took its toll time-wise. Have you ever tried to cover a hole from the front where all taping must be on the inside of the cupboard wall? Think about it...its very tricky and we are yet to find a simple solution.

Anyway, they were all covered and ready for painting.

The second undercoat was then sprayed and went on in one afternoon, much to everyone's amazement. Two days later, it was back to the sanding and this time using 180grit paper. At long last, we were nearly ready for the topcoat.

----- : -----

...breathing the 'isocynate paint concoction'...

The choice of final coat has been rather controversial. Our preference has been to use a two-pack coat both internally and externally because of it's hard wearing attributes.

However, the chemicals used in two-pack have some rather interesting side effects, worse case being inhalation of the fumes causing loss of consciousness.

Coming in contact with the skin, the paint has carcinogenic qualities. All good stuff for mid-forty spring chickens like ourselves. The resolve was to purchase correct masks and wear protective clothing.

Wanting to use the gravity-feed spray gun presented some more issues. We had to find a finer nozzle (1.5mm - 2mm) to get the finer finishing coat..

Back to 'discount trade tools' people, we were told that it would be cheaper to buy a whole new unit than the three bits required to change the current gun to the smaller nozzle.

During all the sanding and undercoating periods, we were always faced with the removal of dust problem. How does one ensure the removal of all the dust, so it was onto the phone again to Peter Snell.

...was to us a waste of valuable time and effort...

The resolve was to vacuum as much as possible, then using a few cloths well soaked in cheap Thinners (or Methylated spirits) wipe down all surfaces to be painted.

It did come up squeaky clean but took half a day. It wasn't until the following day when we tried to re-use the previous days cloths (now dry), that you realised the amount of dust left by the vacuum cleaner.

A quick surface rewipe and the second undercoat went on in one day (much to our surprise).

It was also the first day using a full-on Respirator system. The decision was made to spend more cash and buy a full-face mask with separate filter, quality throwaway overalls and decent gloves that come up to your elbows.

We could not find reason to reduce ones life by possibly breathing the 'isocynate paint concoction' and it has been money well spent. We chose a full-face mask that has a replaceable front viewing section so as to be able to continually have clear vision.

We were unable to find a mask that had a lens that could be wiped clean without the thinners damaging the plastic. To this we stretched over some gladwrap and it worked a treat.

Because of the airflow required (2psi - 5psi constant flow) the respirator had to operate off a second compressor and it provided a very cool fresh airflow over your face. Quiet a relief on the hot day making an unpleasant job a little cooler.

The respirator unit took a little getting used too, but we now would not have it any other way. This day we sprayed 8 litres of undercoat and 2 litres of topcoat and went home with no ill breathing effects, worth every cent.

While not as smooth and a little rough in patches, it was to be 'final-coat-day' for the forward hull lockers and bow-lockers too.

The work here in these lockers was nearing completion. All that had to be done with the lockers was the winch-cut-out and glassing/painting of the hatch tops and doors.

Finally, light at the end of the tunnel. While only a small achievement, there was an extra skip in our step this day.

Trying to get a perfectly dead smooth surface on areas where it would normally not be seen, was to us a waste of valuable time and effort.

For this reason we looked at alternatives for painting these surfaces.

These 'waste-of-time' surfaces included the motor pod wells, underneath the lower bridge deck, the saloon ceiling and cockpit ceiling.

Refer to '**Painting - Exterior Undercoat**' for more information on this alternative painting method.

----- ⦂ -----

A Sailing Catamaran Building Project

Pointers:

1. Get a helper.

2. Start early and 'Be Prepared' before you start.

3. Your helper should be familiar with keeping paint stirred & ready.

Traps:

1. Not sieving the paint prior to use.

2. Applying too much paint causing 'runs'.

3. 'Runs' take longer to clean up and respray than doing two coats initially.

Chapter Twelve:
Upper Bridge deck

At this stage of the build we must say that the painting was getting us 'bogged down'.

Having completed 90% of the internal painting, it was put aside till the deck and turret was on and that did put a step in our stride.

To preserve all our hard work in painting the internal, we taped plastic painters drop sheets to all the walls and bench tops which provided some sort of protection from glue spills, nail drops etc. and this worked very well, too.

Dusting off the book of plans, it was onto the timber shops for delivery of plywood and the good old hoop pine, enough to hopefully complete the project.

Only problem was that for the 'Turret', thinner plywood is required and my supplier was out until the end of the month (18 days away).

...planning holes for cables at this early stage...

We were very glad that we considered this at this stage and not the day before it was required, suppose we could have tried another supplier.

The first project was to cut the notches to take the fore aft deck timbers called 'Stringers'.

In one of those magic thought days, we had decided to pre-cut them prior to painting, and we are very glad we did.

No sawdust over the newly painted surfaces and no chance of accidental drops of the saw on these surfaces, too. Next was to install the bracing to support the deck floor in the main bedrooms.

While we had the paint out, we conveniently painted these pieces in the hope to reduce upside down painting after they were installed; this appears to have worked well too.

Following this came the trial and cutting of the stringer lengths to run fore / aft below the deck floor.

With the length of our yacht, the stringers were not long enough to run in a single piece from the fore to the aft, this meant more time scarfing.

We chose not to do this, but double up on stringers over the joint, then glue and screw. Yes, we knew the aesthetics of this type of join were not very pleasing to the eye, but it would be hidden at all times.

Above the forward single beds in each hull, we have chosen to re-enforce the roof/deck floor timber and in the process, provide easy fastening points for the false ceiling we intended putting in there.

Additionally, a quirky little storage area has also been built in and pre-painted prior to putting the deck on.

It was our original intention to use a lot of Velcro to hold many of our non-structural light panels on

(such as some of the ceiling panels), but this never eventuated.

The advantages are that it is cheap, requires no screwing and can be easily removed for maintenance.

It's now, too, that if any difficult electrical cabling had to be done, the holes needed to be drilled prior to the deck being glued. This opened another 'can-of-worms' so to speak.

"ELECTRICAL ?"

"We know nothing about electric's"

"Worse still - 12V. Is that AC or DC?".

While this topic had been deferred and deferred, it was time to take our heads out of the 'well-worn sand patch' and face reality.

- Where were the lights going to be going?

- Does one use Halogen, florescent or standard 12V bulbs?

- What's this LED stuff, apparently saving up to 90% on electrical light power?

----- : -----

"Hi Peter, its James again............" and we got the same cheerful response.

'How are you? Where are you up to now?'.

Settling the 'electrical nerves', he even praised 'our thoughts of planning holes for cables at this early stage'.

Being 'spoon-fed' does little to help ones-self. Show initiative and ask questions.

Upper bridge deck stringers in place

Positioning plywood for gluing and screwing

For the uninitiated, most of the electrical cabling in our particular design are held within the deck floor, quite a smart idea when you think of it.

One big lesson we take away at this stage is to always double the hole size for electrical cables.

This makes for easy (excuse the pun) access if required and allows the build of the boat to proceed reasonably quickly to an advanced stage prior to cabling.

All in all, there were 17 lights planned (excluding those external - except the two cockpit lights). This is covered in more detail in the 'Electrical' section.

...finances at this stage do not allow for this luxury...

It's not until almost complete that the pattern of one's hard work is shown.

----- : -----

We have chosen to include five 'Weaver windows' in our deck floor:
- One each in the main rooms having a 510mm x 510mm,

- A 300mm x 300mm galley window, forward opening as well, and

- Two 300mm x 300mm aft opening windows above the two forward single beds.

It's at this stage that the framework for these items is built in. Next on the list is the fitting of the deck panels.

All the preparation of the internal bits including the painting have all been done prior to the deck being glued in place, for a big reason. The internal space, while it looks large, is not so when one is trying to carry sheets of ply down the stairs with the deck screwed down.

The confined work area would test the patience of many and we are very happy that we chose to do all the fiddly bits first (including painting) before the deck went on.

The deck panel's fit rather well fore/aft, you would think the design was planned around the plywood sheet size.

----- : -----

We started on the forward port hull first then worked across to the starboard side.

A word of caution came a little too late for us. The hatch cut-outs would have been best left till the whole deck top was on to prevent an accidental step-back and premature thump into one of the double beds (with broken bones to-boot).

Apparently, the designer has experience and appropriate words to discourage the willing.

Then out of the blue...

"Dad, can I have this wall purple please, there's too much white", was the first request.

"Why is her room bigger than mine?" came soon after.

So while we pondered these requests, their ownership of a bit of space meant we were making positive psychological headway too.

Apart from the two panels that covered the forward single bed areas of each hull, all the panels were cut and predrilled, then given a coat of resin a day before gluing and screwing.

On one of the panels, we thought we could save time by just cutting and gluing.

...double the hole size for
electrical cables...

The time spent resining the under sides once the panels were on, was twice that, had it been done prior to gluing.

Also, we missed the stringers a few times during the screwing phase by not having the panel predrilled (this is clearly suggested on the plans, too, by the way, so call us silly - we know).

The two panels over each forward

single bed area were also not resined, so it was decided to resin these just prior to gluing.

The reason for this is that there is a very defined downward curve and pre-resined panels (that have dried) may not form a water resistant seal if bent. This was our theory anyway.

A few things left from this point of construction are the filling of the screw holes and painting of the corners, the latter being left to a later stage.

Additionally, the 'fairing' of the corners will be left until the cockpit is complete, when we will have a few solid days of 'fairing & sanding'.

Next on the 'to do' list, is the rope storage compartments adjacent to the deck winches.

----- : -----

Pointers:

1. Plan the days, cut and predrill, then resin all undersides prior to securing.

2. Secure within a day of resining underside.

3. Don't allow runs on newly painted work.

Traps:

1. Cutting hatch access ports too early, safety issues.

Chapter Thirteen:
The Turret and Davits

The turret turns out to be a little more than just the completion of the main structure of the yacht; it defines the final lines of the yacht and the aesthetic appeal of the final product.

The streamlined shape does in itself provide a challenge or two to the uninitiated such as ourselves. Twisting plywood both horizontally and vertically out of a single sheet cannot be done.

We found this in the cutting of the sides for the turret, arching over the deck and then also peeling inward from the top sections.

After some trial and error we ended up cutting a horizontal arc

out of the lower section, which made the whole lot much easier to work. Prior to this, some stringers were planed at 30 degrees to secure the lower face of the sides too (where it joins the deck), then glued and screwed in place,.

Once cut, all pieces fell into place relatively easily.

Next came the securing of the thinner ply sheets to form the underside of the turret roof.

Before this could be done, four lengths of raw garden edging (5m in length and 19mm x 200mm) were purchased to be used as the frame on which the turret would finally be built.

Starting the turret window build.

Sizing plywood for the turret roof

Turret just before solar cable installation.

Plinths are 10mm pieces of ply, cut to size with a 10mm overlap and routed around the external edge.

These lengths were all cut at the same arc as the top of Main Door Frame, to form the final arc of the turret roof. These were then braced in place by strong pieces of vertical timber to the lower bridge deck.

Having four frames now in place allowed for the construction to start.

----- : -----

The intention with our construction was to extend the turret roof to the rear of the yacht to provide for additional shelter.

Re-enforcing some of the turret stringers with 68mm x 19mm, provided additional support. Two solid 68mm x 42mm sections of timber were glued and screwed vertically against the Aft Frame.

As will be seen later, the strength here would be twofold, being also used in strengthening the davits (the arms that secure the dingy above the water at the rear of the boat) and providing strength for the extended turret roof.

----- : -----

A serious approach had now to be taken toward our electrical requirements, because the wiring (as well as the base for securing of the solar panels) had to be installed before the turret top could be completed.

- How many panels?
- How many Watts per panel?
- What sort of 'Smart Charger' would we buy?
- What is a 'Smart Charger', and

- Where does it have to go?

The questions went on and on and the more we investigated and tried to understand, the more complicated it got.

A line had to be drawn in the sand as to the complexity of the system required and this was difficult, after all we are trying to maintain the 'KISS' formula discussed in the 'Electrical' section.

----- : -----

Regarding the davits, the plan was to have them stationed in a position to carry the dingy high above water level.

...additional free insurance as we see it...

The lowest level should allow full water flow up to the lower bridge deck floor. In other words if a wave washes the lower bridge deck, it should not hit the dingy. This is the starting point for the build. The next question was 'what dingy?'

Here we checked various brands and took an average in dimensions. From this, an idea for the retrieval rope/pulleys system was hatched and the height of the davits calculated.

Davits can be purchased or in our case, made from timber. The trick is to keep them light. This must be achieved as they act as an arm aft of the centre-of-gravity.

The purchased units are normally stainless steel and are bolted straight onto the aft frame.

Like father...

...like son.

Turret window lips. Important in preventing water ingress

Finishing inside the turret

The designer should provide some great simple ideas here.

----- : -----

They are used to place under deck fittings (normally on the horizontal), and their primary function is to reduce water ingress around the screw and bolt points.

The water run-off being forced to move away from the fitting and sit elsewhere.

While this may appear a little eccentric, for those who are not in a real hurry, these can prove very useful and remove the possibility of repairs at a later stage, additional free insurance as we see it.

...photos taken earlier during the turret construction, came in very handy...

This, too, unravelled its own set of questions:
* How many stanchions per side?

* Where will the water inlet be laid?

* On the lockers, which side do we lay the hinges and why?

* Where will the winches go?

The latter being tricky, as the turret hatch we have installed will directly affect the number of winches on that side.

Where were the tracks to be laid? Here we followed the plans being careful not to pierce the turret sections that carry the pre-laid electrical cables.

This is where the photos taken earlier during the turret construction, came in very handy. Having made this decision, it was not until we got started making these plinths that we realised how many there were.

* Locker/turret hatch hinges (two per hinge - twelve in total),

* Under the cleats (three per side - six all up),

* Under the mast electrical connection (one),

* Water filler neck (one),

* Stanchions (eight),

* Winches (five),

* Tracks (three),

* Turning blocks (four),

* Deck hatches (five),

* GPS (one) etc.

* Turret Hatch Hinges (two),

* Rear Swimming Stairs (two), and

* Winch Roller System.

Much of the information about this build is on the Puremajek.com website, so we won't double up on the writing.

----- : -----

Pointers:

1. Our plinths were placed once external fairing was complete.

2. An electrical plan idea should be starting to take shape.

3. Take photos with markers prior to sealing any cavity, to ensure accurate drilling/cutting (if required for power cables etc.) at a later date.

Traps:

1. Plinths are not mandatory.

2. Resin all timber inside and out.

3. Not making the davits high enough.

Davit construction (mid photos), Plinths (lower photos).

Chapter Fourteen:
Glassing and Fairing

This was an area in which we had very little experience. Laying 6 metres by 11 metres of fibreglass in a few hours was a little daunting.

In hindsight, preparation here is extremely important. One needs all the implements, resins, thinners, towels (and most importantly) other helpers, ready in advance.

The whole of the upper bridge deck was lightly sanded and cleaned for this stage.

We had 6 buckets at the ready for the mixing of the resin and had been given a heads-up about using a large 'broom-type' squeegee.

We had one person looking after the resin mixing, one person on the squeegee and a third as a helper with the laying of the glass. The period for the laying had to be planned over a full week in forecast fine conditions.

First day for laying of the fibreglass, days two and three for the fairing and days after that for the sanding.

It is strongly encouraged that the fairing compound be spread as soon as practicably possible after the resin on the glass has set.

There is a chemical reaction that continues for up to seven days after laying and doing the fairing at this early stage allows these layers to react and form a firm bond while curing.

To save on effort, sanding should be done with 1-3 days of laying and not left to a later period.

The fairing compound dries rock-hard and it's a real pain with twice as much effort required for the same sanding finish.

It is important that the fibreglass be laid as flat as possible to minimize fairing and sanding later.

This is where peel-ply may have come in very handy.

It is laid over the glassed surface and flattens any bumps or burrs, almost eliminating sanding later. It is something we would seriously consider next time.

*...preparation here is
extremely important...*

The sheets of fibreglass were first cut to fit the surface, then using the squeegee, resin is poured over the bridge deck and smoothed out.

We rolled the cut pieces of cloth onto a broom handle and slowly unrolled this over the wet resined surface. Pouring more resin over the top of that, it was left to cure.

The following day we lightly sanded any burrs and got muscles warmed up for the fairing.

The fairing mixture was mixed to

toothpaste consistency and then troweled on as smooth as possible. We soon learnt that you can't waste time doing this, the resin starts to cure and soon 'lumps' if played with too much.

The following day the sanding started. We tried every conceivable option to speed up the sanding, but there is no fast way.

The standard elbow grease and long-boards are the only way using the spray-paint or acetone-black techniques. We also did use a compressor sanding board but found it quicker with long- boards.

A long-board is one metre in length and made from 12mm plywood. We screwed some handles to this to make holding easier.

Sandpaper is purchased in a 50-metre roll and the width of the long-board is then cut to fit inside the sandpaper width.

Sandpaper is cut to the 1 metre length, with tab ends. The tab ends are then folded over and screwed to secure.

While they showed the blemishes more easily, it was good old hard work that did the job.

They say the finish here is important as the high build will remove smaller indentations, but not the larger ones, of which we had a few.

----- : -----

Preparing to lay the fibreglass

Glass - day after being laid.

Fairing complete, ready for undercoat

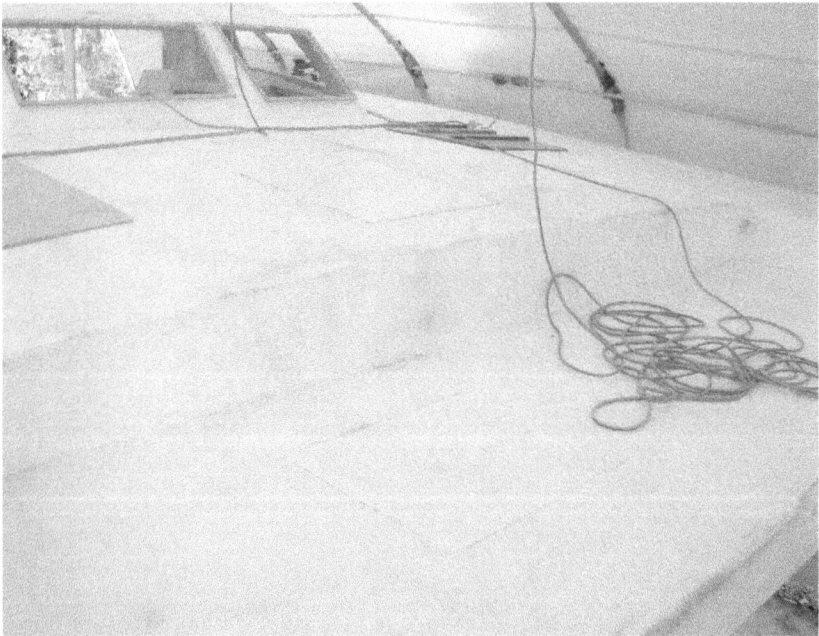

Fairing complete, sanding underway

Chapter Fifteen:
Painting – External

After a visit to the local Bunnings hardware store, a 'stippled' finish was the preferred choice for some parts of the yacht.

This allowed for a relatively unprepared undercoated surface to be finished rather quickly, right up our alley.

The challenge faced (for the external surfaces anyway) was the compatibility of paints, specifically the stippled paint and the two-pack final coat.

We needed the finished surface to be reasonably smooth (as opposed to the coarse rough texture - similar to that on coarse sandpaper).

We also wanted the finish to be very easily washable with no small holes. The small holes would prove prefect breeding grounds for algae especially in the cooler spots of the boat. While additives to paints were an option, none of the local hardware paint manufacturers provided a suitable finish.

Wattyl (the paint brand we were using) also had an additive, which provided a 1 - 3 mm rise, and in individual bumps as opposed to the true stippled finish we were after.

It appeared that no one could provide exactly what we were after.

Wandering through Super Cheap, we spotted a finishing paint that is used on vehicles to reduce stone-chip damage to the under-bodies of vehicles.

It was formulated specifically for two-pack applications and could be cheaply re-applied. Much to our amazement, this normally black type paint also came in white.

----- : -----

Painting Stippled Finish

We tracked down three brands and only two gave the textured finish we wanted. The first painted well, but shrunk as it dried leaving a very flattish finish.

The second made by K & H was the paint we settled on.

The undersides of the cockpit and the saloon ceiling would be finished with this paint and its off-white colour was just enough to make a visible split between it and the white two-pack used in all the coving.

*...issue being that a decision
on the brand of instruments
had yet to be made...*

----- : -----

The efforts in getting a suitable surface that would present well against white reflected light, were a real chore and ended up being a very prolonged affair. In fact, one of the least favoured sections of the build to date.

The plinths definitely did add to the increased build time. This forced us to start laying out the positions of electronics (depth, speed, wind, autopilot and multifunction unit), winches, blocks and tracks.

The main issue being that a decision on the brand of instruments had yet to be made.

We have since gone with Navman Instruments and Multifunction Unit with a Raymarine S1 autopilot.

Having accomplished the 'plinth patch', it was onto the topcoat preparation.

Our procrastination with the painting took a few months and this led into our 'wet season'. From mid November 2007 through to mid December 2007, we achieved only three painting days.

As our build is heavily prone to the elements, moisture would settle on the yacht surfaces including the undersides of the shed tarpaulin after rain. This damp musty condition took at least two days to dry and the reason for our stalling.

----- : -----

Painting Topcoat

The last sand prior to the topcoat was done by hand with 240grit paper.

The deck was marked with pencil lines providing a 50 - 80mm border around the plinths, hatches and lockers for the topcoat.

The remaining areas would be later in-filled with Tredgrip, a rubber-chlorinated-granule water based paint.

To provide nice clean lines we moved up to the more expensive 'blue' 3M tape and then edged that tape with 3M PVC fine line tape.

Topcoat spraying

Stippled finish

This provided a very smooth edge with an unnoticeable join once the topcoat had dried.

We started on the deck/ turret and worked toward ground level. There are three coats, with the paint being thinned further and further with each coat, the last one being the key layer providing the smooth glossy finish.

We also chose to do each coat on separate days, providing the best paint adhesion and apparent finish qualities.

----- : -----

Painting Tredgrip

The painting of this area was left to a few weeks before launch. The choice of texture and paint had been a point of contention with builders since Noah's Ark.

There are many takes on what should be done here and most resort to the system of adding media to two-pack paint and rolling it onto the pre-pared surfaces. The finish gives a light smooth-sandy feel, being just 'grippy' enough to prevent slipping when wet.

We walked the marinas asking fellow sailors their opinions and all were different.

One that did strike us was a 'Salty' that kept to himself. With the tempting of the amber fluid, he revealed his preference and what he said did make sense, initially anyway. His yacht was well worn and he was well travelled having a Master-5 (in Australia, this is one of the top Ship's licenses).

"I'm not interested in all that fancy sh**, I wanted something that is quick to get and put on, then just wash the brush off in water. You understand what I mean?"

"It has to be easy on the feet as I don't have shoes, and with this stuff, you have to be upside down before you slip".

The paint he spoke of was 'Tredgrip'. Its made by a company in country Victoria, Australia called DOMINION Plastics.

...something that is quick to get and put on, then just wash the brush off in water...

It is a water based roll-on paint consisting of white rubber particles.

The paint is easy to apply and after four coats, their white had enough off-white colour that it presented well in contrast to our two-pack white.

Over time, this paint has aged in colour to be off-white, slight mustard tinge.

There are a few things we like about it and they are:

• The compound is soft to walk on,

• The surface is definitely NOT slippery when wet,

• The paint has definitely reduced the temperature within the cabin, and

• Provides mild sound insulation, especially from the rain.

Tredgrip patterns

Tredgrip pattern helps direct deck water flow

To repair any damage or worn areas, resurfacing is very easy. They ask you to remove any excess fouling, mask the area and just re-apply.

All-in-all, easy on all accounts for us and to date we are extremely happy with the outcome.

----- : -----

Painting Anti Foul

Painting is painting and antifouling is not painting as far as we are concerned. The method and reason are different.

...done well ahead of the launch, contrary to what some have said ...

The Antifoul painting has been a rainbow of various coats. Given our mooring position and the grounding of the yacht twice a day, we tried to be proactive in the antifouling area.

The muddy bottom where the vessel will rest twice a day is very soft, so we are not expecting much scratching and gradual wear/abrasion of the antifoul surface.

We spoke to a few companies of which two allowed us to make contact with their 'Technicians'.

In the end, we chose to stick with Wattyl, even with their slightly higher and continual price rises. Time will tell if this decision was prudent.

The plan involved fairing the hulls to a reasonable level. It was then lightly sanded and the process began.

The waterline became a talking point as this was the guide for the Antifoul limit.

We chose to go an additional 100mm above the designer's waterline to cover for the additional weight we planned to carry and provide a 'wave-buffer' once in the water.

There are four paint variations that we chose to use and were all rolled on.

They were all from Wattyl:
1. Epinamel PR250
   * Two generous coats
   * Using 18Lt

2. Sigma EP Multiguard
   * Lightly sanded, then
   * Painted a 200mm strip on all leading edges, then
   * Two generous coats
   * Using 18Lt

3. Sigma EP Tiecoat
   * Lightly sanded, then
   * Two generous coats
   * Using 10Lt

4. Sigmaplane Ecol HA120 (Red and Blue in colour)
   * Lightly sanded, then
   * Two generous coats in Red , the
   * Two generous coats in Blue
   * Using 10Lt each 20Lt in total.

During the process we taped each third coat and moved the taping line up 2mm each time to provide a smoother gradient of paint coats to the top surface.

Anti foul, initial coats

Lower yacht painting complete

The top edge finished well negating the use of tape to finish off the paintwork cleanly.

This was all done well ahead of the launch, contrary to what some have said about launching soon after painting.

The Wattyl tech-head told us that a light sand will re-activate the antifoul a day or so before launch.

Another option Wattyl gave us was to put another 'last coat' on just prior to launch, building up further antifoul resistance.

After all, antifoul is no good in the tin I suppose.

----- : -----

As a follow-up, we have had great success with this anti foul, please check our website as we have been tracking its progress over the years.

----- : -----

Chapter Sixteen:
Electrical

Please Note: For the purists in 'electrical-know-how', this may not be for you as there are phrases and words used which may not be strictly correct in the 'purist's eyes'.

The attempt here is to provide a simpler approach in understanding the basic electrical installed in Pure Majek.

...a free independent
energy source...

We strongly recommend that a qualified electrician be consulted in the installation and connection of your vessel's appliances.

However, we found that being armed with some knowledge and pre-purchased components helped speed up our installation and reduce our costs.

This section too, is not just a read-and-all-problems-solved section.

One needs to sit down and plan. Plan, plan and plan again.

----- : -----

This is how we tackled the maze,   piece by piece and it all revolves around the House Bank (the House Bank being the main bank of batteries used in the running of the yacht, sometimes called the Main Bank).

The size of this must be known for without having this knowledge, we cannot go forward

It's at this stage too, we had to make some assumptions to get the ball rolling, understanding that these initial assumptions can be changed later.

These assumptions are discussed in the 'Calculated Risk' and 'Generic Electrical System' sections, further on.

With the ever-increasing price of fuels, 'green power' is climbing up the priority ladder to such an extent that some predictions of fossil fuel costs (scorned at, 10 years ago), are coming home to roost.

Without putting a negative slant on this, we have chosen to be proactive and endeavour to be as reliant as possible on solar power as we possibly can.

...No electrical system is free
from some maintenance...

While this may cost a few more dollars today, it will pay dividends in a few years.

For this reason, when compared to other similar yachts, Pure Majek carries a few more items such as additional solar panels and batteries, which will surprise some and be talked down by others.

The plan here, again, is simplicity.

Having said that, we have found

that an understanding of a few basic philosophies is a definite advantage. Things like:
- Amps,
- Watts,
- 12 Volts,
- Power consumption of Inverter's, and
- On-Board AC Systems,

...will give one a big head start.

----- : -----

In simple terms, Pure Majek's electrical system has Solar Panels developing sufficient energy to charge two of the six Batteries to provide 12vDC power to the vessels 'House Bank'.

In the event of an Emergency or at the times where power consumption may be higher than that planned (i.e. when visitors are staying on board), a petrol generator (separate to the alternators on the engines) is available to 'top up' the batteries.

For us, the budget dictated the terms of our electrical system and KISS (Keep It Simple Stupid) dictated the complexity of our set-up.

No electrical system is free from some maintenance or complexity.

What is important is the time spent doing that maintenance and this is cursed by many a boatperson.

----- : -----

If one watches what is being purchased at the local chandlery, 40% of the goods are electrical items and with today's fast advancing technology, what is a breakthrough today will be superseded tomorrow.

Keeping-up with the installation of this equipment and installing the units correctly, are where the common problems normally start.

Does the unit truly fit into the planned current electrical system? If not,

• What must be changed?

• Are the cable capacities really capable of carrying power to the unit?

• Will the unit be subject to electrical interference?

For this reason we have chosen to place a little more effort and thought in this area and have literally jumped in the deep-end and started swimming.

The more complicated the system was, the more chances there are of something going wrong.

We have chosen to go for some 'top-of-the-line' gadgets too, an example being the solar panel Smart Charger discussed in a later section.

----- : -----

Calculated Risk

A perfect power situation would be having a free independent energy source and in a perfect world, this is possible. One needs an open wallet and a vessel that has no weight boundaries for this to be achieved. Reality places a different perspective on the issue, so how did we tackle this challenge?

The best we can achieve is based on 'calculated risk', with a system

of replenishing energy (electricity) given proven techniques of small vessel power generation.

Careful thought needed to be placed on the requirements of the vessel's power needs as each system is individual and also specific to each yacht including the yacht's planned:

• General use and expected destinations,

• Lighting requirements and refrigeration expectations,

• Creature comforts from the Cooks wish-list, and even

• Autopilot power.

Added to this was the Legal Electrical Avenue, without a legal system, the insurance would be difficult to obtain.

If we did obtain insurance with a 'non-approved system', they have been known to not pay when an incident has occurred.

Our avenues of investigation took us back to James' father who was a qualified Electrician and it's with his guidance that some of this content was written.

----- : -----

The most common forms of power generation on yachts include:
• Solar panels,

• Generator/s (separate portable generator units),

• Alternators (units making power from available and/or separate motors, usually the motors powering the boat),

- Wind generators, and

- Water generators.

A genuine decision had to be made on what we were going to use the boat for as this dictated the requirements.

The Dreamer always says world cruising or cruising to far-away clear water hide-a-ways, but reality drew us to our requirements for non-global enjoyment, the more social-moored-type cruising lifestyle having fun-with-the-family direction.

One thing that should not be forgotten is:
> What if we sell?
> What will deter the buyer?

While this should not be the primary driver on a particular installation, we kept it in mind in the event of a sale.

----- : -----

Power Generation Forms

Water generators - while they have definitely improved, are not yet at a point where they can be relied upon as the main source of power generation, in our circumstance.

For a start, one needs at least a water current of around 6kts (12 - 15 km/hr.) to generate any power at all.

...'unleaded' are not available in many third world countries...

Below surface, water current turns a propeller connected to an internal small generator, developing power, which is fed back to the vessels batteries.

Some experimental versions of this unit are being trailed which develop power as well as drinking water, which would prove a winner in our books.

These types of units are normally trailed behind the vessel with a power/water cable back to the boat. It's also well known to be a predator attractant with certain members of the deep.

Wind generators have proven themselves the world over and have been finely tuned and developed to a point where they can maintain system loads very effectively.

The two drawbacks that we believe will always remain are that they require wind (obviously) somewhere around the 6-9kts (10 - 20 km/hr.) to effectively generate power, and some units do make a noise while spinning.

...solar panels leave the rest for dead...

A few are very noisy - just go down to your local marina and stand next to a unit that's turning for a few minutes, close your eyes and see if you could honestly sleep through the whine throughout the night.

Many say that the Aero4gen is reasonably quiet but only generates 2amps in 11kts of wind (at time of writing anyway).

Advantages however for wind generators are their small surface area required for installation.

Portable generators on the other hand, can be very noisy too, unless one targets boat specific units.

Some other negatives include the use of fuel to operate the portable generator, sometimes that fuel is different to the vessels motor fuel and then comes the storage of the various types of fuels (diesel, unleaded, leaded, kerosene etc.).

Often fuels such as 'unleaded' are not available in many third world countries, making larger trips offshore difficult.

To their credit, the portable generator has instant power at a given rate and does not have to rely on the elements for assistance. These units also recharge batteries a lot quicker than other forms of power (with the exception of 240V AC from a marina berth).

Fixed generators include those units larger than the portable type and normally cooled in some way by water.

...we were yet to use the generator and have taken it home...

Cooling is either via saltwater or freshwater with a few being air-cooled.

They are normally bolted into the vessel and produce double the electrical power of its portable cousin, however often suffer from resultant vibration and noise.

Generating power from the vessel's motors is another option.

While the motors we have are small (2 x 9.9hp), they do have alternators. As you will see further in this section, these will be used to replenish 'starter battery' power only, providing us with a fully charged battery used only for

starting these engines.

The most common power generation units to date on yachts have been Solar Panels, being very quiet and clean.

Some argue that in areas outside the equator and tropics, wind generators are the way to go, however within this region on sunny Queensland Australia, solar panels leave the rest for dead.

One needs to be careful with their installation as shielding from the sails or even the angle of the panel, play a pivotal part in effective use of these panels.

...definitely paid very handsome dividends...

In fact, in calculating their power generation capability, you will find that we have chosen to use only '5 hours of useful light' to be realistic with the sun's position and the boat.

In summary, Pure Majek utilises solar panels and a portable generator.

When and if the opportunity arises, we will install a wind generator and the cabling has been built in to cover this possible inclusion.

----- : -----

Six months after the yacht launch, we were yet to use the generator and have taken it home to remove it from the salty environment.

When extended cruising is on the cards, it will be taken back. We are also yet to connect to shore-power, the solar charging as detailed below has been more than ample to maintain the ships-batteries with the fridge and 'the toys' continually running.

The forward planning detailed here has definitely paid very handsome dividends.

----- : -----

Generic electrical system/diagram

Why is it that one cannot locate a generic electrical system/diagram that can be used for one's own electrical system on one's own boat?

The answer is simple - all electrical systems are individual to each boat and normally cannot be duplicated unless you intend building an exact duplicate of another with the exact components each time.

...blaming ignorance during the build stage would really hurt...

A similar analogy would be like asking a butcher 'how to plan all the food for Christmas day'. They will sell you meat that is on special that day and give you a tip on how to cook it, but that does not answer your original question.

Electrical circuitry is very individual as each yacht is different and more importantly, each owner is different.

Some new owners (with little or no electrical experience) will argue as to why they need a particular item, not realising the implications on the overall 12vDC electrical 'Big Picture'.

Or why they believe a particular component to be suitable when they are unaware of regulatory requirements that may cause this unit to be unsuitable and therefore void any warranty.

More importantly, not receiving an insurance payout after paying insurance premiums for the last ten years, blaming ignorance during the build stage would really hurt.

Remember that, if Electrics were that easy, there would be no marine specialists or electricians spending four years training to understand this topic and charging as they do.

Owner builders build for a reason and the normal reason is due to budget restrictions.

...non-ignition switches should be purchased...

This in turn drives the owner builder to find the cheapest avenue to meet their goal and as in business, cutback-cutback-cutback is the result.

The electrical system though is one area where very careful consideration needs to be placed with 'cutbacks'.

If one wants a cheap electrical system, don't try and include a laptop or autopilot requiring steady current flow, it will falter at some stage, normally up in smoke.

To calculate the initial electrical budget for the first time electrical builder, jot down all the components, items (including wiring) and try and get an accurate honest figure.

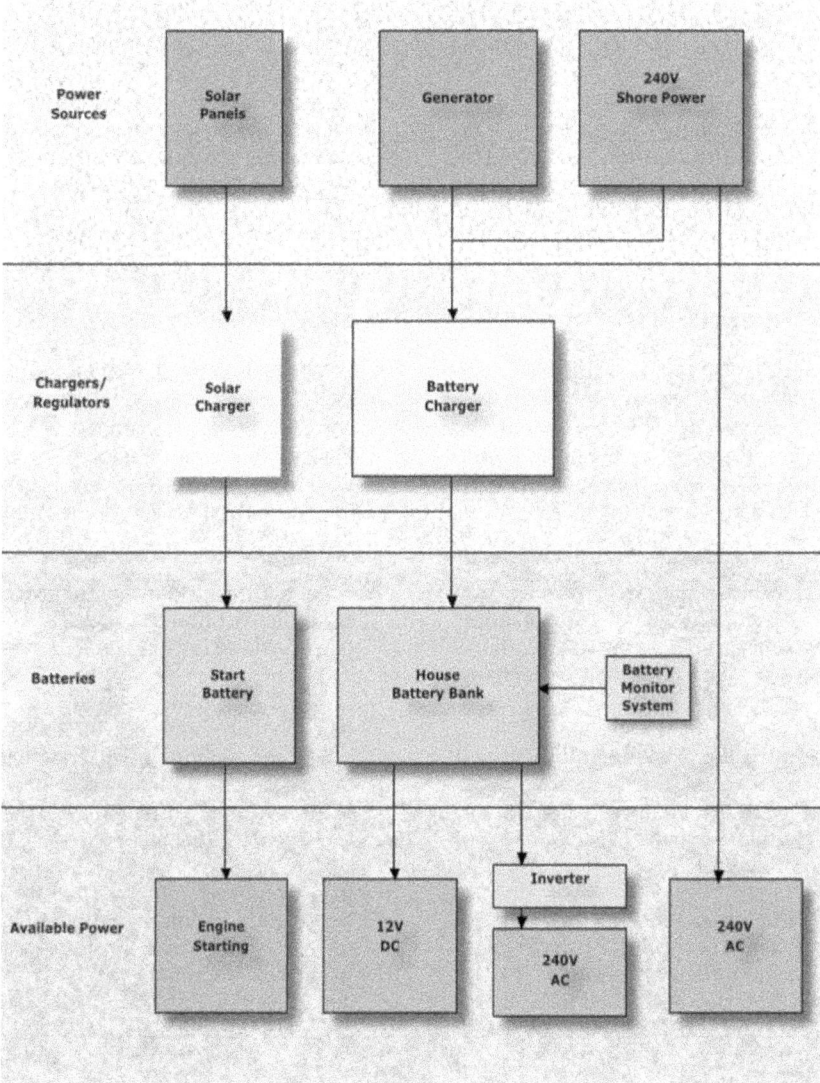

How all the major components come together

Bite your tongue...then double that figure and that is the guide you should be using with your electrical budget.

We were told this and immediately saw red, but have to admit that the person who said this (a qualified marine electrician) was right.

We (like many) found cheap ways and substitutes for various items or directions, only to be reasoned back to this now 'doubled electrical budget'.

The answers as to why, will be answered through this section.

----- : -----

Electrical Switches should be carefully chosen. The normal units sold in automotive shops we found to not be suitable.

Some were not even marked with the correct current (Amp) carrying capacities, if at all. As we know, many switches arc and this is caused by current resistance change.

This is the prime ignition source of fumes from the batteries, gas or fuel and for this reason alone, non-ignition switches should be purchased.

From the no-current-flow situation (when the switch is off) to a maximum-current-flow situation (when the switch is on) takes a split second. The type of switch and quality of manufacture, will dictate the arc.

With most common household switches, a spring is installed to assist the 'switch changeover'.

It's during this switch position changeover (from on-to-off or off-to-on) that heat builds up and without the help of a good spring, could get so hot that the contacts weld together.

Good switch brands have good quality springs making changeover fast. Even with a fast changeover, the contact points do get hot and continual 'flicking' of the switch only exacerbates the problem.

Continual arcing will damage or corrode the switch contact points, leaving a black to grey residue around the switch.

While high voltage systems utilise their power advantage to keep the contact points residue free by design, the same cannot be done with low voltage switches. These contact points are normally made of brass.

Next is the consideration of switch position within the vessel and could include the following data:

1. LPG gas - the escaped gas is heavier-than-air and will sink to the lower sections of the boat (in our case, this is below the lower bridge deck height, so all switches are above this height).

2. Battery Gas - consists mainly of hydrogen and this is lighter-than-air, so should rise (in our case using sealed Calcium will limit any gas escaping). Having said that, there are no switches within:
   a. The battery box area, and

   b. 1 metre of the battery box vents.

Navigation Bus (Nav Helm)

Port Distribution Bus (Nav Table)

Starboard Distribution Bus (Galley Bench)

Hot Battery Bus

Inverter

12vDC Main Bus

100A

60A

100A C Breaker

Solar Switch

Main Bus Switch

Hot Battery Bus Switch

Battery Switch

Spare Solar Charger Outlet

40A

120A

30A

30A

30A

HOUSE 1

HOUSE 2

HOUSE 3

Negative Distribution Bus

Shunt

Solar Charger Remote

Solar Charger

Solar Remote Power In

40A

Battery Charger

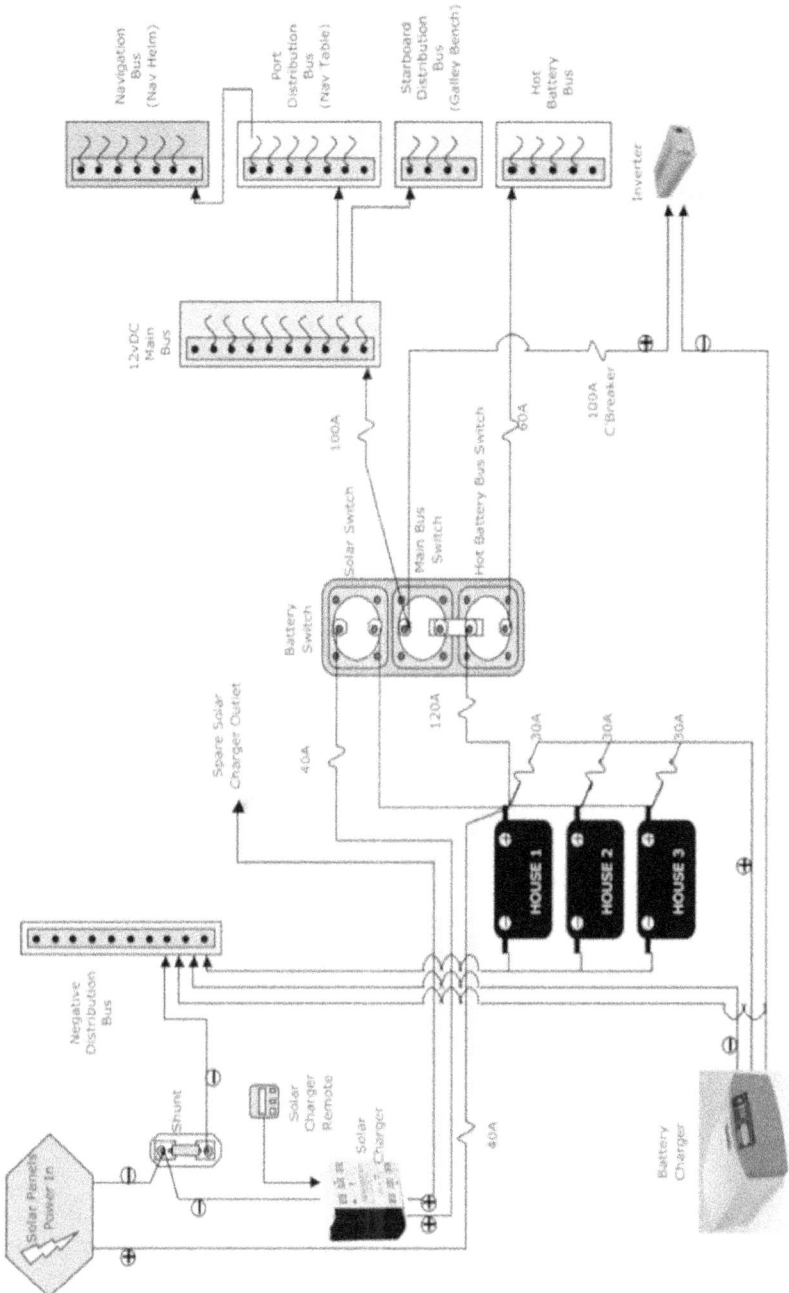

Electrical Diagram

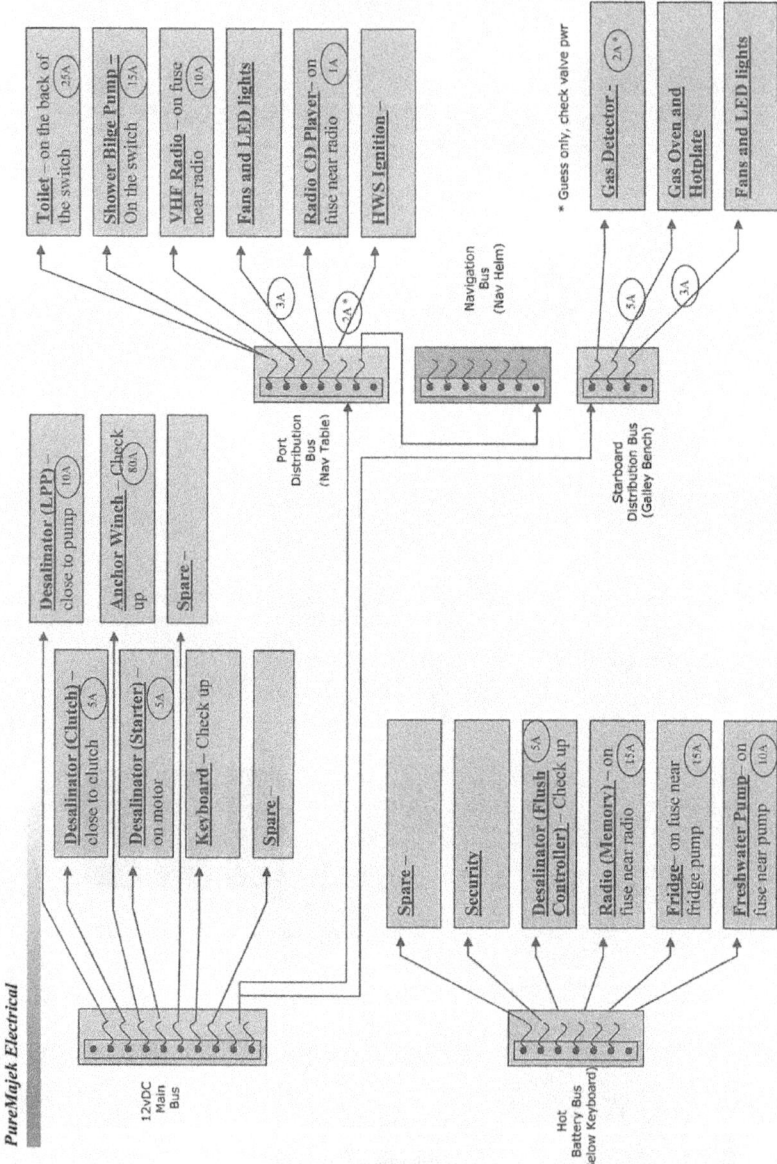

PureMajek Electrical

Toilet – on the back of the switch (25A)

Shower Bilge Pump – On the switch (15A)

VHF Radio – on fuse near radio (10A)

Fans and LED lights

Radio CD Player – on fuse near radio (1A)

HWS Ignition –

* Guess only, check valve pwr

Gas Detector – (2A*)

Gas Oven and Hotplate

Fans and LED lights

Navigation Bus (Nav Helm)

Port Distribution Bus (Nav Table)   3A   2A*

Starboard Distribution Bus (Galley Bench)   5A   3A

Desalinator (LPP) – close to pump (10A)

Anchor Winch – Check up (80A)

Spare –

Desalinator (Clutch) – close to clutch (5A)

Desalinator (Starter) – on motor (5A)

Keyboard – Check up

Spare –

12vDC Main Bus

Spare –

Security –

Desalinator (Flush Controller) – Check up (5A)

Radio (Memory) – on fuse near radio (15A)

Fridge – on fuse near fridge pump (15A)

Freshwater Pump – on fuse near pump (10A)

Hot Battery Bus (Below Keyboard)

Electrical Schematic Overview Ver 4A.doc

Yachts Busses

3. Unleaded Fuel gas - is heavier-than-air and will sink to the lower sections of the fuel chamber (in our case is external in its own fuel chamber vented externally at all times).

Non-ignition type switches have very clean solid contact points that allow for quick firm contact and are constructed from heavier brass components.

These switches also need to be matched to the current (Amp) of the cable to be used and as we found out, they do cost more.

...A clear understanding will save many hours of frustration in problem fixing later...

With the quality switch manufacturers around today, some are purporting the use of their switches for both high and low voltage situations. As long as one is aware of this possible ignition source, all should work well.

----- : -----

Understanding Basic Electrical Jargon - Volts, Amps and Watts

For those who don't understand all the 240-Volt-Amp-12V electrical jargon, here are some simplified explanations – 'DIY style'.

So how does this help?

In working the requirements of a particular appliance (say a Laptop), data is normally supplied on the rear.

It may say DC 15V and 3.0A.

From this, the Wattage can be calculated 45W (15V x 3A).

A clear understanding will save many hours of frustration in problem fixing later on, even when the yacht is on the water.

----- : -----

240/110/ 24/12 V - Understanding the figures

In Australia most houses are connected to the electrical grid and the voltage here is 240V and this is classed as a 'Low Voltage System' (in the United States, their electrical grid house voltage is 110V).

In our cars, the battery voltage is 12V (and in Australia is classed as a 'Very Low Voltage System'), that simple.

The hiccup occurs with AC and DC letters that often suffix these voltages.

You will find that the car's voltage comes from a battery (and not electrical grid or power station as with house power). The letters DC (meaning 'Direct Current' - current that flows in one direction) suffixes all battery voltages.

Most 240V and 110V house power installations are suffixed with AC meaning 'Alternating Current' - current that alternates back and forth in the cable at extremely high speed.

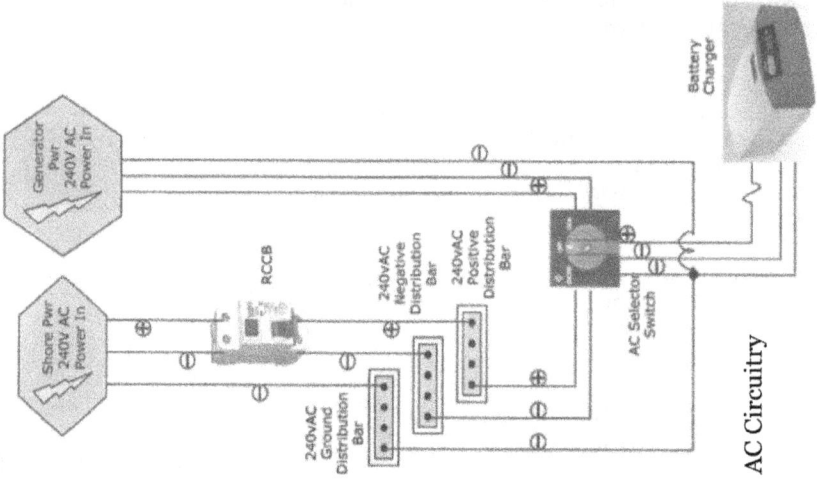

AC Circuitry

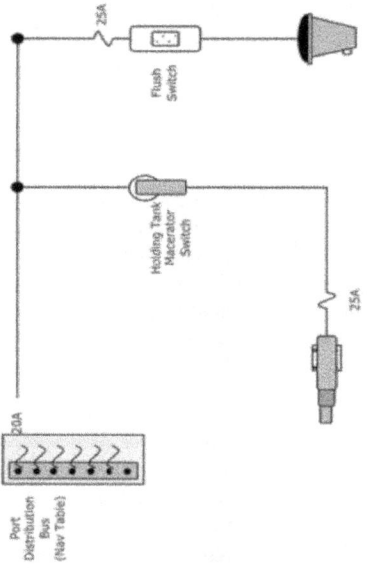

Toilet Wiring

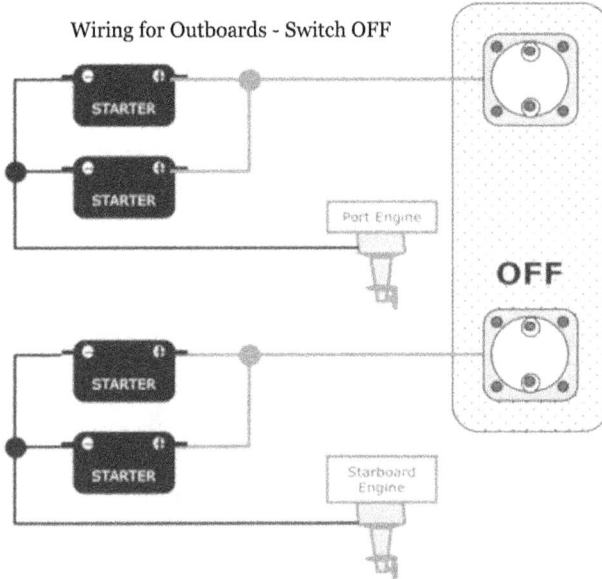

Wiring for Outboards - Switch OFF

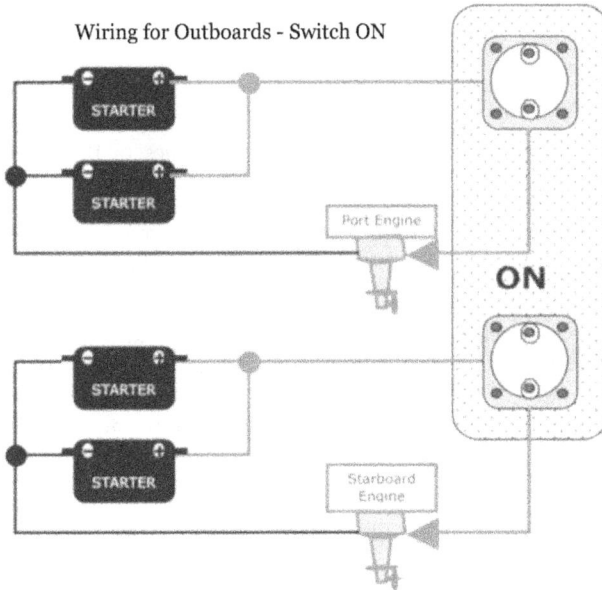

Wiring for Outboards - Switch ON

If you have been brave enough to get a shock from your house power point, you would have felt a 'zzzzapped' sensation.

They use this word because what you are feeling is hundreds of changes in direction of the current at a given instant. While the 'zap' literally gives you a shock, it is normally cool at the point of contact.

The opposite applies to DC current.

...fire and as we know,
'Fire and Boats' don't mix...

As the voltage is much lower the 'shock' will not be as great, but you will feel the heat at the point of contact. Enough heat in fact that you could start a fire and as we know, 'Fire and Boats' don't mix.

As we can't continually be connected to the electrical grid on a yacht, the next best thing is battery power and on most yachts there is a choice of 12V DC or 24 V DC.

A common choice is usually 12V DC as many more appliances and components are available that utilise 12V, lowering building costs.

The Australian Standard AS3000 - Section 7 (in particular 7.5-6-7-9 & 7.14) refers to the design rules that pertain to "Very Low Voltage Systems" such as the 12V system.

There is also mention here to transformers, which does not apply to any DC voltage systems used in our set-up.

One very important note in the Australian Standard relates to clear differentiation between Low (240/415 AC) and Very Low Voltage Systems (12 - 50 volts AC and DC).

The Standard requires the different systems to be clearly identified (marked in some way,) to differentiate between the Low and Very Low voltage systems particularly with switches and power points.

In our case we have overcome this with the use of standard commercially available Low and Very Low voltage light switches, plugs and sockets, which are not compatible (interchangeable).

In other words we cannot plug any 12V DC (Very Low voltage) appliance such as a 12V refrigerator or CD player into a 240V AC (Low voltage Domestic type) socket.

----- : -----

Calculating the power requirements

This is one of the most important topics of the Electrical section as without this, finding the correct battery sizes and therefore appropriate charging systems would be difficult.

We jotted down everything that we thought would require power, even if it sounded silly and then went through a process of elimination, coming up with a 'U-beaut-wish-list'.

We say 'wish-list' as this was normally well over the top and some severe culling was required. Refer to Power Consumption Plot for an idea.

Take a look at the *'Power Consumption Plot'* (in this Chapter). This will help give one an idea of the standard power usage for basic calculations.

Even the kids were involved here and one of their suggestions of a keyboard (as we all play music in some form) has been included in our figures.

Another odd one was a Bread Maker, which doesn't sound like much but try and find a 12V bread maker.

We say, "our boat, not yours"

The market only supplies 110V or 240V bread makers and these units definitely require pure sine wave power, which meant that additional electrical equipment would now be required to power this type of unit. Was the smell and taste of freshly baked bread worth this additional expense?

The electrical items were then placed into AC and DC power requirement sections. This is very important, as it will later dictate the type of inverter (the component that changes DC power to AC power) that would be required. This provided clear direction and choice of the final product/s.

From here we located the power specifications of the items listed. Using the data supplied on Watts, Amps and Volts, it was easy to calculate the 24-hour Amperage Demand.

It's these figures that provide the crux to the minimum power requirements.

Required in these calculations was other data such as the amount of usage (in minutes per day) and at what time of the day that usage would occur. The latter sounds silly but, will provide guidance on when one's heaviest loads are expected and can be used later as a tool to equalise these loads through the day.

In our example it calculated that one needed 113 Ahrs (excluding the desalinator) or 153 (113+40) Ahrs (including a small 12vDC electric type desalinator) to cover this type of set-up for each day ('day' being defined here as a 24 hour period). And yes, this figure is relatively high when compared to others. We say, "our boat not yours".

This can then be weighted against charts similar to what we have made up below:

1. Battery Overview Calculator
This helps assist in finding the correct size battery bank to deliver the required power bank.

2. Solar Panel Overview Calculator
This helps with working out the number of panels needed and the power that they should generate,

3. Generator Overview Calculator
This provides any supplemental power that could help make up the bank to cover ones power consumption, and

4. Power Consumption Overview

This gives an idea of when you can use various components and try and share the load through the day.

(Examples of all these charts can be found in this chapter).

Power Consumption Plot

	Amp	Volts	Watts		Mins Used	Amps Req'd
DC Power						
Anchor Winch	80.00	12	960		4	5.3
Toilet Pump	4.00	12	48		20	1.3
Water Pump	4.00	12	48		140	9.3
Desalinator '	20.00	12	240		120	40.0
Nav - Instruments	0.35	12	4.2		540	3.2
Nav - GPS / Tracke	0.50	12	6		540	4.5
Nav Autopilot	1.50	12	18		540	13.5
Nav - Radar	2.50	12	30		0	0.0
Fridge	4.00	12	48		100	6.7
Freezer	2.00	12	24		100	3.3
Comms - HF	2.00	12	24		30	1.0
Comms - VHF	0.25	12	3		100	0.4
Auto/San System	2.00	12	24		0	0.0
Lgt-Cabin	2.00	12	24		300	10.0
Lgt-Spreader / Nav	10.00	12	20		12	2.0
Ent - TV/Stereo	0.25	12	3		900	3.8
Other 12V	0.00	12	0		0	0.0
Keyboard	0.86	9	7.7		120	1.7
Other	0.00	9	0		0	0.0
AC Power						
Computer	0.43	240	90		120	0.9
Breadmaker	4.79	240	1000		60	4.8
Games Console	0.43	240	90		120	0.9
Other 240V	0.00	240	0		0	0.0

Average	4.7	Ahrs
Maximum	22.8	Ahrs
Minimum	0.0	Ahrs
Total for 24hrs	113	Ahrs

Battery Overview:
1. General:
    a. 2 normal ships batteries, and
    b. 4 x Starting Battery.

2. Starting Battery
    a. Purpose is solely for electric starting of the two engines,
    b. Its recharge is via the engine Alternators
    c. 45Ah Battery (x4) required, and
    d. Must be AGM type, self maintenance and leak free

3. Normal Ships Batteries
    a. Purpose is to provide power for everyday functions,
    b. Is recharged via the Solar Panel System,
    c. 2 x 220Amphour Deep cycle Batteries required,
    d. Must be AGM or Calcium types, self maintenance and leak free, and
    e. Battery discharge **must not exceed 60%** to prolong battery life.
    f. Battery power must be sufficient to provide 1 day @ 24hrs of normal power use with no recharge. This will cover a worstfailure.
       case scenario of no recharge with total recharging

4. House Batteries & Starter Battery Pack Figures

	House Batt's	Start Batt
Number	2	4
Ah per Battery	220	45
Total Battery Ah's	440	180
Less 60% recharge requirement	176	

Available for house bank use per 24hr day

> **In Summary:**
> **176** Ahrs will be available from the House Batteries/24hr day, plus
> **180** Ahrs Engine Battery

Solar Panel Overview:
1. General:
    a. Purpose is to provide recharge for the House Batteries,
    b. System contains   4   Solar Panels,
    c. Each panel is   90   Watt, with output of   5.1   Amps each, and a circuit Voltage of   21.2
    d. Less   Voltage drop of   1   , realistically   20.2   V
    e. Calculations are based on   5   hrs 'useful light' per day.,

2. Solar Panel Charging Figures:

Number	4	
Watts per Panel	90	
Amp Output	5.1	
Circuit Voltage	20.2	
Total Watts per 24hr period	20.2	
Useful sunlight per average day	5	
Expected charge per day	102	Ahrs per day

3. Smart Cherger / Regulator

    MPPT Technology   Improves efficiency by   30 %, conservativly   21 % of manufact. data.

> **In Summary:**
>
>   Panels should generate   **102**   Ahrs
>   MPPT Technology   **21**   more Ahrs
>   TOTAL   **123**   Ahrs per useful day

Generator Overview:

1. General:

a. Purpose is to provide redundancy and supply power recharge shortfall to the House Batteries and as Emergency backup

b. Calculation is based on Honda EU10i and EU201 *(Extracted from Electrical Consumption Min Rqmts 3A.xl file)*

Honda EU10i	
1.79	HP
2.3	Lt
8hr/4hr	
52/58	dB
1000	VA
900	VA
8	Amp
13	kg
Inv	
Eco-Throttle	

Honda EU20i	
4.1	HP
10 - 4hr	Lt
54-59	dB
2000	VA
1600	VA
8	Amp
21	kg
Inv	
Eco-Throttle	

2. Generator Power Figures:

GENERATOR UNIT		EU10i	
1 x		900	VA
Output		8	A
POWER GENERATION DATA			
	1	Hours per day	

GENERATOR UNIT		EU20i	
1 x		1600	VA
Output		8	A
POWER GENERATION DATA			
	1	Hours per day	

In Summary:

EU10i UNIT

V Hours	SubTotal	
1	37.5	
TOTAL	37.5	AH/day

EU20i UNIT

V Hours	SubTotal	
1	66.67	
TOTAL	66.67	AH/day

Power Consumption Overview:

1. General
a. Purpose is to provide adequate power for Coastal Cruising

2. Power Consumption Plot:

24 HOUR POWER DEMAND

DC Power	Amp	V	W	TOTAL Mins
Anchor Winch	80.00	12	960	4
Toilet Pump	4.00	12	48	20
Water Pump	4.00	12	48	140
Desalinator	20.00	12	240	120
Nav - Instruments	0.35	12	4.2	540
Nav - GPS / Tracker	0.50	12	6	540
Nav - Autopilot	1.50	12	18	540
Nav - Radar	2.50	12	30	0
Fridge	4.00	12	48	100
Freezer	2.00	12	24	100
Comms - HF	2.00	12	24	30
Comms - VHF	0.25	12	3	5
AutoScan System	2.00	12	24	0
Lgt-Cabin	2.00	12	24	900
Lgt-Spreader / Nav	10.00	12	20	12
Ent - TV/Stereo	0.25	12	3	900
Other 12V				0
Keyboard	0.86	9	7.7	120
Other	0.00	9	0	0

AC Power	Amp	V	W	TOTAL Mins
Computer	0.43	240	90	120
Breadmaker	4.79	240	1000	60
Games Console	0.43	240	90	120
Other 240V	0.00	240	0	0

24 HOUR AMP DEMAND

DC Power	Amp	V	W	TOTAL Amps
Anchor Winch	80.00	12	960	5.3
Toilet Pump	4.00	12	48	1.3
Water Pump	4.00	12	48	9.3
Desalinator	20.00	12	240	40.0
Nav - Instruments	0.35	12	4.2	3.2
Nav - GPS / Tracker	0.50	12	6	4.5
Nav - Autopilot	1.50	12	18	13.5
Nav - Radar	2.50	12	30	0.0
Fridge	4.00	12	48	3.3
Freezer	2.00	12	24	3.3
Comms - HF	2.00	12	24	1.0
Comms - VHF	0.25	12	3	0.4
AutoScan System	2.00	12	24	0.0
Lgt-Cabin	2.00	12	24	10.0
Lgt-Spreader / Nav	10.00	12	20	2.0
Ent - TV/Stereo	0.25	12	3	3.8
Other 12V				0.0
Keyboard	0.86	9	7.7	1.7
Other	0.00	9	0	0.0

AC Power	Amp	V	W	TOTAL Amps
Computer	0.43	240	90	0.9
Breadmaker	4.79	240	1000	4.8
Games Console	0.43	240	90	0.9
Other 240V	0.00	240	0	0.0
TOTAL				112.5

We suggest you make this in an Excel spreadsheet (similar to our Power Generator Calculator). Check our website for this Calculator, if you are stuck.

Many vessels target a figure of 75 - 110Ahr maximum and achieve this by reducing all unnecessary items and electronics.

...give the old fashioned
Fuse the thumbs up...

Some use diesel power to operate their desalinator, which would lower the figure by 40Amps. However, weighing this cost against installation and maintenance of a diesel generator (plus carrying diesel), we would opt to increase clean solar energy instead, for free too.

We discuss how we get this 'free' extra panel power in the Smart Charger Section.

In line with the information discussed in the 'Batteries Section' and using a daily average battery discharge level of around 40%, one would require roughly 400 Ahrs (200Ahr x 2) of battery storage or more (If this data does not make sense, read the 'Battery section' then return here and continue).

Interestingly is the plot of the forecast usage. The spike is the power being drawn down by the desalinator (if one was to be used).

----- : -----

Fuses vs. Circuit Breakers

What about fuses versus breakers? Each of these serves a purpose in providing over-current protection in electrical circuits. They both have pros and cons.

Circuit breakers can normally be reset when a current problem trips the circuit breaker.

While this appears to be the be-all-and-end-all of protecting circuits, they have a few problems:
1. They have moving internal components which do require checking and can wear over time,

2. They need to be accurately calibrated, and

3. They do cost a bit to buy.

Fuses on the other hand, have:
1. No moving parts,
2. They can't be re-used,
3. Are cheap to buy, and
4. Can never wear out, they just burn out.

At the end of the day, you really have to give the old fashioned Fuse the thumbs up.

Our only exceptions here have been for the AC input circuitry and high amperage units such as the Inverter and Winch

For the lower amperage current users (30Amp or less), we have used the common motor vehicle blade fuses - available in bulk.

For those amperages up to 120Amp, we use a much larger blade fuse (normally sold through electronics stores, such as Jaycar).

We have also made these fuse positions very easily accessible.

The last thing we want to be doing is fumbling around on a dark night trying to replace a Fuse.

----- : -----

Solar Panels

Pure Majek will be using four panels as opposed to one very large or even two large panels.

The reasons here are:
- Our power requirements,

- Redundancy, and importantly

- Allowing the larger spread of panels over the surface, reducing the 'shadow effect' caused by sails, masts and even sun position.

*...Mono-crystalline
are also said to permit
power generation from lower
sun angles...*

Most solar cells are made up of silicon, which becomes the conductor in the cell. To this, other semiconductor layers are added.

Small amounts of electric current are then extracted from the cell once daylight excites their electric field.

Silicon cells are commonly made-up under the headings of mono-crystalline, polycrystalline and amorphous. Silicon (very readily available throughout the world) is melted down and allowed to harden in the shapes required to construct these cells.

In the case on Mono-crystalline, the liquid silicon is poured into a rod of exact dimensions and then very thin slices of the purest silicon are taken and used.

Due to its simple state, effective red spectrum capture and construction technique, they are highly efficient however, costly to make. **Mono-crystalline** are also said to permit power generation from lower sun angles due to this improved red spectrum range capture.

With **Polycrystalline**, the liquid silicon is poured into a block and then sawn into pieces. As the silicon hardens, crystal structures form which by nature have fractured sides. This causes the silicon slice to be less efficient than the monotype, but cheaper to make.

With **Amorphous**, a thin film of silicon is placed on a glass surface 1/75 the thickness of a human hair. These are very cheap to make but are also very inefficient. They are found mostly in the electronics market for solar chargers for smaller batteries, calculators etc. Their efficiency is also said to decrease with time.

These cell types listed above are then normally placed in blocks of 32 - 36 cells per solar panel.

Also included nowadays on most panels are Blocking Diodes and Bypass Diodes. They have two totally different jobs to do and are discussed later.

Most solar panel manufacturers figures are based on an environmentally controlled 25 degrees Celsius test bed called STC (Standard Test Conditions). This test-bed temperature is measured around each panel cell and not the temperature of the whole solar panel with its glass on top.

In fact, the glass encapsulation of the cells acts as an oven making it 30 - 38 degrees Celsius warmer around each cell within that panel, when its 25 degrees Celsius outside the panel.

...higher the temperature, the less efficient the panel will be...

The implications of this are enormous, as the true figures for those days where temperatures are above 25 degrees Celsius have to be addressed by you and I.

It needs to be remembered that the manufacturer panel specifications are there either as a regulatory requirement and display optimum qualities of the product or there to cover litigation issues.

The higher the temperature, the less efficient the panel will be.

An example would be a 38-degree outside temperature (18 degrees above the test-bed temperature of 25 degrees).

Add to this the cell temperature; say 30 degrees and the temperature would now be around 48 degrees higher than the manufacturer test-bed information. This is *'power temperature degradation'.*

A common figure used for power temperature degradation is 0.5% for each degree above the test-bed temperature, making this above example 19% less inefficient with an outside temperature of 38 degrees Celsius, quite remarkable.

For a 12V solar panel (as opposed to 24V solar panel which are available), common current target Amperage ranges are around 6.5 A

- 7.3 A.

To do this economically, the solar cells are linked in series within each solar panel. It's said that each solar cell should generate 0.5V making a 34 solar-cell-panel - 17V (0.5V x 34) and this is called its **'Peak Voltage'**.

The Peak Voltage can be deceiving too as it is:
The best that the panel can generate on the best day in the best climatic conditions.

Of course we never have 'Peak Voltage' on a boat so should rarely see this figure reached. The fact is that the Peak Voltage less 10% in good conditions (less 15% in average conditions and less 20% in poorer conditions) is far more realistic.

Given an example of 17V Peak Voltage, generation figures are closer too:
  > Good conditions - 15.3V
    (17V less 10%)
  > Average conditions - 14.45V
    (17V less 15%)
  > Poor conditions - 13.6V
    (17V less 20%)

Efficiency of a solar panel and contributing power generation factors should now be hitting home. Or be totally confusing.

In summary, we have planned worst case when sizing components such as the solar panels, but there are cabling and Smart Charger considerations too.

----- : ----

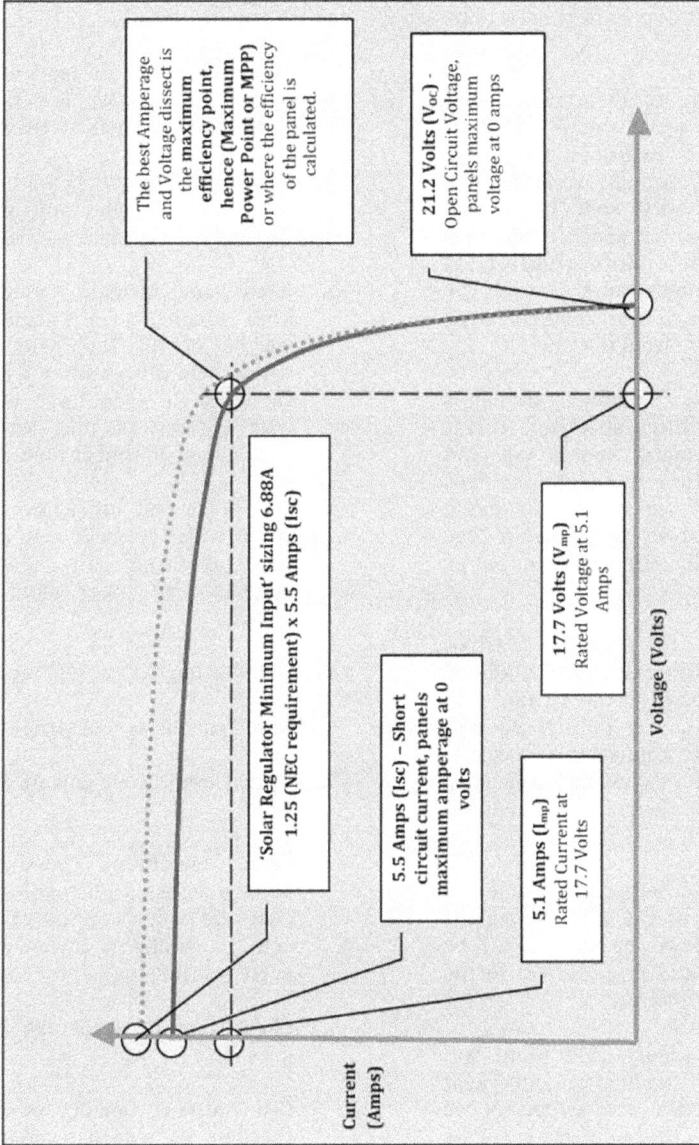

The best Amperage and Voltage dissect is the **maximum efficiency point, hence (Maximum Power Point or MPP)** or where the efficiency of the panel is calculated.

21.2 Volts (V₀ᴄ) - Open Circuit Voltage, panels maximum voltage at 0 amps

'Solar Regulator Minimum Input' sizing 6.88A 1.25 (NEC requirement) x 5.5 Amps (Isc)

5.5 Amps (Isc) – Short circuit current, panels maximum amperage at 0 volts

17.7 Volts (Vₘₚ) Rated Voltage at 5.1 Amps

5.1 Amps (Iₘₚ) Rated Current at 17.7 Volts

Voltage (Volts)

Current (Amps)

NOTE: This is for 1 x 90W solar panel. For 2 same solar panels:
In parallel – double the Amperage figures, maintain the Voltage figures
In Series – double the Voltage figures, maintain the Amperage figures

Understanding Solar Panel figures

There are unusual factors such as **cloud-edge-effect** that can momentarily spike the generation system every now and then, and these worst case buffers need to be built in.

The linking of the panel's solar cells in series does have a downside. **Shading** on any part of the panel, even by covering one solar cell with your hand, will affect the power generation of that single panel. 'Soft shading' is where sunlight can still reach the panel through thin cloud layers, or by reflection from the water.

A majority of shadowing though is classed as 'hard shading'. This is caused by masts, booms, sails and salt accretion to mention a few. The latter type of shading has a high impact on each panel voltage by normally reducing its output by half.

According to Kyocera "Partial-shading even one cell of a 36-cell module, such as the KC120, will reduce its power output. Because all cells are connected in a series string, the weakest cell will bring the others down to its reduced power level.

Therefore, whether 1/2 of one cell is shaded, or 1/2 a row of cells is shaded, the power decrease will be the same and proportional to the percentage of area."

We acknowledge that there will always be shading on our yacht and given the roof extension we have made, the boom swing will be 500mm outside the solar panel area reducing further our averages of boom shading.

The panels will also be variable with installation however; will normally follow the general contour of the turret shape, making it possible to pick up mid morning and afternoon sun as well as that from overhead.

The panels we chose to use were SunPower SPR - 90W. For the more adventurous, their statistics include:

1. Cells are mono-crystalline silicon solar cells and are covered with tempered glass,

2. Each panel weights 7.4 kg. This 29.6kg weight (total weight of all the panels) which may now answer why we chose to re enforce the rear 400mm of the turret roof with solid timber pieces,

3. The solar cell efficiency at 16.5% which we believe to be reasonably efficient when compared to other similar brands,

4. Rated voltage is 17.7V (Vmp)

5. Rated current is 5.1A (Imp),

6. Open Circuit Voltage is 21.2V (Voc),

    (The maximum possible voltage across a photovoltaic cell; the voltage across the cell in sunlight when no current is flowing), and

7. Short Circuit Amperage is 5.5A (Isc)

    (The current flowing freely through an external circuit that has no load or resistance; the maximum current possible).

Don't understand all this stuff? Well, nor did we.

----- : -----

If you have a few minutes, refer to the '90W SunPower Solar Panel' diagram (this chapter), as understanding the specifications now will go a real long way, shortly.

Using the STC (Standard Test Conditions) figures, the authorities require a safety margin to be added and in most cases, the panel figures should be multiplied by 1.25 to determine amperages, sizes and output.

We have taken this further and multiplied by an additional 1.25 for fuses and conductors, total of 1.56 would be very safe and cover all aspects, which is what we used.

----- : -----

Electrical - Solar Panel Understanding

We have used four panels, not only for redundancy, but more importantly, allowing the larger spread of panels over the surface, reducing the 'shadow effect' caused by sails, masts even sun position.

Accepting that there will always be shadowing, we set about trying to improve our odds when this did occur. Having said this, the panels are wired in parallel, reducing the cabling in the turret cavity from eight to two.

As you will see, voltage and/or amperage requirements vary with solar panel make-up and this is directly related to the way the panels are connected together.

This is the first hurdle that needs to be clearly understood as it defines the remainder of the power generation make-up.

Before we made a start here, we assessed the suitability of the panels for two must have characteristics:
> Reverse Polarity (using built-in Blocking Diodes), and
> Bypass Diodes.

The **Blocking Diodes** prevent reverse current mainly at night. If not placed in the system at the end of the panel, small amounts of power will flow back to the now cooler cells, draining valuable power from the battery.

They also serve to stop reverse current during periods of power generation, when other panels in parallel are developing differing amounts of Voltage.

Power will also flow to the area of least resistance; so blocking diodes is a must.

Bypass Diodes on the other hand, are used across each panel. This assists during periods of shading or damage to part or all of the panel.

If a set of panels in series is generating power and one panel falls to shading, some of the power will be redirected to that shaded or damaged section. This does cause overheating and if not addressed immediately, can burnout that piece of shaded or damaged panel, resulting in a replacement panel being needed.

This is not an issue with a parallel panel system, but it definitely affects the 24V, 36V and 48V series system arrays.

Our panels provide both these two features as standard. While we would have preferred bypass diodes at each 'cell', this was cost inhibitive and also not available from SunPower.

----- : -----

Joining Panels to form an Array

There are three options when joining panels to form an array.

Option one - all panels linked in series where the connections ('+'ive of one panel is linked to the '-'ive of the next panel) until all panels are linked.

Manufacturer specifications should be checked here, for example, SunPower permit four of our SPR - 90 panels in series but not five as this exceeds the maximum series panel voltage of 120V.

The advantages of this SERIES type system are:
• Voltage can be increased and assist with units such as MPPT controllers (Smart Charger) making power generation more effective (can be 24 V, 36V, 48V or even more if you can find a controller large enough), where the voltage increases by the sum of the panels,

• Units in series provide low amperage, so thinner conductors (wires/cables) can be used, where the amperage is the average of the panels, and

• The positioning of the panels allow for an increased power generation period throughout the day.

The disadvantages of this SERIES type system include:
1. Purely for the purposes of sizing a Smart Charger, the system may be classed as 48V (4 panels x 12V), but the Smart Charger will need to be capable of handling a much higher voltage rate. With our panels - 84.8V, (21.2Voc x 4 panels). The Amperage required here would be 6.9A (5.5 Isc x 1.25 safety margin)

2. Should one panel fail, the 'connection' will be broken rendering all panels ineffective in power generation, and

3. More expensive 'controllers' are usually needed to be able to accept the higher voltages and change that to a lower output voltage to the battery.

This power output example - four 12V x 5.1A panels, would produce:
> Voltage - 48V
> Amperage - 5.1A

----- : -----

Option two - is linking all panels in parallel where the connections - all '+'ive wires are linked together and all the '-'ive wires are linked together.

The advantages of this PARALLEL type system is:
1. Voltages are low allowing smaller cheaper quality Smart Charger units to be used, and

2. Should one panel fail, the 'connection' will not be broken rendering the remaining panels effective in power generation.

The disadvantages of this PARALLEL type system include:

1. Purely for the purposes of sizing a Smart Charger, the system may be classed as 12V (4 panels x 12V), but the Smart Charger will need to be capable of handling a much higher amperage rate. With our panels - 21.2Voc, (21.2Voc x 1 panels).

2. The Amperage required here would be 27.5A (5.5 Isc x 4 x 1.25 safety margin),

3. Parallel units have higher amperage output (which results in larger cables required).

This power output example - four 12V x 5.1A panels, would produce
> Voltage - 12V
> Amperage - 20.4A

----- : -----

Option three - is linking panels in parallel and series. Obviously one needs more than two panels(preferably four). Pairs of series panels are then linked in parallel.

This provides a happy medium between the advantages and disadvantages of the series and parallel systems, while also providing redundancy in the event of a 'panel pair failure'.

This power output example - four 12V x 5.1A panels, would produce:
> Voltage - 24
> Amperage - 10.2

Using this third option by linking panels in parallel and series does however present another challenge that must be taken into account.

The current (Amps) on both sides of the controller must be considered. 13.75A PV input (at the 24V input point), will be doubled to 27.5A, if it is to be 12V at the output point.

Therefore the consideration here for smart charger selection needs to be capable of handling the output Amperage (and safety margin of 1.25).

----- : -----

We chose Option Two.

This meant we needed a charger that could handle 21.2V and 27.5A.

This option does have the drawback of cable size required. It should be remembered here too that buying thicker cable will definitely be cheaper than buying a larger, higher quality controller (Smart Charger).

Our panels are wired in parallel and run via two 25.7 mm2 copper conductor cables (one positive and one negative), reducing the cable numbers in the turret cavity from eight to just two, down 8.5m to the battery via the Smart Charger (controller).

When measuring and making your calculation of cable length, it must be from the panels to the charger and back.

Voltage Drop should not exceed 2% in a good 12Vdc system. Using the Australian AS3000 calculator, the expected Voltage Drop in our case will not exceed 1% (see this Chapter - 'Wiring and Cables') for expanded information on Voltage Drop - fairly important.

The chosen cable has a nominal

shop size of 10mm (conductor size of 25.7mm2 - see chart below) and is sold as 4/5 B&S (battery and starting) in Australia.

Some may scoff at this detail that we have gone to here, however, this allows us to attain every bit of solar power we can.

By the way, there is another larger cable sold locally which can halve this voltage drop again, but one starts to see weight penalties and cost blow-out, defeating the initial goal of reasonably priced power generation.

Calculating the requirements and getting them right is fairly important for those up to the 'turret-building-stage' of their vessel, as the cables being installed here are permanent fixtures. There will be no more access, even to change the cables, so it has to be right the first time

----- : -----

Smart Chargers

Having now spent good money on the quality solar panels and batteries, it would be very silly to rely on a cheap 'Smart Charger'. The Smart Charger (which has many other names, Intelligent Regulator, solar charger, solar regulator etc.) regulates the flow of charge to the batteries and at the very least, should contain a three-stage battery charge regulation. Many have other options such as over voltage protection; reverse current protection, auto discharge functions and trickle charge functions, all geared to make life easier.

We needed to sit down and look at exactly whether we wanted to have

some control in this area or have this partially automated.

This decision is a costly one and is where some draw the line in the sand and choose to go the cheaper avenue. This decision sometimes costing them dearly down the line, with the replacement of batteries at a more frequent interval than what should normally be required.

A solar charger is basically a regulator, which monitors power to the battery bank. This regulator switches off and on as demand dictates and while power availability exists. It's also here that other solar charger whiz-bang gadgetry is utilised, that:
- Improves efficiency,

- Assists in various stages of charging, and

- Offers circuit protection.

An Australian company Plasmatronic, has designed a 'middle-of-the-road' unit called the Plasmatronic PL20.

The PL20 is a simple quality unit however, does require manual intervention in some areas. What we liked about this unit was its ability to be controlled remotely (at an additional cost).

With the correct set-up, one can monitor and even change charging values from home, very good value for money. Xantrex is another quality brand.

In our case, a higher expense in this area was warranted considering the use of four quality 90W solar panels and two quality 220Ahr batteries.

There are two key areas where power losses occur during power generation:

- Cable current losses, and

- The components used (their associated transformers, electronics and switches).

Regarding the cable current (which is discussed in more detail later), the higher the current (i.e. parallel panels 12V input/12V output), and the higher the cable power loss.

In fact, heat loss is proportional to the square of the current. So if one can cut the current down by say 1/2 (i.e. 24V input/12V output), the heat loss will be 75% less.

A second power loss point is within the Smart Charger itself, power is converted from solar panel DC, to AC, then back to DC again. This all eats away at valuable power before it even gets to the batteries.

Smart Charger - three stage charging.

Given technology today, 3-stage charging is the least that one should source. The charging stages include:

1. Bulk Charging
This is where the majority of the battery charging takes place and is usually when the battery is at its lowest point of charge. It's here too that MPPT technology 'clicks-in', which is discussed later.

This charges the battery to a rough capacity of 70% - 75%.

2. Acceptance Charging
It's here that the battery temperature sensor is an asset, the charging voltage is constant and

the battery continues it's charging to 93% - 95%.

3. Float Charging
Once the 95% mark is reached, the float system maintains a constant 13.1V - 14.6V. This figure is strictly set by one's battery type. In essence, a small charge is supplied to replace the small amount of normal battery charge loss.

Some manufacturers include a fourth stage of charging (sometimes listed differently) called Equalisation.

...If you are flipping out, don't worry. We think MPPT chargers are great, stick with the better known brands...

Equalisation replenishes battery cell specific gravity, but needs to be done carefully and in line with the manufacturers data sheet. Not following their guidelines will result in heavy gassing and stratification of one's expensive batteries.

Temperature compensation - this is normally an option, however forms a critical part of correct charging and maintaining optimum performance of one's Smart Charger, especially in climates outside 20 degrees Celsius - 30 degrees Celsius.

Why this does not form part of the unit is beyond us. Charge voltage changes with temperature, the lower the temperature, the higher the charge or visa-versa.

One should be fully aware of the implications of overcharging a good quality battery on a hot day. Overcharging and Undercharging are discussed further in the Battery section.

MPPT Technology

Maximum Power Point Tracking (MPPT) is an algorithm which when programmed into the Smart Charger,
allows the maximum voltage to be used in the generation of power, given the conditions at that time.

While this technology has proved very impressive in the cooler climate areas, the 25-30% power gain (simply by installing this technology) was what attracted us.

This technology alone, would allow us to generate all the power we needed from the solar panels and keep the generator as a backup. Brands that we considered here included Blue Sky Solar Boost and the Outback MX60 and Xantrex XW.

...using MPPT would be a cheaper option than buying a fifth panel and using a standard PWM controller...

To understand MPPT technology, one needs to be aware of Pulse Width Modulation (or PWM). PWM is a constant voltage means of battery charging by switching the actual controller's power devices during the charge mode. This PWM charge decreases as the batteries charging condition improves.

One problem with constant voltage is that any excess power (that may be generated above that required by the solar charger) is lost, specifically during the 'Bulk Charging' stage.

It is this wasted excess charge that MPPT harnesses and uses by increasing the controller output

amperage (still at the same voltage).

Units available to date, appear to be less effective in charging when the solar panel array is less than 250W - 300W (the total of all solar panel wattage's).

Also, the power taken to operate the controller units is taken from the panel array and not the batteries and the MPPT units are very hungry in this area.

Given the Outback MX-60 as an example uses 10W to operate and that's before any wattage can be passed onto the batteries. MPPT technology also comes at a much higher purchase cost (more than double in some cases) when compared to a high quality PWM controllers.

Another consideration that must be included in Smart Charger selection is a strange phenomenon called 'edge-of-cloud effect', where there are sporadic spikes in current levels and this could exceed your Smart Chargers input limitations.

This needs to be accounted for, usually done by increasing the Smart Charger input amperage level above that required from your solar panel calculations.
An example of 'edge-of-cloud effect' could be where sunlight reflected by the water, illuminates a solar module that was cooled under the cloud's shadow and momentarily spiking the power system.

Many authorities, such as Australian (ISO/AS 3000:2001) and US (UL - 1703) Regulatory departments require safety margins to be added to the required amperage of the controller of 1.25 or 25% to cover 'edge-of-cloud effect'.

They state that the Smart Charger one selects must be capable of handling amperage of the panels plus the safety margin above.

They then go on to say that 'components' need to then be matched to this with a further 1.25 or 25% buffer. While the law does not dictate, we have chosen to use a factor of 1.56% and this covers all possible scenarios or contingencies.

----- : -----

The MPPT argument- is it a 'goer' or not?

Get a pen and paper and draw diagrams to follow this through.

The 'theoretical - Jill Genius' says that Pure Majek's panels produce 360W (4 x 90W).

The standard PWM controller can only handle somewhere around the 13V and the rest goes out the window. Multiplying the 13V by our 20.4A (5.1 x 4 panels) equates to 265W (of the original 360W) going to the batteries.

That's a loss of 95W or one whole panel's worth - now that we have your attention, how does MPPT improve this?

The newer technology (MPPT) takes advantage of that loss (or 95W in the above example).

It does this by increasing the OUTPUT amperage of the Smart Charger while still keeping the voltage at a constant of 13V.

The MPPT amperage actually increases by a whopping 7.3A (95W/13V) or 36%.

This is great news for 'theoretical Jill Genius' as MPPT has to be the go, given this data.

Along comes 'simple - Jack Amateur' with his proposed new Outback MX60 Smart Charger with the following cumulative challenges:

Challenge 1:

The blurb states that one needs 10W to operate the MX 60 unit. Using the 95W excess calculated by Jill, the **units operating power** is then subtracted from the excess wattage (95W - 10W), resulting in an 85W excess.

Still a good gain with this MPPT unit.

This in turn drops the amperage to +6.5A (85W/13V) or a 31% MPPT gain.

5% of the original gain was lost in operating the unit.

Keep this in mind if you intend using less panels or panels with less wattage.

Challenge 2:

Outback MX60 quote:

Power Conversion Efficiency. *96% typical @ 28 Volt 24 Amp Output*

These numbers, put another way, equate to a 26.9W (28V x 24A x 0.04) loss from a 672W (28V x 24A) system.

In the Pure Majek system, this

could mean a loss of another 10.6W (13V x 20.4A x 0.04).

This figure when subtracted from the excess wattage we calculated in 'Challenge 1' (85W - 10.6W), resulting in 74W excess, still not a bad gain.

The amperage drops further to +5.7A (74W/13V).

The gain now stands at 28%.

Challenge 3:

The MX60 is a 'sweep and sleep' technology gadget, the interval of which is user programmable. This technology programs the unit to do a scan at particular intervals and **amend MPPT charge settings for that particular scan instant**.

The Blue-Sky controllers are even simpler; they use a percentage of the voltage at power-up to guess what the voltage maximum power (Vmp) point will be. This can provide incorrect data to the unit.

An example could include shadowing caused by the yacht rocking at the exact instant a cloud passes by. Or a sailboat that is randomly placing shadows on the panels, such as a monohull or multihull in a swell. Neither situation is favourable.

While there is no figure that can be used here, it can affect the unit by limiting correct current by as much as 7%.

We chose to use a loss of 3%.

74W excess (from Challenge 2), less 3% (74 x 0.97) leaves us finally with 72W of excess power.

MPPT Considerations::
1. Units operating power (up to 10W),
2. Units Power Conversion Efficiency (up to 10.6W),
3. Scan charge settings (averaging 3%).

----- : -----

Jill Genius' pessimistic approach relates to the cost of the technology. Quality PWM controllers retail around AUD$250 verse the MPPT counterpart of AUD$700.

In our example above, this equates to AUD$6.25 for each extra Watt ($450/72W).

Jack optimistically then says that $450 will go a long way toward a generator that would provide a lot more than 72 Watts too, to which Jill adds 'but think of the extra weight and the fuel that you would have to carry'.

Our 'Optimistic Spin' says that MPPT technology would basically provide us additional power, equivalent to a fifth solar panel.

Considering that MPPT smart chargers cost between 3 - 4 times more than a quality PWM controller, using MPPT would be a cheaper option than buying a fifth panel and using a standard PWM controller.

MPPT Summary : MPPT technology (in our situation) would cost us 23W of power and be a fantastic option.

----- : ----

Other Solar Controller challenges include (whether PWM or MPPT):

Sun Angle:

All the above assume that the sun will be directly overhead at the perfect angle for the full 'bulk charge' period and that the MPPT/PWM are performing at their peak...wrong.

The fact is that these irregularities will cause a power degradation to the power conversion efficiency of the unit, but one needs to draw a line in the sand.

We have assumed here with 'sun angle' that the reduction will be 6% of the power conversion efficiency.

In our system, this could mean a further loss of another 15.9W (13V x 20.4A x 0.06) as a result of sun angle.

This figure when subtracted again from the excess wattage we calculated in 'Challenge 3' (72W - 15.9W), resulted in 56W excess. The gain is now 22% with MPPT.

Excessive temperatures:

If the yacht happens to be stationed in an area where the temperatures are normally 38 degrees Celsius or more, further efficiency challenges exist.

Conductor resistance increases with this increase in temperature, resulting in a voltage drop and the controllers themselves cannot remain cool and some shutdown automatically (called Thermal Shutdown) until a more suitable temperature is reached.

The moral here is to ensure that the controller is very well ventilated and in a cooler area of the yacht. See also the section in Solar Panels for temperature degradation.

----- : -----

Finding cable suitable for the Controller:

We located our cable length (from the panels to the smart charger, plus to the battery area) and added an additional 3%. This came to 8.5m of required cable.

For these calculations, the solar panel Short Circuit Current (5.5A) figures are used.

Using theory from the 'Solar Panel' section, panel set-up and values are:

- Series - 34.32A ((5.5A x 4) x 1.56),
- Parallel - 8.58A ((5.5A x 1) x 1.56), and
- Series / parallel - 17.16A ((5.5A x 2) x 1.56).

In our case, the latter (8.58A) figure has been used. We could safely assume from these deductions that a Solar Charger with 20A rating or more would suffice.

----- : -----

We chose to go with the Blue Sky Solar Boost 3024i. Additionally, we chose to obtain the temperature sensor and the IPN Pro-remote.

The temperature sensor will improve battery life by providing the Smart Charger with valuable data to modify the charging rate of the expensive batteries.

The IPN Pro-remote was purchased primarily for easy panel control and the ability to download all electrical data for future reference and power budgeting.

Advantages of this unit include an auxiliary output for 20A load control or a second battery charger. The latter will be our preference in providing power to the starter battery (which is independent to the main battery bank).

An important note is located in small writing at the base of our 'Blue Sky Specification Sheet', which is extremely important in matching an appropriate Smart Charger.

It states that:

Solar Panel voltage must be greater than or equal to battery voltage.

The Voc should always be less than the Smart Charger rating by 25% (or divide by 1.25).

For those who have not lost the plot yet, you may see a link between 'the above' and the 1.56 figure used in our solar calculations.

This is one of the safety factors already accounted for in our previous workings.

Having said that, the Blue Sky Solar Boost 3024i has a maximum 30A rating, (less the 25% from above), results in 24A.

This figure is well above the 17.16A solar panel value in our panel configuration.

----- : -----

If you are flipping out, don't worry.

We think MPPT chargers are great, just stick with the better known brands.

MPPT Solar Charger

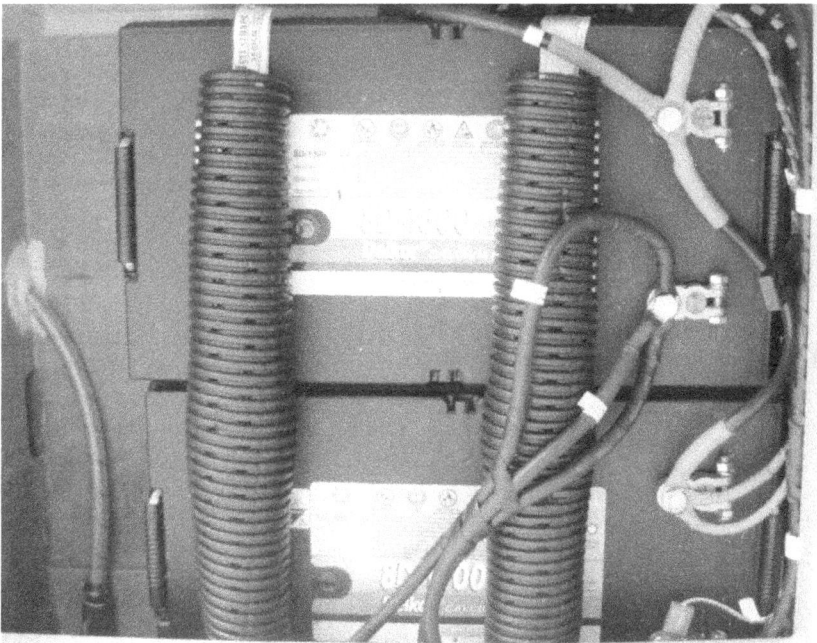

Battery Bank (or House Batteries)

Batteries

Solely relying on the elements to provide power at any given instant is risky and foolish, especially in our case, with the use of an autopilot. For this reason good battery storage is critical.

Our best endeavours to get our mind around this topic can be summarised below.

There has been a lot written about batteries and their advancing technology. Given this technology, 'deep-cycle-batteries' are said to be the choice of boat owners for many reasons.

The confusion arises in the various types and how they are differentiated from each other.

...'Cruising Configuration' as this is the most power demanding...

Basically we have found there are four common battery types being geared toward the yachting/boating market and they all contain lead-acid in some form.

It is how this lead-acid is maintained that causes some confusion. LIFELINE, a highly recommended marine battery manufacturer explains this well, having:
> Flooded acid type batteries,
> Calcium batteries,
> Gelled type batteries, an
> Advanced AGM type batteries.

Flooded acid batteries While this type has proven to be reliable, they can spill and need to be vented externally making it difficult to keep the battery weight over the yacht's centre of gravity (in our case).

These batteries also require regular maintenance and top-ups and given the qualities of the other types, were considered, but not used.

Calcium Batteries are on the uptake at the moment and the direction we have gone for the House Bank. They have very low rates of self-discharge and are maintenance free.

However, they can be temperamental with overcharging, so a very good charger (solar or battery) is required.

They have 4.5% more capacity than their gel type counterparts, allow a higher charging rate and have nearly twice the expected life.

They are however more temperamental on the undercharging and overcharging issues, making it very important to have some form of undercharging and overcharging protection built into the circuit.

----- : -----

The Battery Trade-off Challenge

We can't have the best of both worlds in the battery equation, so a trade-off needs to be found. These may help that decision as each case needs to be taken on its own merit.

Design Lifespan - is very dependant on the way the battery is used and recharged. This area is critical...that simple.

Discharge Rate - The rate at

which a battery will deplete its energy storage over a particular period with no recharging.

Plate Thickness - The thicker the plate, the better for deep cycle properties. The 'corrosion' of the plates again is strongly dependant on the way the battery is used and charged. Additionally, the sponge plate type batteries corrode faster with the higher surface area they carry, see below.

Plate Life - does vary with battery type:
> Automobile types have thin plates providing maximum charge exposure.

Their plates are compressed together forming a sponge type high surface area, allowing for short high current demands.

> Deep cycle battery types on the other hand have solid thicker plates, some 'Marine Batteries' even have a mixture of both. They have a plastic lattice type enclosure around each plate - some cheaper units have no enclosure at all.

> AGM's and Gel's have spongy to hard plates (depending on price normally).

Charging Critical Rating - How critical the charge control is during charging.

High quality charge controllers (specific to those types) are strongly recommended for those batteries in the High to Very High range, especially with the GEL type batteries. GEL batteries charge slower than similar AGM types.

Efficiency Rating - Based on use in a marine type environment with 300Ah - 600Ahr battery banks.

Additionally the effective use of charging and discharging energy given the 'heat gain/loss issues' with these types during that charging period. Other concerns here include the Voltage variation from the charged to non-charged state.

Recombinant Quality - the ability to conduct electrolysis internally without loss of battery water.

Temperature Critical - all batteries are temperature critical for their charging capacity. The higher the battery environment, the higher the battery maximum capacity - the lower the battery environment, the lower the battery maximum capacity.

...it is said that if you buy cheap, you get cheap...

Which is why temperature probes are so important on the charger. Unfortunately, battery life also decreases with higher environmental conditions.

Some Smart Chargers have this type of protection as standard within their units, but this all comes at a price.

If AGM's are left to stand for a few weeks, their discharge rate is said to be less than 3% per month and are maintenance free. We have chosen to use these for our Engine Starter Batteries.

----- : -----

Battery Life

Cutting to the chase here, there are normally two areas that will not prolong battery life and they are:

153

1. The use of the battery, draining it to a value less than 55% on a regular basis, and

2. The use of a cheap 'Smart Charger / Regulator' that has little manual intervention.

It has been proven in many a study that batteries used in the cruising marine environment (namely Deep Cycle Batteries) are best used on a regular basis down to 65% of their capacity, then recharged.

Sulfation (internal damage caused by continuous draining of power levels below 50-60% of the battery) is the result if used lower than 50-60%.
Specifically, sulfation of batteries starts when specific gravity falls below 1.23 or voltage measures less than 12.4 in a 12v battery.

'You never know when Murphy is on board though.'

Sulfation hardens the battery plates reducing and eventually destroying the ability of the battery to generate Volts and Amps. Further information can be found on the Internet from most of the quality battery suppliers.

With batteries too, it is said that if you buy cheap, you get cheap, so we chose to go for the better end of the market.

We chose 2 x 220 Ahr Delkor Calcium batteries, which will form our main 'house battery bank'.

4 small motorbike 45 Ahr AGM batteries are used solely as a 'starting battery' or cranking battery as it is sometimes known.

The reason for this split in batteries is that one can then guarantee a starting battery and reduce cabling.

We would have the solar panels to provide some charge to depleted house batteries and if that was not available, then the portable generator.

The House Batteries are also in the saloon area under the bench seat.

Here they are easily accessed and very close to the Electrical Panel (ours being accessible from the port hull with lots of room to move and good ventilation).

The Starter Battery is stowed 600mm away from the port engine (which is the one we always start first).

The battery is still within the cockpit area but nice and close to the engine, negating the use of thick cable due to the 'voltage drop' discussed further on.

Remember that this cable, once the start is complete, then acts as the charging cable to recharge the starter battery. This type of isolation from the main battery system will ensure that this battery is always charged to its capacity.

One idea that was continually discussed was the distance from the batteries to the anchor winch and the power that the winch needs to operate.

The cables here would have had to be very thick and this all comes at a cost and weight penalty.

Is it easier to place the battery near the winch and have the charging cables running all the way back? Should a second 33Ahr battery (solely used for the anchor winch) be positioned close to the anchor winch?

If this was done, maybe it could be used to power the emergency equipment , too. We did not follow through on this idea.

As a safety backup, our power storage banks could easily stretch power in a 'Cruising Configuration' over two days, using critical components only, should no charging power be available or generated, a comforting thought.

We mention 'Cruising Configuration' as this is the most power demanding part of sailing.

...the fatter the copper area within the cable, the better the carrying ability...

This is where the electronics, autopilot, lights, radios and other electrical equipment are draining the most power.

Here we also assume that the solar panels are not generating power and the generator is unserviceable.

----- : ----

Wiring and cable

Many an amateur boatperson has come unstuck at some stage in the electrical 'black-hole' regarding components or equipment not living up to their specifications.

One buys a component expecting a particular performance, to find

that it just does not happen.

Apart from the obvious of advertising, two other reasons are normally to blame:
• Inadequate component knowledge, and

• Incorrect cable and soldering.

It is the incorrect cable size and soldering that we can overcome once we grasp a basic understanding of the some of the facts.

While this understanding will slightly increase your establishment cost, the return of performance of that equipment will soon out-weigh this cost.

Cable size (in particular, copper conductor size), verse the distance from equipment, is also very important and it directly affects the voltage (the measure of 'pressure' within an electrical cable).

The way the cable is secured to a component (and sealed from the marine environment) will also affect that voltage.

Many appliances come with a metre or so of cable and if one chooses to add an extension cable or change the length, other items should be considered to maintain efficiency of that item.

The manufacturer will no longer guarantee its efficiency and in some cases the warranties become void.

Confusion starts in the Pacific area with the various standards of cable, we find AWG type wire (American Wire Gauge) often listed in American wiring diagrams

155

which differs to that in the Pacific region.

The British system often sees 'csa' (or cross sectional area) used. All have their own positive attributes and yes in Australia/New Zealand we have our own too, which thankfully conforms to the ISO (International Standards Organization) rating system.

This all sounds a bit much but in essence standardises Australian cable size and is best for obtaining and maintaining regulatory compliance for any Australian or New Zealand vessel.

The wire sold by some Pacific chandlers and motor vehicle stores can be rated differently to the Australian ISO standard and unless you know exactly what you are doing, can be the wrong buy, purely because of the way they are rated.

The cable size in the Pacific 'motor vehicle case' is sometimes sold in thickness of the cable (insulation and copper internal conductor), while the Australian ISO standard calls for

cross-sectional copper conductor (NO insulation), a big difference.

This brings many, unaware of this issue unstuck and its here that the problems start.

Remember: the fatter the copper area within the cable, the better the carrying ability of that cable for a given distance.

In wiring there is a situation called Voltage Drop, which is the drop in voltage verse the length/thickness of the cable (or copper conductor

to be precise).

One may start with 14V and by the time it reaches an appliance it may be as low as 9V, which in turn makes the appliance strain and even falter.

The drop is calculated using Ohms Law (which in summary says that Volts = Resistance in Ohms x Current in Amps) and this is the 'pure way' to mathematically understand and explain voltage (or in our case, Voltage Drop).

However, this comes with one big flaw and that is that the result is based on a perfect 20 degree Celsius environment and as one could imagine, this will definitely not be the case in the turret or vessel wall cavity.

Conductor resistance increases with an increase in temperature (resulting in Voltage drop).

Basically, this means that the cable carrying capacity in our application is heavily reduced due to its length and being partially surrounded by 'thermal type insulation', (referring to Australian Standards 3000 Table B2 for this case), hot air trapped in the turret cavities around the cable.

Even when we bunch the cables together, we get the same effect while on a smaller scale.

Given that the heat within the cables cannot escape, (or hot air around the wire does not allow the cable to disperse its heat energy) it reduces the carrying capacity of the cable and we therefore have a further Voltage loss.

All joints sealed from the elements

Wiring Stats Example   (These cables are tin coated and multistrand)

Nominal Size (mm)	Another Name	Conductor size (mm$^{2)}$	Roll size (m)	AS3000 Conductor Comparison
4		1.84	50	Exceeds
6		4.59	50	Exceeds
8	8 B&S	7.91	30	Exceeds
10	45 B&S	25.7	25	Exceeds
12	2 B&S	49.45	25	Exceeds

The cable being used in the marine environment also needs to be protected against corrosion. Certain elements in salt water act very aggressively when brought in contact with the copper internal conductor of the cable.

This corrosion (which is not immediately noticeable) will eat away at the cable causing a weak point, often seen as a green/whitish powder found around the cable where it has been cut, scarred or even soldered.

It is here that the electricity (for the want of an easier explanation) bleeds and is lost. This decay in power increases over time with the cable eventually failing.

...Conductor resistance increases with an increase in temperature...

One can see that not being aware of this event can be costly (or on a grander scale to those with little electrical knowledge, can be the $1000 repair). So...how do we reduce or minimise this corrosion?

We have found three ways to overcome this challenge.

The first is to always buy new cable that is protected by insulation and as soon as it's cut-to-size it is soldered then sealed around the weld, as well as 1cm back over the bare copper section and insulation with clear silicone (or similar).

This seals and protects the cable from the surrounding air and prevents corrosion.

It's that simple, but one needs to be disciplined in sealing the exposed areas as soon as possible, better over-done with the silicone (or similar) than underdone.

Better still, the use of 'heat-shrink' will improve this even further.

For those unfamiliar, 'heat-shrink' is similar to plastic and is tubular, this is then slipped over the join (the greater the overlap, the better) and using a heat-gun, (hair dryer or similar) is heated, causing the sleeve to shrink around the join or soldered area, resulting in an airtight finish.

The second is to purchase 'tinned-coated' cable. This cable has been coated in tin, which resists corrosion around the tinned areas (but does not resist corrosion around the solder-point of that same cable).

...always purchase 'tinned-coated' cable...

The third is the securing of the cable, especially near the joints or connections. Any minute movement either by vessel motion or that being caused by current in the actual cable will cause corrosion and/or loss of some power, as it ages.

The use of Stainless Steel bolts, nuts and washers (correctly matched to the size of the hole) is crucial.

Fitting a smaller bolt through a largish hole will work fine for a few months/years however, it will work itself loose causing arcing (normally a million miles from anywhere).

There are many accounts in various magazines of boat electrical fires/smoke resulting from this very small oversight.

Last items on the list are overall cable thickness and crimping. With cable thickness, the worst offender here is single core cable (cable that has only a single strand of copper conductor), which is normally found in housing wire.

The flexibility required for our set-up due to the continual vibration environment, requires the use of multi-strand cable. Even when selecting multi strand cable, there are some better than others.

As an example, seven laid strand cable (compared to four core circular cable) is half the overall thickness when compared to each other and is important when cable space is a premium.

...acceptable maximum voltage drop for this type of system is 5%...

Additionally, the 7-laid strand is tough and resists flexing better than its counterpart, great for systems such as yachts (the more strands, the better).

It's this type of purchase decision that can save on cable fatigue and size.

Lastly, cables should be supported at 400mm intervals for many reasons and the 'crimping' of electrical ends was used on all our cables. It was worth the money to buy our own crimping tool.

Put all the above points together and corrosion (and therefore resultant power loss) will be very minimal for the life of the vessel.

Other items that directly influenced the type and thickness of cable were the use of 'Fuses' (a rewire-able type of fuse) or MCB's (circuit breakers that allow slightly higher current capacity).

This is further explained in the section 'Cable Voltage Drop given ISO/AS3000'.

----- : -----

Cable Voltage Drop

(Using Australian Standard ISO/AS 3000:2001)

The whole system at the start of each circuit is protected by Circuit Breakers (MCB's) as they allow a slightly higher current capacity for any selected cable size.
Another strong recommendation made to us was to ensure we used circular bunched cable.

In the case of the solar panel cabling, ensure the correct Current Carrying Capacity.

This was strongly advised because the cables housed below the turret outer skin will always be naturally heated by the indirect action of the sun on the turret roof during daylight hours when the Solar panels and cables will be carrying their maximum charging current.

----- : -----

The quickest way to calculate Voltage Drop (but very technical) is using a formula where certain values are known.

Refer next page.

> **For the 'Tech Heads', the formula reads:**
> $$E = V_c \times L \times I / 1000$$
> Where:
> ➤ E is the Circuit Volt Drop,
> ➤ V_c is the conductor milli-volt drop per amp metre for the conductor size,
> ➤ L is cable run in metres, and
> ➤ I is circuit load in Amps.

These known values must include:
> The type of resistor within the cable where copper value
  = 0.017, aluminium value
  = 0.028, steel value = 0.18 (R)
> The maximum short circuit amperage of the solar panel (Isc),
> Length of the cable from panel to battery - not controller
  (L),
> Safety Margin of 1.25 (S)
> The cross sectional area of the cable (A).

Voltage drop = (((2 x L) x Isc) x (R x S))/A

In our case:
= (((2 x 8.5) x 22*) x (0.01 x 1.25)) /25)
          (*22 = 5.5A x 4 panels)
= ((17 x 22) x 0.02125) / 2
= (374 x 0.02125) / 25
= 7.9475 / 25
= 0.318 Volt

They say that acceptable maximum voltage drop for this type of system is 5% of the nominal battery voltage. Pure Majek's comes in at less than 2%.

For the theoretical gurus, another formula helped us unravel some of the mystery in Voltage Drop and is based on available data supplied by Australian Standard ISO/AS 3000.

From Table B2 of this writing, a realistic variable figure that accounts for heat loss in the conductor/cable.

Other data we needed to bring this together included the distance in metres from the panel to the battery (not the Smart Charger by the way),the maximum amperage, and conductor size (the copper centre in mm2).

Using previously stated data from the SunSolar Solar Panel data sheet, the Short Circuit Amperage and Open Circuit Voltage were extracted and used here to calculate the expected loss or voltage drop.

A chart (in this Chapter) provides a reasonably quick guide for cable selection with 5% and 2% voltage drops. While it is at 24V, follow the 'Notes' for other voltage systems.

----- : -----

Bus Bars

A Bus Bar is used as a distribution point for power, either on the positive or negative side of the electrical circuit.

They are normally made of good metal resistor types such as copper. Used correctly in a circuit, they can save on weight and electrical cable.

When in the circuit, they are normally insulated from all other surfaces and in our case being screwed into timber worked a real treat.

The thickness of these bus Bars depends on the current flow expected. They are very cheap if one has the time.

...thickness of these bus Bars depends on the current flow expected...

We have used two of these in our Electrical Circuitry, one at the Port Bus (negative side) and the other at the Main Switch Board Panel (Negative side).

They proved their weight in gold (literally) as this allowed all negative terminals (35 at Port Bus and 38 at Main Switch Board Panel) to be linked to a single point.

One cable runs from the Map Table Bus Bar to the MSBP and then to the battery negative.

This allowed for a single cable back to the battery and we have chosen to not have any form of switching on the negative wiring in our yacht. This includes fuses or circuit breakers; they are all on the positive side of the circuitry.

(It's noted - ABYC and some other groups are now insisting on protection in both the positive and negative cables.)

----- : -----

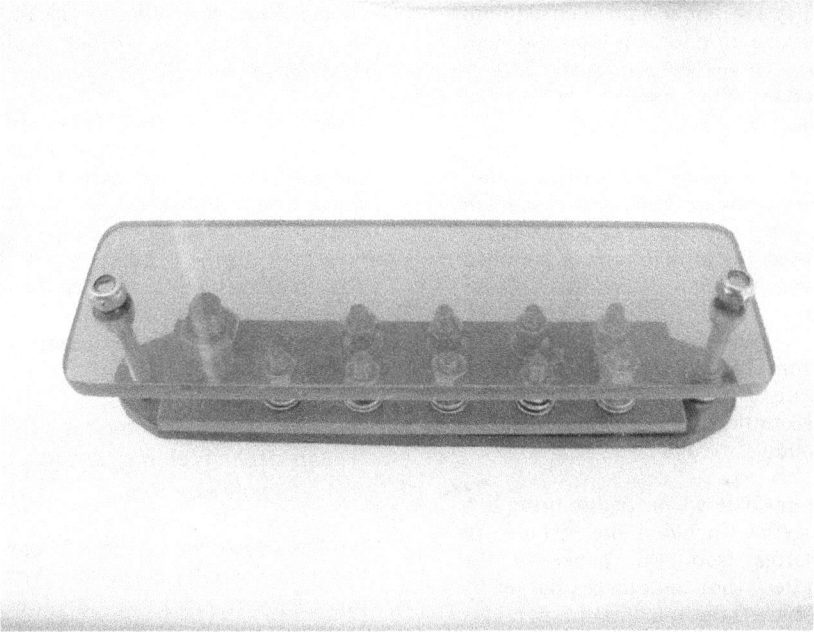

Homemade Bus Bar. See the diycatamaran.com website for details

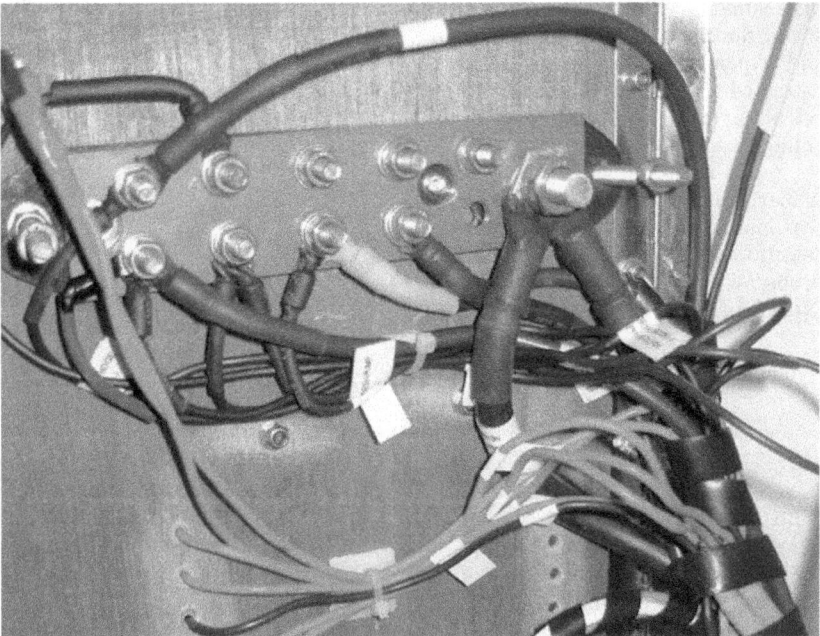

Installed Bus Bar unit

----- : -----

Lighting

It's here that you realise to what extent we rely on power and how easily, given some guidance, this 'green-power' can be developed, especially now with the onset of the LED /CCFL bulb age.

The light switches are mostly located at each light fitting. Two that have different points on Pure Majek are located together inside the entry door.

They have been placed there specifically for ease of use and they operate the cockpit and saloon main lights.

This has saved many hours of wiring, weight and frustration.

...LED's emit only small amounts of light ...

Lighting is all about Lumens and a Lumen is the measure of light against the power used (normally Watts).

The more lumens from a Watt of power, the better (or energy efficient) the bulb is said to be. While one can get very technically involved in comparison data here, we chose to simplify our information in simple English for the purposes of making a reasonably informed choice.

In the low voltage marine environment, light bulbs can be broken down into four common areas:
1. Fluorescent Bulbs
2. LED's
3. Incandescent Bulbs, and
4. Quartz Halogen.

Fluorescent Bulbs
The long bulb contains an argon and mercury vapour (or gas). The inside of the tube is lined with phosphor that when activated by ultra violet light, shines white.

In simple terms there is an electron interaction when power is applied within the vapour.

Their Lumen rating is between 50 and 100 lumens per watt, four times better than incandescent bulbs and lower heat, too.

These bulbs do lose efficiency over about two years and a change will do wonders in any environment.

Early 2000 saw a blossoming in the florescent age with the aid of electronic advancement. This helps cement the now common **compact fluorescent lamp** (or CFL) or sometimes called the energy saving bulb.

The catch has been the cost of this technology.

The lifespan of this type of bulb is now 8,000 and 15,000 hours, making it a viable alternative to the current incandescent bulb (lasting 8 to 15 times longer) with the plus of a much lower and cooler operating temperature.

The CCFL **(Cold Cathode Fluorescent Light)** is the latest of the CFL range.

The difference here is the amount of current they use when compared to their CFL counterparts, at around 8 to 12 times less.

The lifespan of CCFL bulbs has jumped to 50,000 hours however;

the lumen value has been cut by 1/3 when compared to their CFL counterparts.

This is the price one pays for the extended life they forecast.

----- : -----

LED's

LED's (Light Emitting Diodes) have no filament and are illuminated solely by the movement of electrons in a semiconductor material.

LED don't force your eyes to re-adjust every time you use them and makes getting around in the dark much easier.

Because of their low power consumption, LED's emit only small amounts of light and are therefore normally clustered (have more than one diode) in each bulb. Lumen rating is still very low around 15-20 lumens per Watt.

Technology has advanced in this area and in some instances; clustered LED's have been electronically modified to switch off and on automatically at such a fast rate that the human eye cannot detect this switching.

"So what?" you say

Well, this increases the life of the LED and halves its power consumption. In effect making it a 30-40 lumen per Watt device.

This technology is moving very fast and approved clustered LED's are now available for navigation and anchor lights. To be certified here, they need to be seen from at least

2-3 nm, not bad for a few pulsating diodes.

----- : -----

Incandescent Bulbs

These bulbs have a very thin tungsten filament that is housed inside a glass bulb.

When power passes through the very thin filament, it causes heat (which one can feel) and glows white hot, seen as light.

They are very inefficient in that much power is given off as heat. Their Lumen rating is commonly 15-17 lumen per Watt. The life span is typically 750 hours to 1000 hours.

----- : -----

Quartz Halogen

Quartz (or tungsten-halogen) bulbs are basically incandescent units that have more 'grunt', a better quality light and are brighter.

The tungsten filaments are operated at higher temperatures than incandescent and their efficiency is said to be better by 15%. However, this comes at a cost in heat, which is where a majority of the valuable power is wasted.

Over extended periods (30 minutes or more), the heat build-up is noticeable and in warm climates, not the asset we sought.

----- : -----

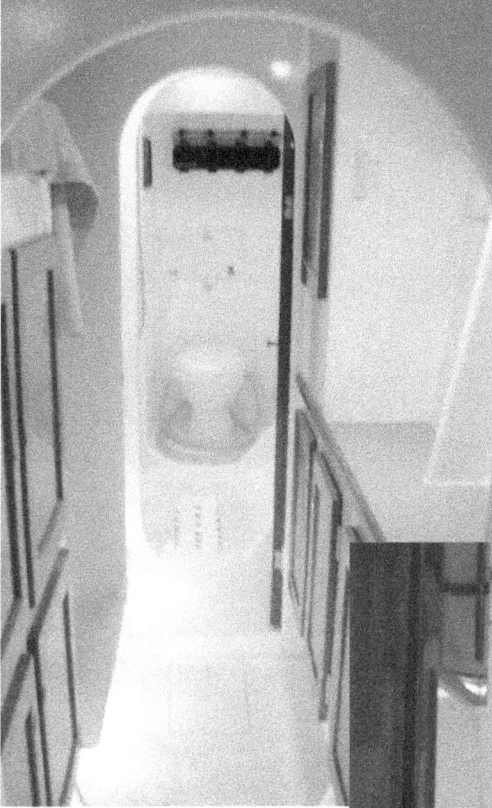

Forward to the port front room with floor and ceiling lights on.

Using LED floor and ceiling lighting at night. There is more than enough light.

So in a race to the finish of **Lumens per Watt**:
1. Fluorescent's (50 and 100 lumens),
2. CCFL's (65 - 75 lumens
3. LED's (15-20 lumens),
4. Quartz Halogen (15 – 25 lumens), and
5. Incandescent (15-17 lumens).

In the race for **least heat** omitted:
1. LED's
2. CCFL's
3. Fluorescent's
4. Incandescent
5. Quartz Halogen

In the race for **bulb life**:
1. CCFL's - 50,000 hours
2. LED's - 50,000 hours
3. CFL's - 8000 to 15,000 hours
4. Incandescent bulbs - 750 to 1000 hour
5. Quartz Halogen - 750 to 1000 hours or less

In summary:
The CFL/CCFL's and LED's have their place in our boat with specific uses.

---- : ----

Internal Lighting

It was decided that a total of 9 single type spot reading lights, all movable and containing their own switches, were needed at:
- Each bed position,
- One stationed at the keyboard (near the port hull steps), and
- In the crux of the settee area in the saloon.

White Overhead lights were to be positioned:
- Four in each hull, for general passageway lighting. The galley and shower lights being specifically placed to provide best lighting for each purpose, and

- Two in the saloon area (one overhead the table and the second overhead the map table).

The map table light will be a two-position light, one side white light and the second side red light.

The latter being for night navigation.

----- : -----

External Lighting

Vessel navigation/position lighting include:
- White light (top of the mast),
- Spreader light (on the mast)
- Berthing lights (x2) on the fore beam, and
- Position lights (Red and green either side.

In the cockpit, there are:
- Two stairway lights positioned overhead in the turret extension, and
- General cockpit light.

----- : -----

Internal Power Points

Why so many 'general use' outlets you will soon ask?

Well apart from a few yachters wishing they had more power points, we intend to use these points for general battery charging but most importantly for the portable emergency bilge pump.

...power-eating switch systems, nice and close to the battery...

We need easy access to a central point fast without hindrance in the unlikely event of 'holing' the yacht.

240v outlets:

- Four doubles ('general purpose' - double in the galley and starboard rear room, double at the port steps and Main Switch Board Panel),

12V outlets:

- One in the forward starboard hull at knee height in the forward room
- This will be used for a portable freezer when and if any extended trips will be done (just getting ready),

- Two at the map table (two for 'general use' and two for TV and Video),

- Two in the galley (two being for 'general use' and one each for the gas oven and cook top ignition), and

- Two in the central electrical position behind the keyboard (one for 'general use' and the others for keyboard, radio etc.).

---- : ----

External Power Points

240v inlet point:
- Under turret roof area (port side) out of the weather, can be easily secured for long term berthing (not that we would have the cash to do that), and

- There are no 240V external outlets.

12V outlets:
- One for the gas hot water ignition, and

- One for the gas BBQ ignition.

Having now established a basic plan for the lighting and power points, cabling began in earnest. One 50m roll lead to a second and then a third, its amazing how quickly it disappears.

It was our intention to not solder

any cables until all the wiring was installed. This meant that once the cable was cut, the ends were quickly folded and taped to provide little chance of any corrosion.

The smallest possible holes were drilled to take the cable lengths and while not mandated in any manuals or regulatory marine authority, we chose to fasten the cable to the stringers at 200mm sections.

This does two things:
• Prevents movement of the cable and therefore cable deterioration, and

• Prevents knocking of cables with boat movement.

Nothing worse than a cable quietly tapping the ceiling as the swell moves below and 'the cook' pondering the thought of mice. That leads to the inevitable as you could imagine

With some left over waterproofing sealant, all holes through timber sections were then sealed on either side to prevent weathering and movement of the cable within the access hole.

All-in-all, very firm and secure.

----- : -----

Main Switch Board Panel (MSBP)

A '**Main Switch Board Panel**' provides a single point for control of the general electrical system components and is located in the centre of the port hull alongside the stairs.

Controlled from here are:
1. Inverter,
2. Battery Charger Unit,
3. AC Switching,
4. Main Bus Circuit Breakers, and
5. Solar Charger Unit.

A second smaller 'Port Bus' is located in the saloon adjacent the chart table.

Controlled from here are:
1. Port Bus Circuit Breakers,
2. Solar Charger controlling,
3. Battery Charger controlling,
4. VHF Radio, and
5. Entertainment Radio

----- : -----

The 'Main Master Battery Switch' (MMBS)

This is located at the rear of the saloon bench for:

• Easier access with a cold vessel, and
• Security reasons

Controlled from here are:
1. Winch Cut-off Switch,
2. Solar Panel Master Switch,
3. Inverter CB & switching,
4. Main Bus Master Switch, and
5. Hot Battery Master Switch.

As can be seen, these are the power eating switch systems, nice and close to the battery. Improving safety by limiting the cable run required, especially within the Inverter.

The main wiring for connection to the 'Main Master Battery Switch' is detailed in this section.

----- : -----

Main Switch Board Panel (MSBP)

Carries all the main circuit breakers, including junction to the
two other Switch Busses shown on this page.

**Main Master
Battery Switch' (MMBS)**
The main control of power to
the vessel, discussed on previous
page.

Port Bus
On the map table containing most of
the day-to-day switching.

Starboard Bus
Small panel on the starboard side in the
galley.

Inverter

During your planning stages, we are sure this AC power challenge must have been looked at.

With our yacht, we have chosen to have only one Inverter AC outlet. And no...this is not connected to all the other AC outlets.

To connect the Inverter to all the other AC outlets, there is much more needed by way of AC wiring circuitry and protection, and we believe this to be unnecessary for our circumstances.

If one is that desperate to have 240vAC (other than the Inverter) while Cruising, start the Generator and plug into that - solved.

Our use for the Inverter is limited to 380W Pure Sine Wave maximum.

If you are unfamiliar with Pure Sine Wave and intend using AC Electronics such as laptops etc., do some research as this type of Inverter can save you money in electronic replacement costs.

This allows us to use computers, kids game consoles etc., just a token amount.

In the electrical diagram you will also see a huge circuit breaker right next to the Inverter, solely for the Inverter.

Because this unit draws such a large amount of power from the DC side, this is a strong recommendation.

Mandatory considerations in line with marine ABYC best practice when choosing an Inverter include:
1. Conformal coating,
2. Non trickle charge type units, and
3. Independent AC and DC internal components.

The **conformal coating** is there to provide further resistance to corrosion of circuit board components as a result of the salt-water environment.

This is done normally by using a spray similar to MIL-1-46058C. While this does not stop the ingress, it certainly extends the component life

The internal Inverter AC components need to be totally separate to the DC components, normally by **two isolated coil types**.

Less expensive units use autotransformers.

The reason is that some current can and does pass to the vessel and when high, poses a shock issue and is linked to galvanic corrosion, especially when dockside with other vessels.

----- : -----

Pointers:

1. Plan your install (on butchers paper) and keep it.

2. Be realistic with what you REALLY need.

3. Always use tin coated multistrand cable.

4. Choose the best batteries you can afford.

5. Choose the largest solar array you can.

Traps:

1. Not keeping a detailed plan of the wiring.

2. Not labelling the wires.

3. Damaging cable during install.

4. Installing too much for the vessel's purpose.

5. Complicating the build with too many fancy gadgets.

6. Not selecting a quality solar charger.

A Sailing Catamaran Building Project

Chapter Seventeen: Gas

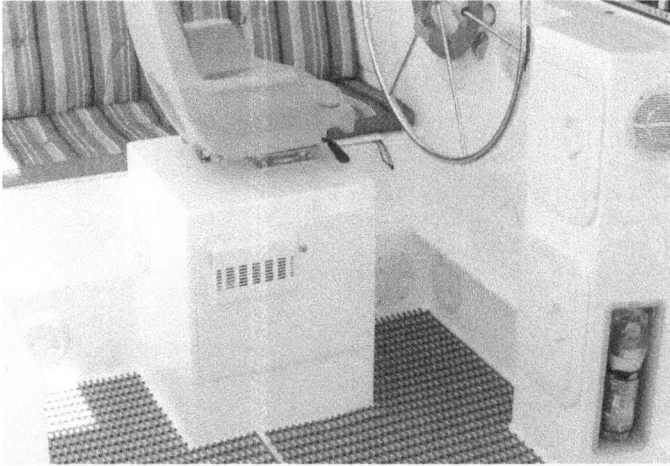

Well...what a topic. What could be so simple has been complicated by the bureaucratic powers-that-be.

In an effort to speed compliance processes up, they have formed various committees over the years which have slowed (if not stalled) the process of reform and compliance in this area.

Each state having their own compliance groups which, in some instances, are in contradiction of the Australian Gas Industries counterparts on policy requirements.

This makes our amateur build that more difficult.

Do you require regulatory approval for a gas system; in Queensland you do, however in Victoria on a private sailboat you don't (at time of writing).

In Queensland, registration forms ask the question and require a 3-week old Gas Certificate to follow.

This brief cannot fulfil the changing requirements in this area and professional guidance was our only avenue.

There are however a few items that place one on the better side of the law in most states, which include:

1. A totally separate, well vented, externally accessed, bottle compartment,

2. Gas lines that do not go through any living quarters,

3. Use appliances that are approved for Australia (and

carry the AUS Gas Sticker),

4. Heaters are an issue,

5. Heaters and Instant Hot Water systems MUST BE externally vented, and

6. Keeping gas and un/leaded fuels at least one metre apart.

----- : -----

This is at least a start. It took a lot of searching, but we finally located a plumber that would do the job for us and we chose a four-pronged attack.

We got the fellow in for an appraisal and advised him where our preferred positions for items would be and thankfully, got his approval.

The second visit, we got all the internal welding and pipes in prior to painting internally.

On the third visit, we got the appliances installed and connected during the fit-out stage, then lastly just before launch, got him in to give the all-OK with that crucial bit of paper. There is a fee and they don't mind charging either.

----- : ------

Our Gas-Locker is positioned on the fore starboard hull, which can only be accessed from deck level.

The floor in that locker was made with a fall to the large vent hole allowing any gas (being heavier than air and thus at the base of the locker) to vent overboard.

Two gas bottle lines run to a joiner and selector valve (either left or right), this then flows to the Gas detector electric shut-off valve (discussed later), through the Gas Regulator (which regulates the pressure to around 3psi) and into the pipes feeding the appliances.

Various state authorities have their own requirements for connections within this compartment and definitely the security of the bottles.

Some states even require fire proof lining or fire resistance compartments that allow a 'safe-burn' for 10 minutes.

The gas line then runs through the hull to the galley (with no joins) where it divides into three:
• One for the gas cooker,
• One for the oven, and
• The last out to the cockpit to feed the gas hot water heater and BBQ.

We chose to install a Gas Detector with an automatic shut-off valve. The valve is a key feature not only for safety, but also as a means of turning gas off when leaving the vessel.

The 12V DC valve is only powered when power is available and opens on command allowing gas through the entire system.

Switching off, or losing power closes the valve automatically, disengaging gas right at the bottle source. The system (DVK Marine Gas Alarm) uses minimal current while operating, a key feature we chased when buying the unit.

----- : -----

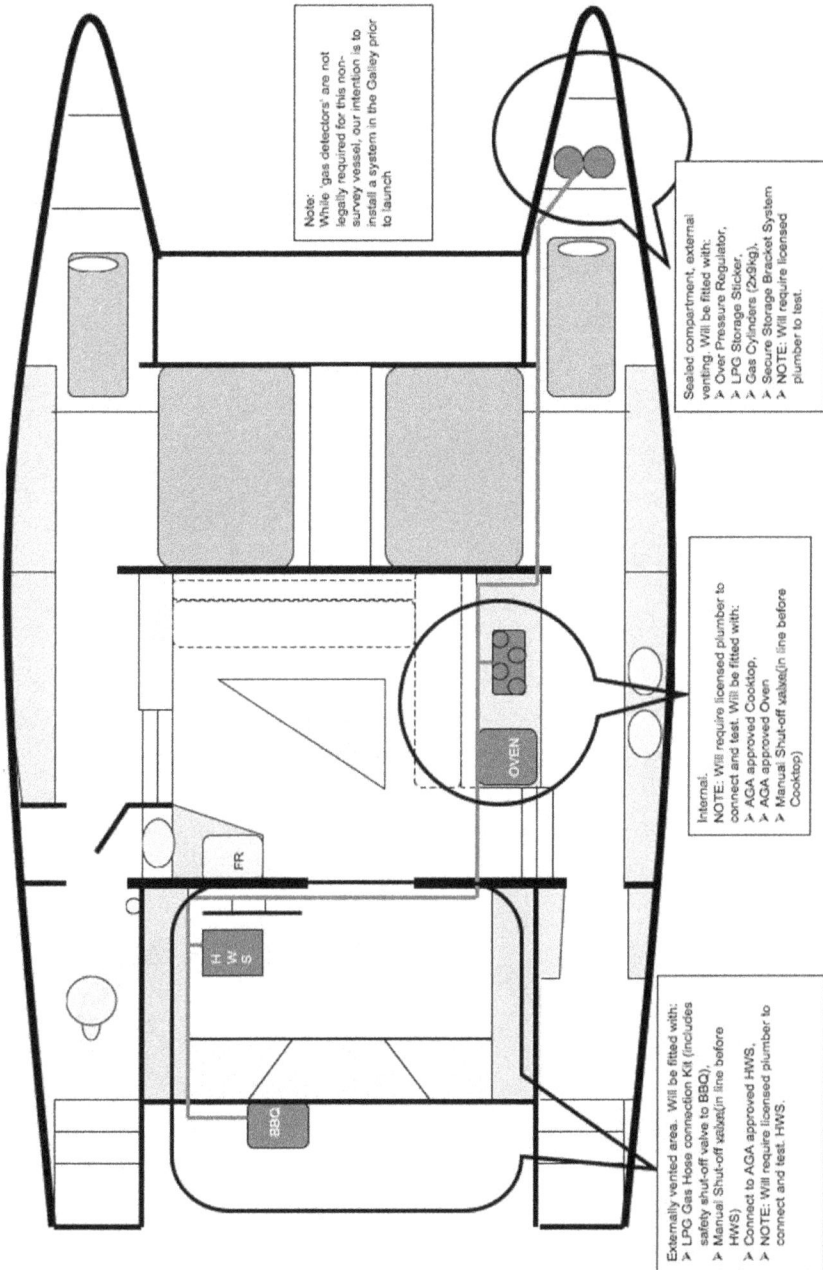

Note:
While 'gas detectors' are not legally required for this non-survey vessel, our intention is to install a system in the Galley prior to launch

Sealed compartment, external venting. Will be fitted with:
➤ Over Pressure Regulator,
➤ LPG Storage Sticker,
➤ Gas Cylinders (2x9kg),
➤ Secure Storage Bracket System
➤ NOTE: Will require licensed plumber to test.

Internal.
NOTE: Will require licensed plumber to connect and test. Will be fitted with:
➤ AGA approved Cooktop,
➤ AGA approved Oven.
➤ Manual Shut-off valve(in line before Cooktop)

Externally vented area. Will be fitted with:
➤ LPG Gas Hose connection Kit (includes safety shut-off valve to BBQ),
➤ Manual Shut-off valve(in line before HWS)
➤ Connect to AGA approved HWS,
➤ NOTE: Will require licensed plumber to connect and test. HWS.

Gas Installation Diagram

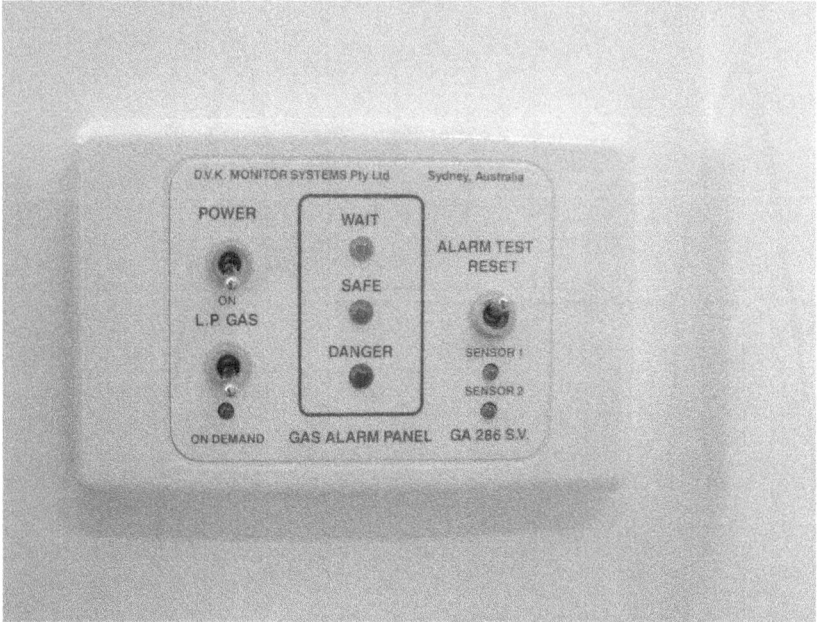

Gas Detector Switching

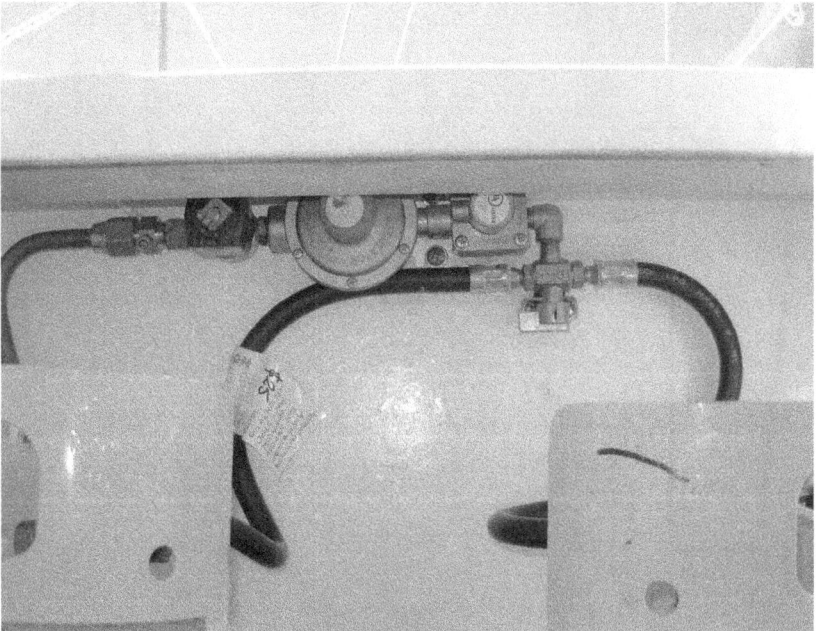

Gas selector and automatic shutoff valve in the gas locker

Chapter Eighteen:
Freshwater and Saltwater Systems

The water system carries three types of water - saltwater, freshwater (drinkable) and freshwater (non-drinkable).

The saltwater outlets include:
- The toilet,
- Deck-wash, and
- Desalinator (not discussed here)

Freshwater outlets include:
- The hot water system,
- Showers (Internal and external),
- Vanity Water, and
- Galley Water (drinkable and non-drinkable water types).

The freshwater system is made up of three basic sections:
- Desalinator (not discussed here),
- Freshwater drinkable (having being filtered), and
- Freshwater non-drinkable.

There are two tanks (one of 200L called the Main and a second of 100L called the Reserve) that provide the freshwater needs for the yacht.

The intention is to have the Main Tank used only and when required, the Reserve Tank filled and used - normally left empty.

Based on our planned water use, these sizes should prove more than suitable. The tanks are the collapsible type and can be individually filled and emptied.

Tank water flow control is via ball valves stationed in the saloon, below the main seating area. From here a single water line leads to the main water pump and accumulator, in the Vanity, under the sink.

We have purposely chosen the vanity position for three reasons:
- Positive water pressure,
- Easy maintenance access, and
- Single 'wet area' on the yacht.

Our intention is to be proactive in the maintenance with the system and this meant easy access is a must and the pump units must be easy to work on.

This however does have its own drawbacks in that additional plumbing and forward planning is needed.

Freshwater from the tanks are piped to this area with the pump purposely being positioned lower than tank level, making pumping more effective.

The positive pressure reduces the workload of the pump, extending pump life. As a result, an additional ball valve has been placed in the line to the pump (below the port steps) to prevent backflow shutoff during maintenance.

Below the vanity sink, the system is also pressurised. Together with an accumulator, the on/off cycling of the main pump is reduced and a more constant system pressure exists.

The pump chosen is a common Shurflo unit to allow for cheaper spares and replacement.

We will also carry a spare Shurflo pump which may seem over the top, but provide immediate replacement in the event of a malfunction. It too is needed for the desalinator auto-flush-function (when we are away from the yacht), making its serviceability rather important, in our case.

In the vanity area, the pressurised water now goes two ways:
Back to the 'water tank area', which supplies:
- The galley, and
- The desalinator.
- To the Vanity, which supplies:
- Vanity basin,
- Internal Shower
- External shower (cold only), and
- Hot Water system

----- : -----

Vanity and Hot Water System (HWS) Plumbing

The yacht has a single tap for the shower. The main reason for this is that we want to control the water use.

This control in turn reduces water waste (by those who use their big toe trying to find a suitable temperature before jumping in, at start-up), reduces plumbing costs and also provides a single temperature for all showers.

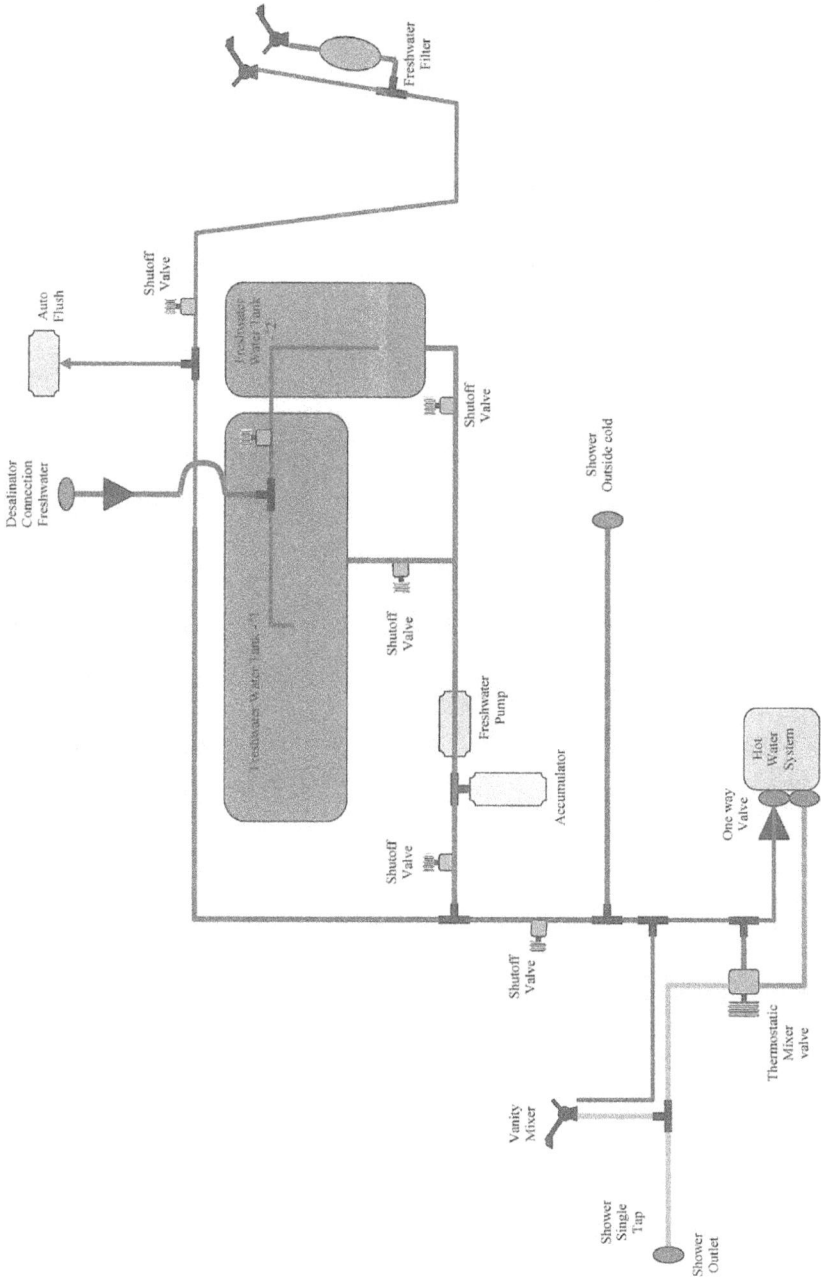

Water Plumbing Diagram

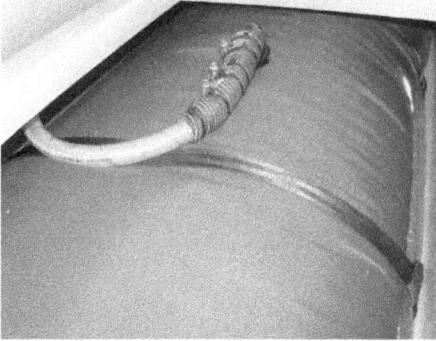

200 litre water bladder - one of three

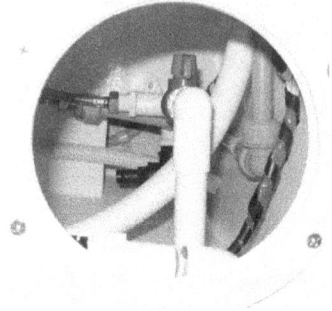

Valve selector to Hot Water
System - Quick access

Freshwater Pump
and Accumulator

Vanity Bilge - Saltwater
Inlet, Transducer
paddle-wheel, filter and
Bilge

We pre-set the control and mixing, closer to the Hot Water system. Cold pressurised water is sent to the HWS where it is heated and then returned.

At the exit from the HWS tank, we have a mixer valve that reintroduces cold water and its here that we control the temperature. This warm water then goes to the vanity and shower.

An additional separate cold water line is run to the vanity sink.

----- : -----

Galley Plumbing

The second pressurised return line (that runs back to the 'tank area') is split two ways:
- One line to the Galley, and
- The Desalinator system.

A 'flickmaster' has been placed in the galley to provide this fresh water through a filter on one side (even although the water should be clean from the desalinator) and standard freshwater on the other.

The amount of vessel use, specifically the periods and type of sailing we intend doing, will mean that freshwater will be sitting in the freshwater tank for extended periods between uses.

While every effort will be made to 'turn-over' the water being used, one cannot guarantee that water made 12 months ago has been all used.

The last thing we want is to be buckled-over with gut aches caused by bacteria in the freshwater system three or four hours into a weekend away.

This outlet has its own tap and the filters are down to 5 micron. To keep the filter systems full, a one-way valve will be placed in the line below the filter too.

----- : -----

Saltwater

There are two saltwater inlets on the yacht:
- Desalinator , and
- Toilet/Deckwash.

The toilet/deckwash inlet detail is listed in the toilet section, from where we continue.

The saltwater pump is located in the vanity area above the freshwater pump. This is for the same reasons mentioned for the freshwater pump location.

There are two saltwater filters in this system (given that the water could be contaminated with plant matter).

The deckwash pump has only one outlet (above the shower area) and a hose pipe is used to wash the entire yacht.

We do not have saltwater to the galley.

----- : -----

Pointers:

1. Plan your install (on butchers paper) and keep it.

2. Get gas compliance certificate.

3. Be aware that access may be needed near all joints after install.

Traps:

1. Not using approved appliances.

Chapter Nineteen:
Final Fit-out, nearly Launch Time

It's an exciting, yet nervous, time for us. We have waffled on about many things to date and put in place many ideas that theoretically make life that bit easier.

This was all incorporated in the design/build phase and now we try and make the bits fit.

Many of the cosmetic faces went on quickly such as the access hatches for the stowage lockers.

This aesthetically made the cockpit look a million bucks with that professional touch.

The hatches open a particular way to allow easy access and keep arms/hands at bay from the steering spokes. While at rest this wouldn't prove an issue, but under sail, the steering moves port/starboard continually, making access through these spokes very dangerous.

Navigation Instruments

We have chosen to go with Navman Compass, Wind, Depth and Speed gauges as well as the Raymarine S1 Autopilot.

The Depth and Speed instruments provide clear 65mm (backlit at night) readings, which can be seen from any position in the cockpit including the rear steps and winch areas.

The navigation instruments are being installed down a centre section of the cockpit door.

External Scuppers

Cockpit Steering and Instrumentation

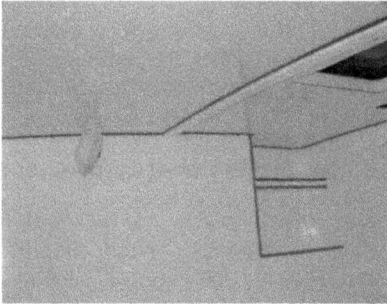

Ceiling and Fan Fit-out

Seating and external floor covers

We originally built the frame to take the full width of the navigation instrument nuts, which hold them onto the frame.

Access to the gauges is from the saloon where the cables are fed back down (hidden from view), behind the map table and join the myriad of other cables in the starboard hull.

The instruments will then all be linked via NMEA and appropriate units to chat to each other and provide data on our Navman 8084 8" Multifunction unit.

The radar, while not having its own instrument, can be either separate or overlaid using the Multifunction unit.

...run all night using no more than 0.8 Amps, a real winner...

Additionally, the Fuel-sender-unit will provide charted data that can be used for optimum power assessment.

The GPS aerial also fell into place easily, the pre-laid 15mm plastic conduit within the turret roof proving a great success. This too then feeds behind the map table against frame 7 to the instruments.

The high-speed fairing unit that takes the transducer as been mounted fore of the port keel, yet high enough from the lowest part of the hull in that area.

We are sure that there are many of those who have and those who are going to, sail over a rope or cable accidentally and we want this fairing to miss being torn off. To add more piece of mind, the forward part of the fairing has a

12mm bolt securely attached through the hull to provide for that additional holding power.

The transducer is a Navman 1kw unit (for those not in the know - this is huge) and provides for more accurate surface definition and the good-old fish finding.

----- : -----

Steering and controls

The steering too, slotted in well. It proved that hard work in the planning stages is vital and worth all the effort and headaches, in the end.

----- : -----

Cockpit Drainage

The drainage is done at four points using plastic household 80mm bathroom drains. These were then set in place in pre-resined holes. They have also been strategically placed to prevent the odd foot falling on them and mindful of the best water capture points with fore/aft and port/starboard movement.

----- : -----

Fairing's for external outlets/vents

We have chosen to cover all external holes/vents with a fairing of some sort.

The advantages here are to prevent any backwash caused by waves or movement of the boat through the water.

Many a story has been told of wet pants in the cockpit on a cold day or even fountains of water coming from the sink drain. While the fairings will not stop the backflow, it will definitely help in preventing 90% of the backflow.

The fairings we made out of 50, 90 and 100mm plumbers pipe. A word of caution here in that some plastics do not adhere to resin.

A try out would be strongly suggested. We then cut these at an angle to suit, trying to get the same angle throughout.

Then with very careful placement and clever use of Sikaflex, the normal stain-runs, that one sees down the sides of the yachts, have been prevented using these fairings.

To paint, we lightly sanded, undercoated and top coated with two layers of polyurethane. With those beneath the hull, they were stippled to follow the underneath stippling effect.

----- : -----

Internal Fit-out
Front opening Windows

The leading edge to where the windows were to be hinged did provide a headache.

Given that the front is curved very slightly, hinging had to be spot-on. We chose to go with four smaller hinges as opposed to two large ones. This provided for more security and strength in the actual window frame/pane.

The holes here were predrilled oversize and filled with resin, left to cure overnight, then drilled to take the appropriate screw. The extra effort taken, hoping to

prevent water ingress that occurs with age.

Two Weaver handles are used to secure the window internally and the window can be held ajar with two heavy-duty hatch stays.

----- : -----

Ceilings, Lights and Fans

Before we could continue with the internal fit-out, the ceilings had to be up.

To do this all external bolt-on attachments (winches, cleats, some navigation lights etc.) needed to be in place to prevent doing the ceiling-job more than once.

Having finished that, the ceilings were tested and some more changes made to the panels.

We chose to add a few more LED lights in the galley and had wiring in place for the fans, an additional item that we chose to add given our experience with the sleeping quarters, on a hot day.

The three speed Caframo - Bora fans on high, use very little power, which fits our power schematic perfectly. All four fans could be comfortably run all night using no more than 0.8Amps, a real winner.

While these units suit us, they are not very strong and should be tried before purchasing.

All the lights are LED's with the exception of a few bulbs on the mast.

The LED selections took a long time and at the time of purchase, were at the expensive end of the price bracket. It is hoped that they will come down in price in the near future.

....creates a visual feel of space in the cockpit...

All of the main lights were purchased from the United States.

The reading lights, we put together (being a little more complicated than originally thought as resistors had to be added to meet the lower voltage level required for the bulb. There is a lot more on this topic in the 'Electrical section'.

The main and exterior cockpit lights were 48 LED cluster types, which should prove valuable.

We checked these out on a friends boat and the light was above satisfactory for the power being consumed.

Lining all the hulls at ankle height (and hidden from view) are other smaller LED clusters, which should provide sufficient light for walking down the hulls at night without the normal lights on, again saving on some more power.

With these in place and wiring set, it was time to raise the ceilings. We have diverted from our original thoughts of using Velcro due to its cost.

Instead the panels are held in place with capped screws and French polished trim. While on the ceiling panels, we chose not to clear varnish the hidden side.

This may prove an asset at a later stage if there are any leaks. We are told that the location can be found much quicker and sooner as only

the porous part (as opposed to pooling and running out on the edges) will discolour and can be seen from below making repair location a lot easier.

----- : -----

Cockpit doors and Trim

The main cockpit door is bi-fold and the extra effort to build it this way we hope will pay dividends once cruising.

It has been designed to open up half way for those cold or windy days or completely when in normal use. The door folds inwards and tucks behind the centre upright inside.

This definitely creates a visual feel of space in the cockpit area whilst opening the saloon.

The bi-fold pair has been glassed faired and painted. This did add a little weight, but worth the effort.

The panes were polycarbonate leftovers, which we may live to regret as they are already scratched. It is here too that 'Murphy' decided to pay us a visit.

Once re-assembled, the gap above and below the pair of doors varied. We remeasured the cut out and it was plumb.

So during the door fairing stage, the extra few millimetres all added up to now be out by 0 - 5mm. Not much in the grand scheme of things, but bad for a door gap.

As we would have it, we intended to fit an aluminium strip at the base of the doorframe as this is an area of high 'trampling'.

Internal Doors, carpets and trim

External hinges, solar fan and hatches

We chose to trim the required height here, which meant a re-resin of that section a few times prior to Sikaflexing the strip down. All is well that ends well.

Cupboard doors have been made to fit either side of the galley. The rooms will remain door-less.

A single door normally covers two hatch holes and is latched by a 'push button door latch'. The hinges are 316 stainless steel and were picked up at half the price of retail from Ebay, $3.20 for the 85mm 'hirline hinges'.

To allow the doors to remain flat on the surface, the hirline hinges were all flattened slightly and once screwed in place, leave a 1-2mm gap, just enough to allow air to circulate within the cupboards.

All the Surian Cedar timber (also called Toona calantas syn.) trim and doors are now in place. We could carry all the doors and trim in two hands, the timber being extremely lightweight and paints very well too.

*...Total interior cupboard
door weight came in at 16kg...*

With a little elbow grease and some French-polishing, the finish is fantastic. Given that the reddish timber will fade a little with time, this should bring out the deeper timber-red finish.

The pieces were all lathe-moulded to suit, then painted with 2 - 3 coats of clear polyurethane before being lightly polished.

While it may seem to be a small amount, each main room took close to 25 metre of trim with

100m being used in total.

Total interior cupboard door weight came in at 16kg with hinges and latches with other interior trim made of the same timber, weighing just 7kg.

This was a real timber winner given the additions we had already made to the boat in other areas.

Of the 21 doors, 6 had Perspex panes. These doors were above the galley, the upright glass cabinet and electronics cabinet.

Given the cost of Perspex, we looked elsewhere and were lucky enough to pick some up where James worked. Their building renovations saw a large piece of Perspex being discarded and while badly scratched, did the job.

The door panes were cut using a jigsaw and then sandblasted on one side to give a hazy appearance. These were then installed using rubber strips and stainless steel staples.

Our original thoughts were to use a silicon based glue to install all the trim, instead of resin and/or nails. In fact we had already started doing this until a seasoned builder on the issues caused by using silicone kindly picked us up.

Being aware that silicone seals anything it touches, it makes repainting a very difficult task.

The reason being that the already dried silicone, instead of sanding off, spreads and fills even more pores on the surface spreading like dropped mercury.

Finding a suitable alternative to silicone that carried the same qualities was an uphill battle. We finally settled on Sikaflex, even if it does have a tendency to yellow with age and cost a lot more.

Doors were then screwed in place and trim fitted. Avoiding nails made heavy going as all the strips had to be help in place with strips of timber until dry.

The final view will be shown once the yacht is complete and ready for launch and that will be yet another story or video.

----- : -----

Genoa and Main Track installation

All holes were again predrilled oversize and filled with resin. They were later redrilled to take the appropriate fasteners.

We are told that this in another area of water ingress with age and have tried to be proactive in prevention, using two tubes of Sikaflex here alone.

----- : -----

Pointers:

1.   Test motors before launch.

2.   Having a non-flexible fit-out timetable.

Traps:

1.   Not completing the whole fit-out.

2.   Hastily completing the fit-out.

Chapter Twenty:
The Mast

The mast design and build presented some fast learning of new words and a few headaches along the way.

The team at All Yacht Spars were kind enough to supply most of the equipment and while their plans were rather scant, our preferences in equipment position soon resolved the positioning problem.

What also provided a great deal of help was a morning with a friend on his EASY and he kindly went through all the fitting positions, the do's and don'ts, and preferences.

We took their preferences and canvassed a few others then made our own call.

We quickly found, too, that there was many fancy words, and saying 'rope' is a definite no-no (used only when one talks about the raw material or about the piece of 'rope' below the ships bell).

It's a halyard (used to haul up something and comes from 'Haul yards') or sheets.

The mast blank had to be positioned below the bridge deck and stuck out past the front fence during its build stages.

This provided protection from the elements and allowed work to be done at ground level (on a chair too).

Looking back, planning is crucial and the equipment needed for the mast had to be purchased and available during the build process.

This included the radar, decision on television aerial, radio (VHF) types of sails to be used, navigation lights etc.

...get the help of someone else who has been there and done that...

To our advantage, we had two friends who had built a few masts in their time. It appears to be one of those things that when done once, can be done again with the new found experience.

All the cut-outs were marked using masking tape in an effort to help keep the mast-blank clean from marks and scratches.

This worked very well. After double-checking all positions, the rather noisy cutting began in earnest.

The router and some good files proved handy and having friends with experience here, expedited the process.

Given that two different metal surfaces are used with the components (aluminium and stainless steel), additional

precautions had to be taken.

There are various compounds on the market and ours proved invaluable, we used Duralac. Under the winches, we also used a quality-strengthened tape.

The production drawings need to be checked by your designer or at the least, need to checked by someone qualified in this area. There are numerous accounts of Insurance payout's not being fully paid due incorrectly built masts.

The measurements listed in the drawings are only a guide. We marked the mast with a texta and tape and made sure that all components could be fitted prior to starting the cutting.

This meant that some of these figures were modified. At the end of the day, the fittings are totally reliant on the sail types you intend using.

In hindsight, if it's your first shot at a mast build, grab your camera and a tape measure, and ask a friend if you could get all the dimensions and photos and have a good look at where all the bits go.

Then ask questions why items are placed in particular positions and write the answers down (you would have forgotten by the time you get home).

Check that this fits in with your own sail design and start drawing. Better still, **get the help of someone else who has been there and done that,** even if it costs for his or her time, it's worth every cent.

Brace yourself, the list of components is extensive.

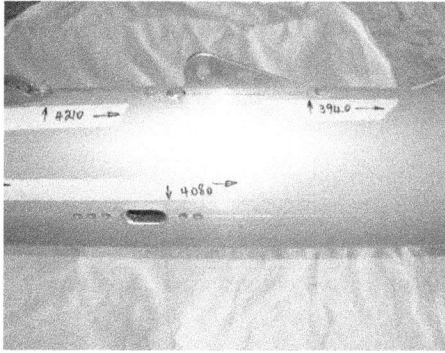

Marking with tape

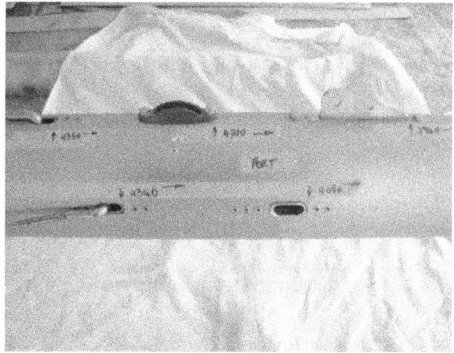

All fittings strategically placed

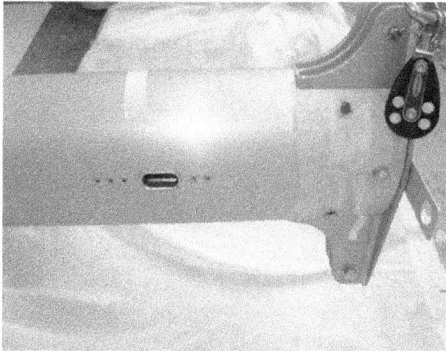

Rope Cleat installation

Installing radar plate

Completing build prior to stepping

Pointers:

1. Get a camera and get photos of other masts.

2. Ask others what works and what doesn't.

3. Install a permanent mast 'pull-wire' internally.

4. Do ALL the work before you 'stand' mast.

5. Negotiate a 'build-plan' when buying parts from extrusion supplier. No *'build-plan - no buy'*.

6. Get all parts from one supplier.

7. Price getting the mast built for you, it may be *'worth the money in time'*.

Traps:

1. Using a second hand mast.

2. Damaging cables during the install.

Tweaking the stays prior to launch

Crane lifting the mast

Boom and sheets/halyards in place

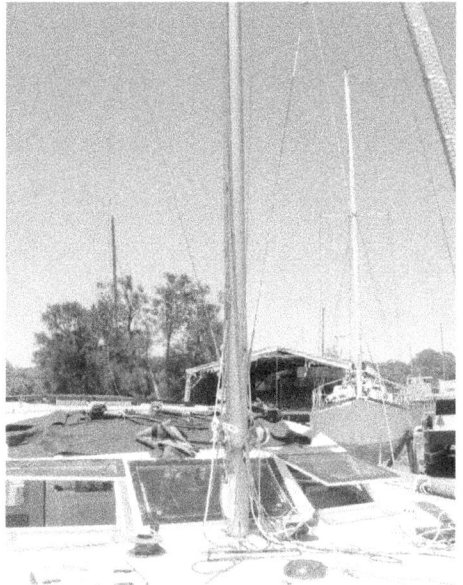

Cables everywhere

A Sailing Catamaran Building Project

Chapter Twenty One:
Navigation and Electronics (Upgrade)

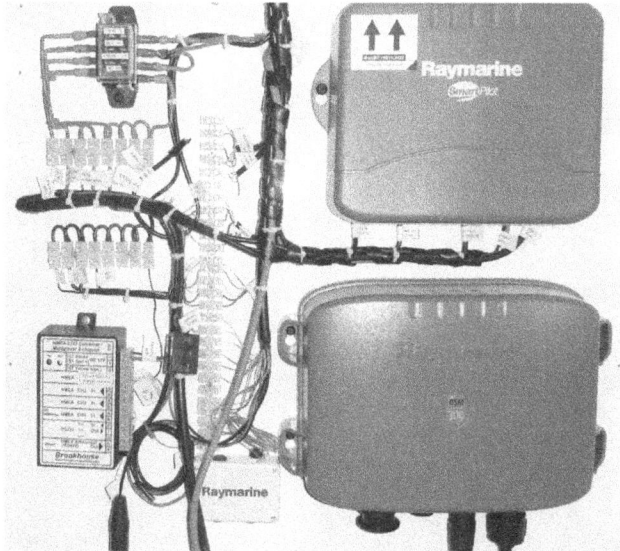

There is information here that may seem like 'gobble-dee-gook'. Don't let it scare you, it's a slightly in-depth peek at some of the electronic workings and how they chat to each other.

Most certainly not 'must know' information.

----- : -----

With the advent of Wi-Fi, NMEA 2000 and new 'wide screen' technology, our system has been upgraded to take advantage of these qualities.

This included faster data transfer streams between instruments and enhanced redundancy, with 'power saving' manual switching introduced.

Initially, the primary switching was changed to affect two key areas; redundancy and power saving functions (when not required or not in use).

----- : -----

Power saving switching

While the vessel was underway, smart switching was installed to reduce the drain on battery reserves when one or more components were not in use (or needed).

With the use of a Laptop or iPad and Multiplexer (MUX), various areas could be de-energised while allowing for basic navigation and autopilot use.

The major navigation power consumers are:
1. Airmar DSM300/P60 Transducer,
2. Raymarine C90W MFD (Multifunction Display),
3. ICOM 422 VHF Radio, and
4. Raymarine ST6001 Autopilot.

----- : -----

To provide options to isolate components when not needed and build in some sort of redundancy, Navigation switching is by way of:
1. **Autopilot Switch**,

2. **C90W Switch**,

3. **Sail Instruments & Brookhouse Multiplexer Switch**, and

4. **Radar Switch**.

----- : -----

Autopilot Switch

This allows the powering of the:
* Raymarine autopilot head,
* Raymarine Wheelpilot, and
* Raymarine autopilot computer.

This also has its own two fuses, one on the navigation wiring panel and a second within the Raymarine autopilot computer unit.

In its simplest form (with no other switches ON), the Autopilot Switch allows basic autopilot use in the 'auto mode' (that is without the

tracking function).

This is the least power position with basic autopilot help and does not provide depth or any sail instruments.

To engage the 'tracking mode', the autopilot will require heading and GPS data.

This can be provided three ways:
1. Switch the 'Sail Instruments and Brookhouse Multiplexer' switch ON, and use a laptop with navigation data, or

2. Switch the Raymarine C90W ON, or

3. Switch both the Raymarine C90W and Sail Instruments & Brookhouse Multiplexer (without laptop navigation function)' ON.

Redundancy of 'Autopilot Switch' function:

There is none, once any one of these components fails, the autopilot will be unserviceable.

----- : -----

C90W Switch

This allows powering of the:
* Raymarine C90W , DSM300 (and P60 transducer),
* Icom 5000 (AIS), and
* Radar power to the Radar Switch.

It has its own fuse on the navigation-wiring panel.

In its simplest form (with no other switches ON), the C90W Switch allows plotter information to be made available.

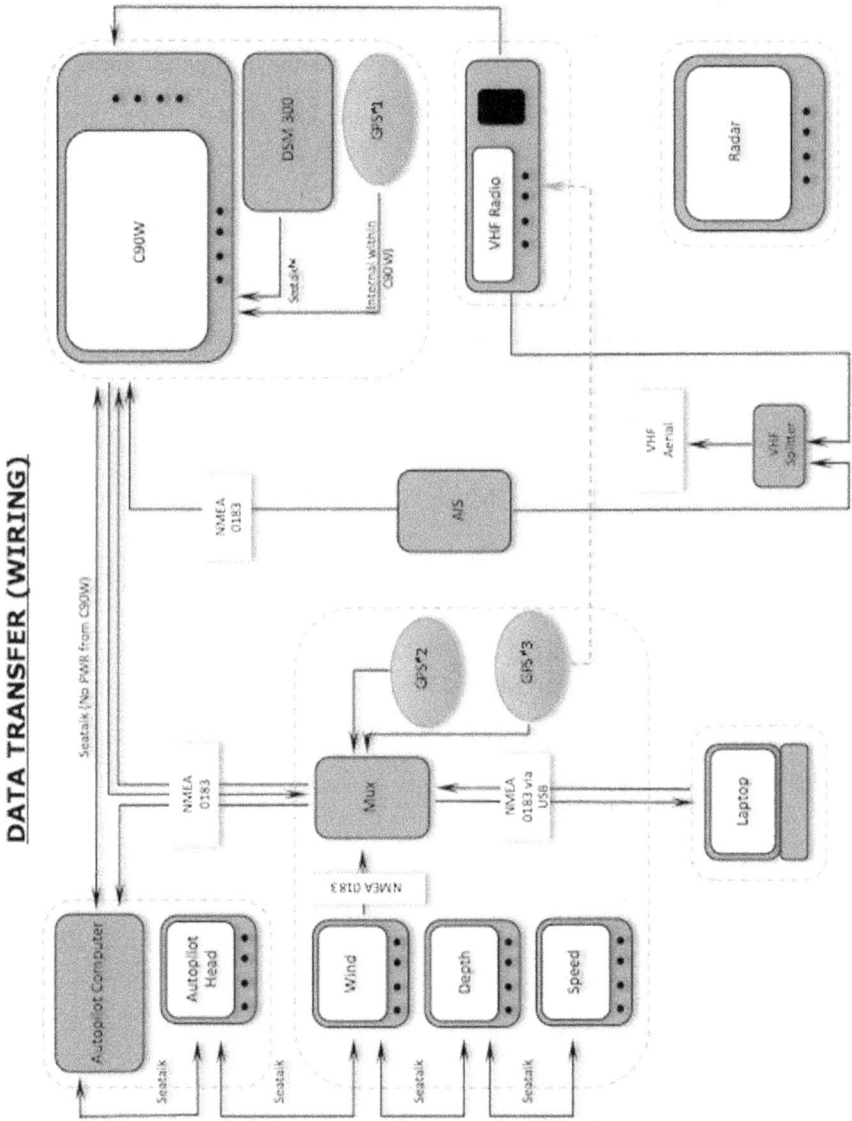

DATA TRANSFER (WIRING)

Basic Navigation Electronics Wiring

This is the least power position for this unit and will not provide autopilot, sail instruments power, AIS and radar. The depth will be shown on the Raymarine C90W.

To engage the autopilot, switch the Autopilot Switch to ON. This will provide basic autopilot functions in both 'auto' and 'tracking' modes.

Redundancy of the 'C90W Switch' function:

Failure of this unit can be supplemented by a Laptop and use of the 'Sail Instruments & Brookhouse Multiplexer Switch' (refer to that switch function for further detail).

However, depth will not be available.

----- : -----

Sail Instruments and Brookhouse Multiplexer Switch

This allows powering of the:
* Raymarine ST60 Sail Instruments (wind, speed and depth),
* Brookhouse Multiplexer,
* Humminbird GPS (to the Brookhouse multiplexer for GPS backup to the C90W) and
* Navman 1240 GPS power (VHF position function).

It has its own fuses (Sail Instr. and MUX) on the navigation-wiring panel.

In its simplest form (with no other switches ON), the Sail Instruments and Brookhouse Multiplexer

Switch allows all sail instruments to be powered (no depth function) and Laptop plotter/navigation information to be made available.

This is the least power position for this unit and will not provide autopilot, C90W, Depth, AIS and radar.

We had found that GPS's do have a tendency to fall over.

Given that our new MFD had an internal GPS and that that GPS could be shaded at times given its installation position, a back up would be a strong advantage.

We have three GPS heads in total:
1. Navman 1240 (external),
2. Hummingbird GR16 (external), and
3. One within the Raymarine C90W MFD (internal).

----- : ------

SWITCHES and FUSES

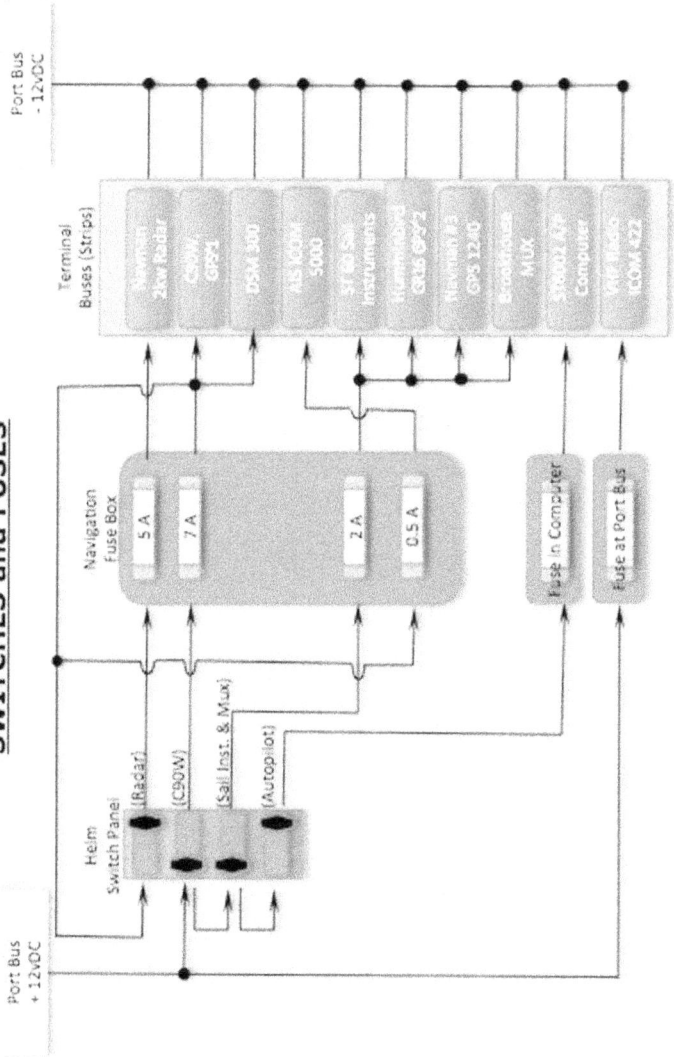

Port Bus
- 12vDC

Terminal
Buses (Strips)

Navintish
2kw Radar

CSW
GPS1

DSM 300

AIS ICOM
5000

ST 60 Sail
Instruments

Humminbird
Chts GPS2

Navintish B3
GPS 1240

Brookhouse
MUX

SR002 A/P
Computer

VHF Radio
ICOM 422

Navigation
Fuse Box

5 A

7 A

2 A

0.5 A

Fuse in Computer

Fuse at Port Bus

Helm
Switch Panel

(Radar)

(CSOW)

(Sail Inst. & Mux)

(Autopilot)

Port Bus
+ 12vDC

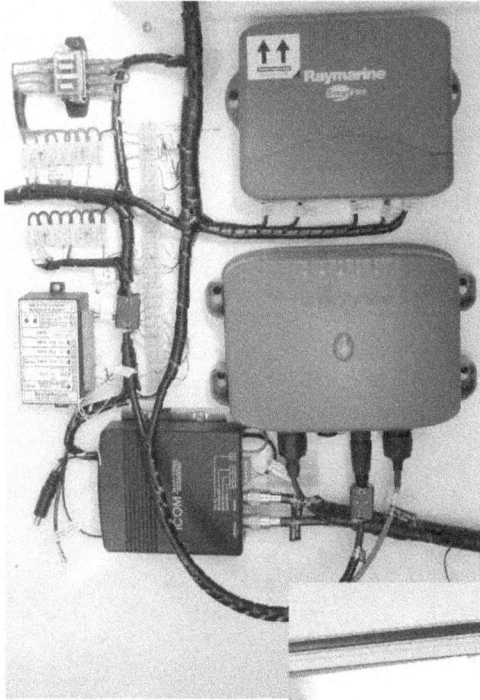

Wiring - all
labelled and
secure

Switches at Helm Station

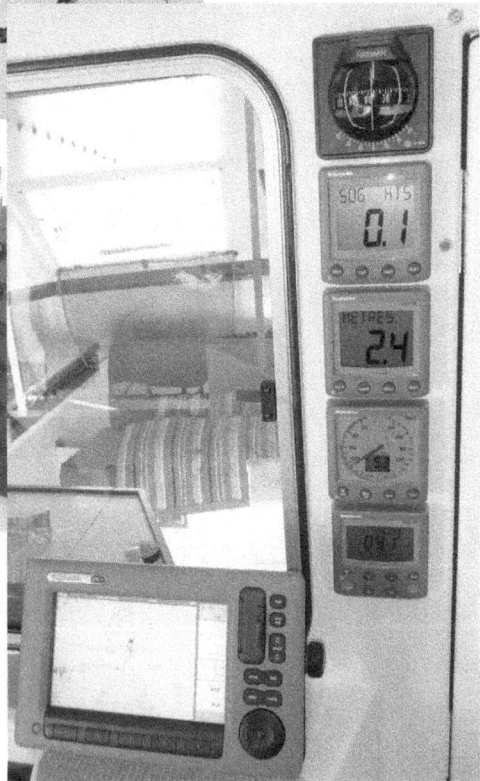

Sail
Instruments
and C90
Plotter

GPS Backup - automatic mode

Using the Brookhouse Multiplexer (MUX), we were able to provide this GPS redundancy automatically.

The Brookhouse MUX has a great feature that assesses the 'GPS related data strings' at regular intervals and when it finds the data missing (i.e. primary internal Raymarine C90W 'GPS strings' not being transmitted), it automatically switches to the alternate GPS (in our case, the Humminbird GR16).

The Humminbird GR16 then continues to supply GPS data until the Brookhouse MUX again senses the 'primary GPS strings'.

The Humminbird GR16 is then reverted back to standby by the Brookhouse MUX.

----- : -----

GPS Backup - manual mode

Should the C90W be switched off for any reason, the Brookhouse Mux will sense a loss in GPS data (as detailed above) and automatically allow Humminbird GR16 data strings.

This can then be used with laptop connection and navigation, allowing the autopilot to navigate without using the Raymarine C90W.

The last line of defence is with the Navman 1240 GPS. This is independently linked to the VHF radio and allows data reading as a last resort.

Redundancy of the 'Sail Instruments and Brookhouse Multiplexer Switch' function.

Failure of this switch will not provide GPS and navigation back-up. GPS data to the VHF radio will be lost.

----- : -----

AIS

Our challenge lay in finding a cost effective compatible AIS unit.

Considerations included:
1. True NMEA 0183 RS422 input and output
2. VHF splitter (built-in),
3. Raymarine C90W compatible (Seatalk, and/or NMEA 0183 and/or NMEA 2000), and
4. USB / Wi-Fi (we did have the Brookhouse MUX USB which could be used).

After much research we brought this down to three units:
- iAIS (from Digital Yacht),
- AIS-Multi (Comar), and
- ICOM 5000.

We settled on the ICOM 5000 and have been pleasantly surprised at its ease of installation and use. Our only gripe is that it gives no indication of its operation. The AIS has been wired into the C90W.

----- : -----

C90W Wiring

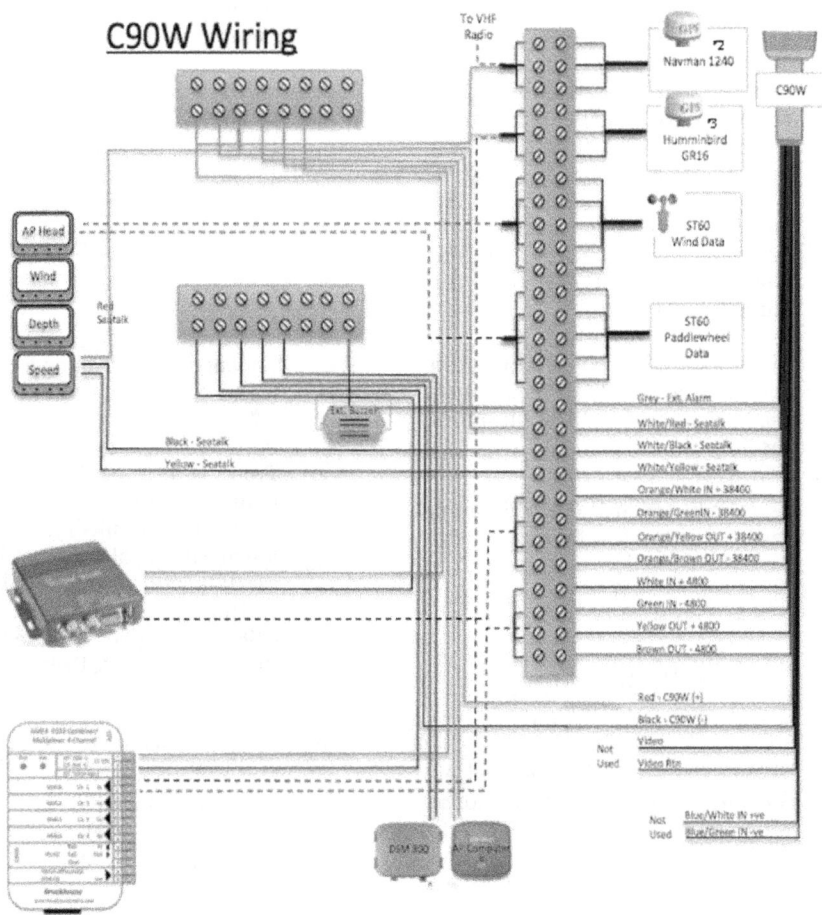

To VHF Radio

Navman 1240

C90W

Humminbird GR16

ST60 Wind Data

ST60 Paddlewheel Data

AP Head
Wind
Depth
Speed

Red Seatalk

Ext. Buzzer

Black - Seatalk
Yellow - Seatalk

Grey - Ext. Alarm
White/Red - Seatalk
White/Black - Seatalk
White/Yellow - Seatalk
Orange/White IN - 38400
Orange/Green IN - 38400
Orange/Yellow OUT + 38400
Orange/Brown OUT - 38400
White IN + 4800
Green IN - 4800
Yellow OUT + 4800
Brown OUT - 4800

Red - C90W (+)
Black - C90W (-)
Not Used   Video
            Video Rtn

Not Used   Blue/White IN +ve
            Blue/Green IN -ve

DSM 300   AIS Computer

Pointers:

1. Try to stick to a single brand.

2. Buy the best you can afford.

3. Have a compatible 'no-nonsense' autopilot.

4. Try to go Wi-Fi.

5. Get large digit instrument gauges.

6. Plan for worst-case scenario and single-pilot operation.

Traps:

1. Buying your electronic equipment too early, then running out of warranty.

2. Buying the cheapest.

3. Not documenting information and wiring.

Chapter Twenty Two:
Anchor Winch Roller

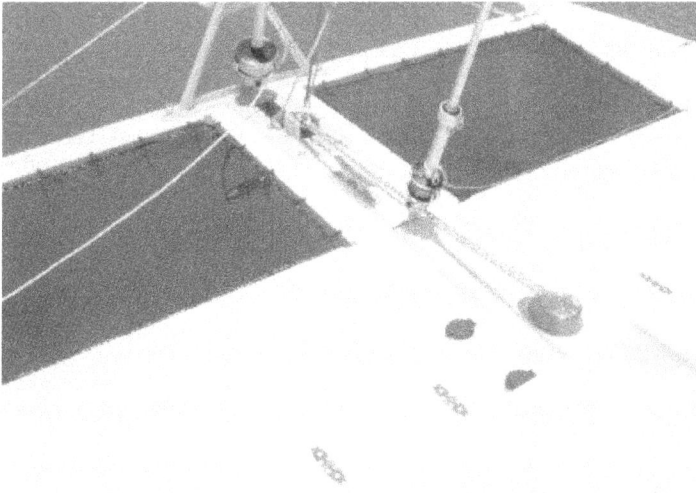

Given the vessel weight and experience of most crew one needs everything to be on one's side when 'Murphy" comes knocking, additional insurance as we saw it.

This is really our last resort point in most of the bad situations. It's in the most inopportune times that the system needs to operate flawlessly and the most critical that comes to mind are:

Loss of all ships power - Highly unlikely as we have two motors and even then a whole wardrobe of sails.

Sounds fine and dandy, but if the skipper is not available (broken arm/leg or even MOB), the remaining crew must be able to

easily and safely be able to at least hold position into wind.

Bad Weather situation – Where conditions have caught one out, or extreme weather requires one to sit tight.

Or where breakages (such as sail, rigging or mast) have occurred and repairs need to be carried out.

Towing – Again another highly unlikely occurrence, but this is really the last resort where we want everything in our favour.

Unless one is aware of one's boundaries during the retrieval process of the anchor, a no nonsense approach here is almost mandatory.

This meant that this particular item had to be beefed-up to take the stresses and movements we would be placing on the beam.

We had been told that one should always winch from straight ahead at all times as the sideways stress movements would eventually cause unnecessary wear on the beam/winch area.

While at anchor, a 'bridle' can be easily used to prevent the swaying by current and/or wind.

The windage and lighter weight of the catamaran makes it prone to swaying off-centre during retrieval.

The above thoughts did unravel many new questions. Horror stories exist of worn roller bushes collapsing at the wrong time, even rollers coming away from the stem during the retrieval process.

The roller system also needed to pull the anchor into the full-up position and not damage the fore beam in any way including 'self-righting' capabilities, where the anchor swings prongs down at the last minute.

This is a function of the roller retrieval system and needs to be assessed at the early build stage.

The latter forced us to make a decision on the primary anchor type that we needed and this ended up being a Sarca.

We say primary as one other

anchor is carried. The Sarca type anchor, while very expensive, is designed to withstand a variety of bottom types including mud, sand, gravel and rock, offering superb holding power in all conditions.

It also happens to have a self-righting arc over the top of the anchor making initial anchoring easier.

The Sarca Anchor 'top arc' also went into the build equation, as it does stand out a little and could easily damage the fore beam if not managed correctly.

Importantly, the Sarca also happened to be one of the physically larger anchor types making the fitting of any other anchor type within the Anchor-winch-assembly practicable.

These all led to a decision of a single anchoring unit, to be one with the:
- Fore beam A-frame,
- Cat walk brackets (front only), and
- Forestay Tang.

----- : -----

Material Use

Using the Stainless Steel for the size of the project would have proved too heavy, so it was to be Aluminium 5083 plate.

Even with this alloy, weight would still be an issue, but one we were very happy to live with.

We found it cheaper to purchase a full 2.4m x 1.2m sheet of 12mm. When you initially see the cost, I suspect you will gasp.

BUT...we also used this material to build our 'chainplates', radar-baseplate and desalinator components instead of 10mm Stainless.

----- : -----

A Plan

These are the three large components and smaller pieces, made and cut to suit.

We started with a cardboard cut-outs, progressing to 10mm plywood, then transposing to the final sheet of aluminium.

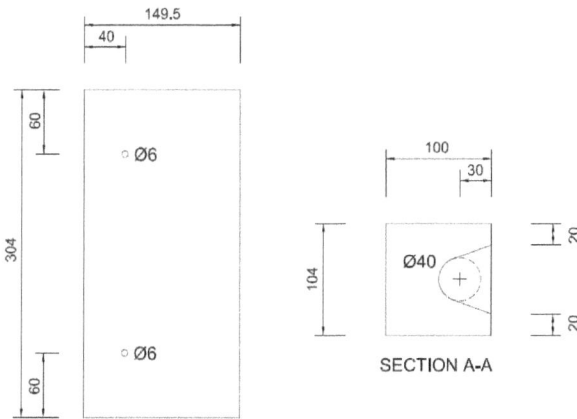

FRONT PLATE (1 No.)

SECTION A-A

TOP SPACER PLATE (1 No.)

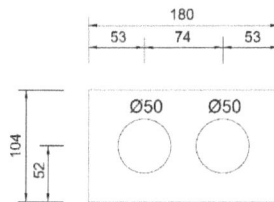

SPACER PLATE (1 No.)

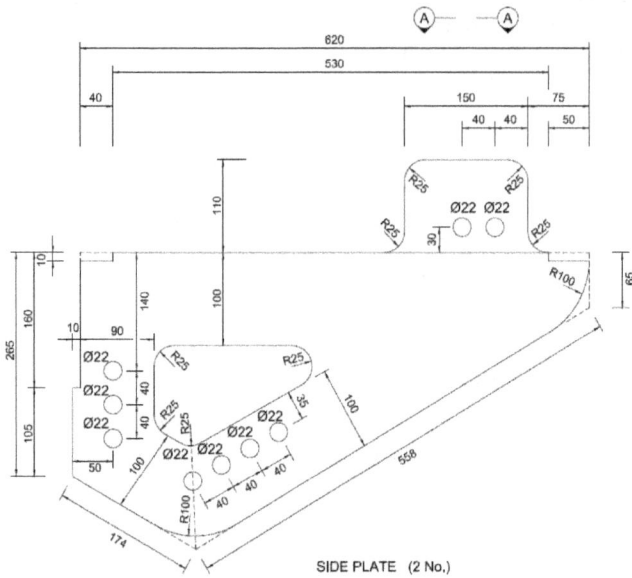

SIDE PLATE (2 No.)

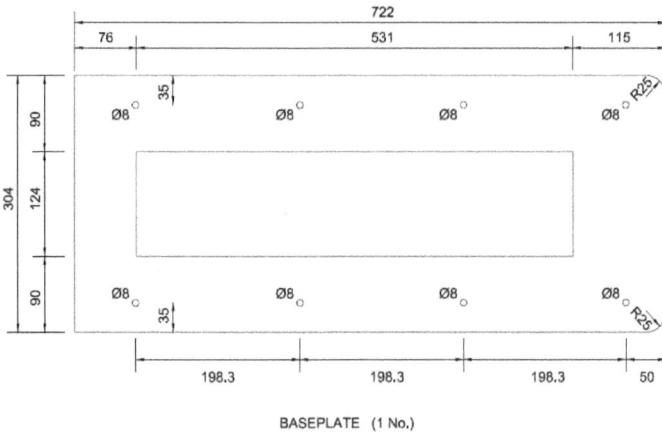

BASEPLATE (1 No.)

Our friends from Outback Dreamer (EASY Sarah) must
take credit for producing these drawings for us.

http://www.outbackdreamer.weebly.com

Components cut from aluminium

The holes were lined with homemade bushes, cut to suit.

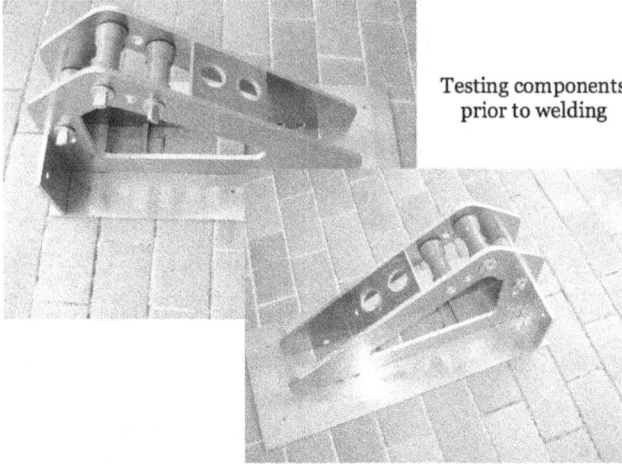

Testing components
prior to welding

We had the unit welded to the A-Frame and then had it powder-coated.

Unit (Installed)

Note the large cleat at the rear of the unit. This cleat is the standard aluminium cleat used on jetties and welded to an aluminium base, then powder coated. Very handy for towing and working on the winch with all chain extended, would definitely do this again.

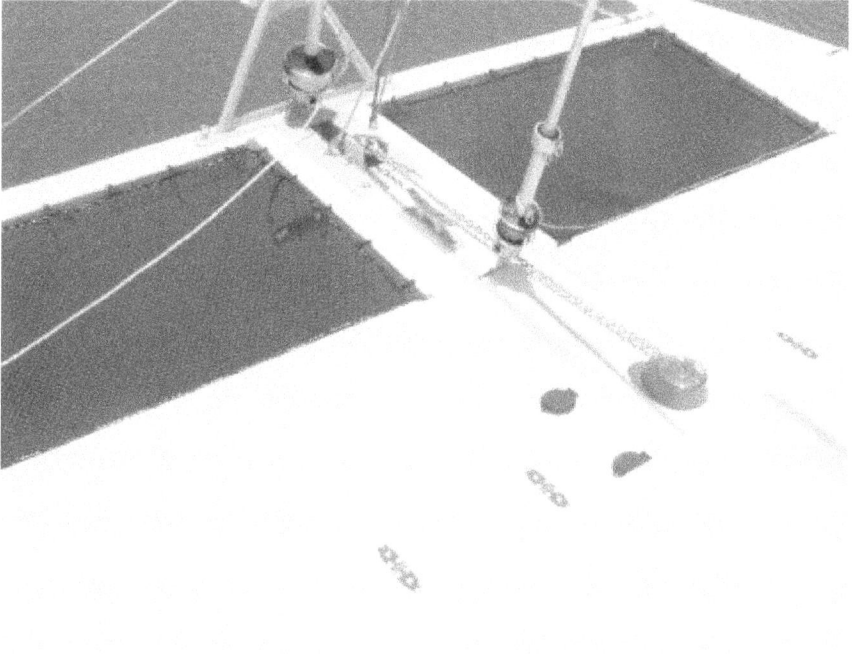

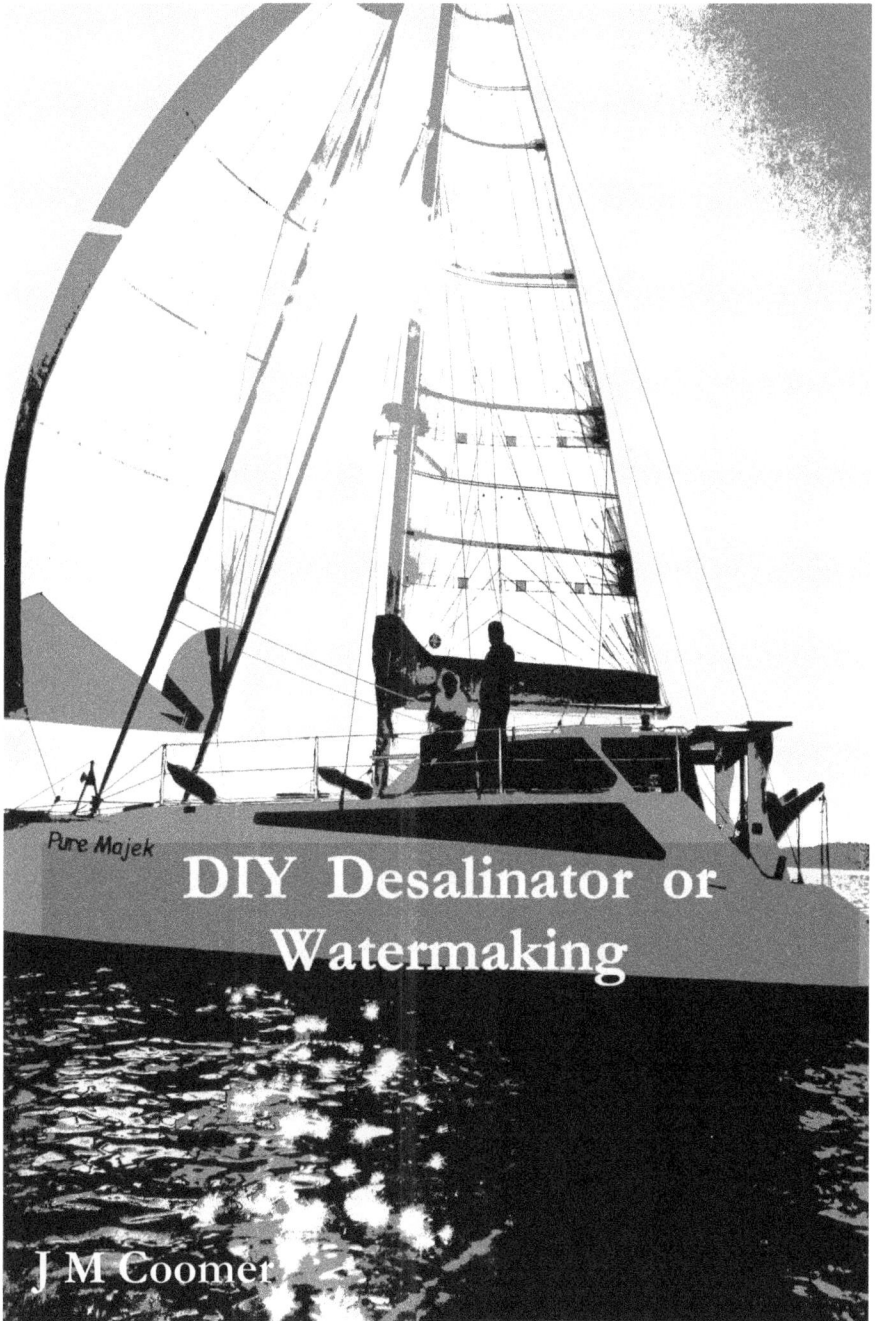

Pure Majek

DIY Desalinator or Watermaking

J M Coomer

Chapter One:
What is Desalination?

Our attempts to find a reasonably priced desalinator unit that delivered large amounts of water over a short 'engine-running' period, did not prove fruitful.

In early 2000, the United States appeared to lead the way with their availability of desalinator components.

This, for the non-US resident, presented another challenge in that postage of these heavy 'complete units' would fast out way the search.

Making our own fresh water seems to supplement the solar energy charging of our batteries. The feeling of self-sufficiency and not being dependent on someone else to survive is a good one.

The Internet age and ability to freight small items worldwide has opened doors for the amateur builder and with a little drive and know-how, a homemade desalinator is within reach. This is our successful attempt of how we went about the challenge.

We have since tackled another project (July 2011) and have successfully restored a 12vDC watermaker that provides 16 litres of water per 6 Amp hours.

It's from the Italian Schenker Watermaker Group and what a win that was. We discuss this in a later section. Please check the website (www.diycatamaran.com) for updates on this desalinator.

----- : -----

We planned to have plenty of freshwater. It meant *re-inventing the wheel* with desalination and trying to recover some of the high expense in this area by building the desalination unit ourselves.

Our original question was '*why was it so expensive?*' The answer lies, we suspect, in the possible litigation issues of malfunctioning units and component compounds used in their construction, both of which we could tackle.

We scoured the Internet for desalinator units, which all ranged between AUD$5000 to AUD$15000 (July 2007), but with many of these packages, there was no generator or battery source as part of that package, only adding to our financial woes.

...become increasingly harder to claim component failure without receipted components...

Building a unit ourselves was the only viable alternative.

----- : -----

So what is it about these components that add to the cost? A 'safety model' put forward by Professor James Reason may help explain this quandary.

His theory of system failure, sometimes called the 'Swiss Cheese Theory', states that overall system failure is more often than not a function of many smaller failures.

These smaller failures may be as minute as a fatigued section caused by simple flexing which on its own, will not normally cause a failure.

But, when many small failures align (like the odd occasion when all the holes aligning in a block of Swiss cheese - the cheese collapses in that aligned area) and this too is the case in some manufactured desalinator units.

This is well documented in the aviation industry where accidents can often be traced back to a small component issue, which finally leads to the accident.

Applying this theory to the desalinator build meant that each component needed to be specifically chosen for its qualities.

Modification of these components, such as switching to a cheaper part or replacing a stainless steel nut with a plastic nut, will add to the holes in our block of 'desalinator Swiss cheese'.

A good example here concerns fittings below the waterline. While plastics development has come forward in leaps and bounds, even reputable pump manufacturers such as Jabsco with their 'cyclone range', state that plastic fittings should not be used below waterline on their pumps.

...designs are built with a certain safety reserve...

It's the continual small vibration of the motor, causing small fatigue lines in the fittings that when aligned with other fatigued components could cause a situation where the boat leaks and heaven forbid, sinks.

----- : -----

By nature, we (human beings) will always try and find an alternative or cheaper way to do or repair an item and this 'calculated risk' needs to be just that...very carefully calculated.

Replacing an elbow with a cheaper alternative may work at the start, but as contaminants fill the filters, the pump works harder and this in turn raises unnecessary pressure within those components.

Variations in water temperature causing expansion and contraction of the component add another hole to the fracture theory and eventually all the hard work comes undone, costs go up and the manufacturer becomes the easiest scapegoat for one's shortcutting.

A good excuse, except insurance assessors are now wise to this and it has become increasingly harder to claim component failure without receipted components.

For the reason mentioned above, many designs are built with a certain safety reserve, such as the motors horsepower - always higher than that actually required or piping that carries 30% higher-pressure ratings than what are actually listed.

...the manufacturer becomes the easiest scapegoat for one's shortcutting...

They do this for a reason.

Those who test these boundaries appear be the minority and are the ones we consistently meet conducting repairs and complaining of how labour intensive the desalination task is.

When you dig a bit further you find the dollars they saved initially during set-up, come home to roost.

Understanding some of this waffle will go a long way in helping grasp why certain items appear to be over-the-top with our choices and as stated previously, there are many ways to skin-a-cat when making a

desalinator, and this is our way.

----- : -----

So, what is Desalination?

Desalination is the removal of impurities (such as salt) from a liquid. This then makes the water potable and/or palatable. Also called a Water Maker (or watermaker) , the desalinator is still fairly expensive due to the limited scope of development.

To date the cheapest way to do this has been by forcing the 'liquid form' through membranes that are small enough to remove the impurities.

This is a lot easier said than done as the pressure that is normally used to do this is around 56bar (around 820psi), fairly high and almost explosive when using inadequate components.

...'our boat – our wish-list'. ..

This then means that the vessel container must carry a higher pressure rating than its membrane, in our case, 68bar (around 1000psi).

We are talking very high compressed water pressures here, and this can be very dangerous in the wrong hands.

----- : -----

Calculating the freshwater needs

The summary of the desalination argument was that we needed to generate sufficient fresh water to cover our use, not that we have anything against those who enjoy the spiritual virtues of salt-water bathing.

DIY Desalinator or Watermaking

For the seasoned sailor, the next few paragraphs are not for you. However, for the amateur builder hoping to win the heart of his water-loving wife/partner and kids, continue reading.

We jotted down the water requirements we thought would be our comfortable minimum per person. In line with Nigel Calders' suggestion we added a further 10% buffer, then multiplied this by the number of members in the family.

Our calculations are based on 4 showers per day plus drinking water. We used 22 litres per person as a guide making our requirements 88 litres per day for four adults.

...only 12-15% of saltwater taken through the high-pressure membrane is returned as fresh water...

We can see some already raising an eyebrow, all we say is 'our boat - our wish-list'.

The other requirement we put in place was the running of a generator to drive the desalinator. It was not to exceed one hour a day - period.

Again, *'our boat - our wish-list'*, and for the sake of peace and quiet too.

This figure then represents a minimum freshwater requirement per day and becomes a key for calculations further on.

To calculate freshwater tank size, we then multiplied the daily figure by two. That would give us a comfortable two days of freshwater or a good six days if rationed supplies with a non-functioning desalinator were that to ever eventuate.

We have also a second 150-litre tank

for the extended trip.

----- : -----

Pointers:

1. Minimum of 820psi pressure is needed for most desalination.

2. Calculate your minimum water quantity per day.

Traps:

1. Not realising the consequences of a burst high-pressure line.

Chapter Two:
Understanding System Make-up

Use the 'Desalination Diagram' (next page), as a mud-map while you read this and the Components Chapters.

----- : -----

Simple System Operation

Saltwater is drawn into a Low Pressure Pump (called LPP here) via a Raw Water Filter.

The Raw water filter (one of three) removes larger debris and smaller crustaceans. This should have a removable filter that can be washed and or replaced easily.

The LPP delivers the water at around 8psi.

----- : -----

This low-pressure seawater is then again filtered before going to the High Pressure Pump (called HPP here).

The filters (two and three of three) are the larger canister household types that carry 5 and 10-micron filters respectively.

----- : -----

Depending on the power source, the HPP is engaged on and off via a Clutch (not shown in the Desalination Diagram). Some units can be purchased without a clutch. We chose the clutch type, the reasons are discussed later.

----- : -----

The high-pressure seawater from the HPP is then forced through Membranes, which separates the contaminants.

Only 10-15% of the HPP water entering the membranes will be returned as fresh water.

This can be measured via a

flowmeter (if installed).

----- : -----

The remaining HPP (80-85% of the intake water - now called brine), is returned to the sea via the High Pressure Regulator and its own Flow meter.

This return 'Brine' flow is very important as it in turn acts as flushing liquid within the membrane, self-cleaning the membrane of contaminants and venting them overboard.

----- : -----

A clear understanding of this basic sequence will help describe the components discussed next.

Another item mentioned shortly is the 'Motor'. Where this term is used, it specifically describes an electric or petrol motor that is used to drive the HPP.

-----: -----

Pointers:

1. Only 10 - 15% of inlet water will be freshwater.

2. The Membrane will need to be flushed at least every 7 days.

Traps:
1. Not ensuring filters are cleaned on a regular basis, especially if not used very often.

2. Not flushing the membrane.

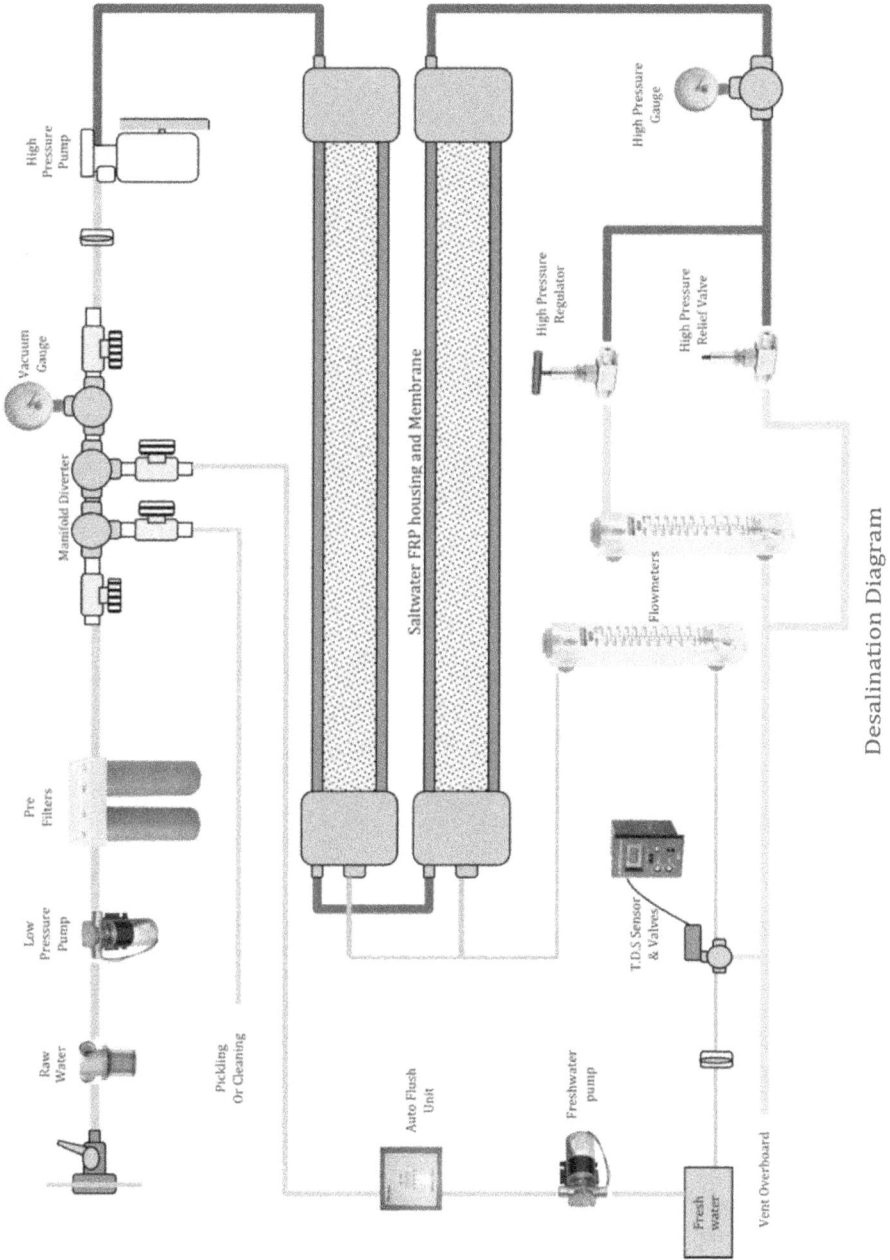

Desalination Diagram

High Pressure Pump

Vacuum Gauge

Manifold Diverter

Pre Filters

Low Pressure Pump

Raw Water

Pickling Or Cleaning

Saltwater FRP housing and Membrane

High Pressure Gauge

High Pressure Regulator

High Pressure Relief Valve

Flowmeters

T.D.S Sensor & Valves

Auto Flush Unit

Freshwater pump

Fresh water

Vent Overboard

Chapter Three:
Basic System Components

Use the 'Desalination Diagram' (previous page), as a mud-map while you read this section. <u>It will help immensely as we go through each component</u> and where it fits in the grand scheme of things.

----- : -----

High Pressure Pump (HPP)

The time that one wishes to have a motor purring (rumbling, vibrating or pumping fumes) needs to be carefully assessed as this will reflect the pump size that needs to be purchased.

Our choice limited this noise to one hour per day.

This meant that in 40 minutes, we had to generate all the water we needed to top up the tanks. The other 20 minutes of the 1-hour run time was to be used for any charging or 240VAC requirements, such as a washing machine.

For those about to start the *'numbers journey'* themselves, you will soon notice the challenges about to be faced in selection of a high pressure pump, pump motor and whether AC or DC motors should be used.

----- : -----

Given that we required 88lt/day. freshwater, we needed a pump that could produce this, plus move an additional 85% more saltwater through the membranes.

Remembering that only 12-15% of

saltwater taken through the high-pressure membrane is returned as fresh water, making our high pressure pump requirements.

If:

15 % = 88lt freshwater, then
100% = 587lt total water needed
(say 600lt/hr.).

This is a lot of water, yet alone in 40 minutes.

----- : -----

We are now starting to talk serious big pumping numbers.

To be able to do this, we used a type of pump is known as a 'high pressure pump' (HPP) as it increases saltwater inlet pressure from low pressure (around 0.55 bar (8psi)) to high pressure (no more than 65 bar (950psi)).

> *...Brass and saltwater*
> *do not mix...*

This is required to force saltwater through the membranes. While 65 bar (950psi) is a little high, we insert a High Pressure Regulator to lower this pressure to around 56 bar (820psi).

This 56 bar (820psi) figure is the magical minimum number required to bring the salinity of the saltwater down to an acceptable drinking water value.

This *drinking-water-value* is around 200 parts per million or less (saltwater being up around the 12,000 parts per million normally).

From these numbers above, it can be seen that a lot of contaminants need to be removed.

----- : -----

The pump used in desalination units is a specialised piece of equipment and needs to be stainless steel or bronze.

Any other material compounds will not be suitable for saltwater use, and yes, this definitely includes brass (found in most high pressure water washers).

Brass and saltwater do not mix.

There are some good and bad high-pressure pump manufacturers out there, too. We narrowed our search down to AR Pumps, Cat Pumps, and General Pumps.

Our final choice was a Cat Pump given that many of the off-the-shelf desalinator companies use Cat equipment.

The decision now was whether to go Stainless Steel or Bronze HPP pump parts.

The Cat Pump Company state that:

> *'Some installations and water conditions may tolerate a liquid-end construction of nickel aluminium bronze. Other locations may demand more corrosion-resistant liquid-end materials such as 316SS, Duplex Stainless Steel or even Super Duplex for the RO pump.*
>
> *A lower speed (rpm) for your RO pumps is highly recommended. When pumping corrosive liquids such as seawater, higher rpm operation further aggravates the corrosion-erosion wear process initiated by seawater'.*

The cost of the various HPP types does vary from vendor to vendor and bronze is cheaper by 20%, so it pays to shop around.

A close search was made for a second hand HPP unit on Ebay and we did find a few. BUT, with all of them:

➤ Do the internal components need replacing?

➤ Has the pump been dropped?

➤ Has the pump seized? (One respondent here stated 'no, I can still turn it with a wrench') etc.

Cat Pump 3-Frame Plunger Pump-Model 241

We could not get a component guarantee for this critical high-pressure part, which is why we chose to buy new (remembering the Swiss Cheese theory discussed earlier).

----- : -----

HPP cavitation is one item that should be considered during this building phase, cavitation being influenced by air seeping into the system plumbing.

...cavitation is one item that should be considered during this building...

Plumbing must contain suitable shutoff valves to prevent air from entering the HPP unit at all costs. This also means that plumbing must be very secure and the use of PTFE liquid or tape is strongly recommended.

Air here definitely does fast-track premature wear and resultant costs as well as frustration with repairs.

We settled on purchasing the Cat Pump 3-Frame Plunger Pump-Model 241 (in Stainless Steel). The specification sheet for the 241 HPP recommended that:

> The unit be driven by a minimum of 3.0hp electric motor

> An operating pressure range is 70bar (1000psi) to 85bar (1200psi) (We chose to use the 70bar figures) and for this pressure,

> The HPP operating RPM of 1725 was needed. This figure will be used later in sizing the motor pulley.

Note too that the manufacturer has made the clear distinction between electric and gas (petrol) engines, electric being their preferred choice for advertising reasons. This leads us onto the next challenge where we discuss the this issue.

----- : -----

Motor to drive the HPP

The motor that drives this HPP unit can be:

> Electric DC (directly connected to the HPP pump),

> Electric AC (directly connected to the HPP pump),

> Belt-drive from an electric motor, or from a

> Belt-drive petrol (diesel) generator.

The choices are varied and can be

very confusing to the uninitiated. One option available to us was to use:

> A petrol (gas) engine, to drive
> An electric motor, to run
> The HPP

We found that the amount of petrol (gas) engine power required to run a largish electric motor (3hp in our case with the 241 Cat pump), was enormous.

In fact, electric motors become very restrictive beyond 1-1.5hp electric motor sizes, which is why many tend toward the belt-drive units.

Another option was the AC Electric Motor on its own. Given that we only have batteries, an Inverter would be needed.

The challenge with AC motors is that they need three times their running power requirement just to break the inertia during their initial start-up.

Don't be fooled by this requirement. There is much written about it. If in doubt, ask any electrician who is familiar with AC electric motors of this size.

----- : -----

As a rough guide, this meant that to start 3hp electric motor, one would need an equivalent 5-6hp AC electric motor 'power-draw' just to get it started (while not strictly correct, this acts as a very good guide).

Then you need to factor in the 1-hour running battery 'power-draw' to make the required water.

We were often asked why we could not use a 2kva Honda power generator to do the job.

We came to the conclusion that it would only be able to drive a small HPP, say 10 - 20lt per hour, making running times a lot longer (for our requirements) and in some cases more expensive.

----- : -----

Other avenues we did look at were 'soft-starters' which proved well in theory, but as we found out would not be suitable for an amateur desalinator build.

We finally agreed that we needed a non-electric motor with a belt-drive system. Searching for this took some time.

Our decision to minimise holes in the hull meant that saltwater cooling became a last resort and left freshwater or fan cooled motors our preferred option.

Given that our HPP needed a 2.5HP Electric Motor, an increase of 20% is needed for the petrol (gas) equivalent, making our Petrol Motor minimum size of 3HP.

This was stipulated in the manufacturers data sheet downloaded from the Internet.

To this, one needs to consider how hard they want the motor to work and do they want to use the same motor for other applications.

Finally, our choice was between the industrial diesel fresh water-cooled generators from a Yanmar (TF60 - 67kg) or the unleaded air-cooled industrial Honda (GX200QXE - 26kg).

Weight and cooling requirements dictated the direction here as they were the same price.

Motor - Honda GX200QXE

Motor - Yanmar TF60

The Honda GX200QXE is a common unit and parts are very readily available and are cheap to buy. It also has electric start, which could come in handy depending on the automation level that one desires.

We went with the Honda.

It has a maximum shaft RPM (with no load) of 3900RPM. As we do not want maximum RPM and given that petrol (gas) engines struggle with torque below 50% of their normal operating range, we chose 60% of this value - 2400RPM.

According to Honda dealership, this happens to be:
> The most fuel economic range for the motor,
> Reduces wear and tear of the motor components,
> Allows the motor to run cooler, and
> Reduces the noise level by 15%.

This '2400-RPM' figure will be used later to calculate the motor pulley size.

----- : -----

12vDC Clutch/Pulley

Options were available for a:
> Direct-drive 'pulley belt' system, or
> Clutch-drive 'pulley belt' system.

We chose the Cat Pumps Industrial Clutch - Model 34961, which has a 7" OD (outer diameter).

This is an important OD number needed for calculating the Motor Pulley size in the next section.

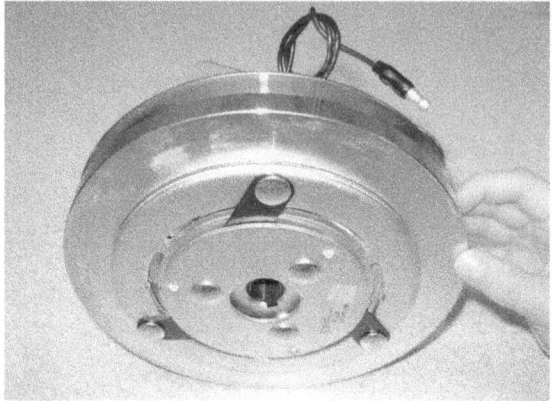

Cat Pumps Industrial Clutch - Model 34961

The clutch is a real asset and allows the motor to be run without the HPP engaged making the motor available as a generous generator (alternator actually) and could also be used to:
> Power (240V) in times of need (thinking of a washing machine here - remembering now that fresh water will not be a issue),
> The far reaching 'wish-list' item for air-compressor ability for scuba units,
> Provide power for a small air conditioner/ heater, and/or
> As back up for those overcast days for the batteries.

----- : -----

Clutch engagement occurs when a small amount of 12vDC power is applied via a separate switch from the battery.

While ever this switched battery power is available the clutch will remain engaged running the HPP.

Cut the switched power and the clutch will disengage stopping the HPP. The motor will continue to run until switched off separately.

This leads into our next

consideration, HPP pump protection via automatic shutdown.

----- : -----

This is not mandatory - but a nice-to-have. Inserting a pressure switch in the salt water feed line from the LPP to the filters, will detect:
> A failed LPP (pump could fail or, pump could not be switched on), and
> Low water pressure (the inlet or raw water strainer could have blocked with debris).

This 'pressure switch' would cut electrical power to the 12vDC clutch achieving the automatic disconnection; thereby stopping the HPP unit from running.

The motor will continue to run and the worst it can do is run out of petrol, which is fine. It's all about saving the HPP unit from water starvation.

...clutch is a real asset and allows the motor to be run without the HPP engaged...

This HPP decision was one of the stumbling blocks that took a few months to remedy and now having resolved the water requirements and HPP guidelines, the planning for the remainder of the items took off.

----- : -----

Pulley; Motor Calculations

To calculate the motor pulley size, three figures are required from the previous data:
> Desired Motor RPM - 2400,
> Clutch/Pulley OD - 7", an
> HPP 70bar (1000psi) RPM - 1725.

Jabsco 12vDC Puppy

Motor Pulley OD
$$= \frac{(\text{HPP Pulley OD} \times \text{HPP RPM})}{\text{Motor RPM}}$$
$$= \frac{(7 \times 1725)}{2400}$$
$$= 5.0"$$

To summarise:
Operating the motor at 2400RPM, will turn the 5.0" and 7" belt pulley system.

This in turn will drive the HPP at 1725RPM producing 68bar (1000psi) of saltwater pressure to the membranes.

Accidental overpressure is covered in the 'Pressure Regulator' section later.

----- : -----

Low Pressure Pump (LPP)

This would be the second most critical component in the whole desalinator system.

Cheap alternative LPP's, will increase costs in future years in replacement parts.

The unit must be capable of providing a positive flow of corrosive fluid at a rate higher than that required by the manufacturer of the HPP.

During the planning stages, the flow rate should be calculated at a value, plus 15%. This 15% then covers:
> Filtration losses as the filter progressively fouls,
> Saltwater temperature variations,
> Desalinator height above the waterline, and
>Aging of components, both within the LPP and upstream of the strainer.

Note that we talk of a high flow rate here, not a high-pressure rate.

A pressure rate around 0.55 bar (8 psi) would be sufficient as long as up-line, the filters are regularly cleaned and there are at least two in series.

Failure of the LPP at any stage could cost in repair as the feed source of the whole system now stops.

The HPP will end up trying to operate with a negative pressure, have possible air ingestion, and damage the pumping components, specifically the membranes.

This means that while the HPP is operating, someone must continually be in attendance at all times or, a safety feature installed (such as a pressure switch) that can initiate automatic shutdown of the HPP unit should the LPP fail.

----- : -----

This too is not mandatory, however we chose to install a pressure switch/sensor.

At low LPP pressure, a sensor cuts the 12vDC circuit to the clutch,

disengaging the clutch to the HPP. Simple yet effective.

LPP line pressure greater than 0.1 bar (1.5 psi) closes the 12vDC clutch electrical circuit via the pressure switch.

Once the clutch power switch is switched to on, power flows through the pressure switch to the clutch and engages the clutch. This in turn allows the HPP to operate until either:
> The clutch power is switched off , or,
> The pressure switch is < 1.5psi.

The petrol/diesel motor will continue to run with no damage to any components until:
> It runs out of fuel (gas), or
> It is switched off.

For those really keen, another pressure switch could be installed in the freshwater tank, so that a filled tank would disengage the clutch once again.

----- : -----

Two LPP pump types are available here:
>A centrifugal type pump, or
>A self-priming non-centrifugal unit.

The self-priming units (positioned above the waterline) normally require twice as much preventative maintenance due the wear on the impeller.

Centrifugal pumps however, must be installed below waterline and for this reason, do not require priming and there is a lot less impeller maintenance required.

We chose Jabsco 12vDC Puppy Pump for this purpose and while expensive, forms a key component in the set-up that can have minimal maintenance.

Centrifugal pumps can be run normally with little to no flow. This can be a huge advantage as the LPP can be used to purge the pipes to the HPP without the HPP running.

This prevents air from entering the HPP system, saving on the life of the membranes.

...continual opening and closing, will take its toll on the seacock unless correctly installed ...

----- : -----

Seacock

So do we use stainless steel, bronze or plastic?

As far as we were concerned, in our situation, stainless steel or bronze would be fine.

Our frequent use at this inlet required the seacock to be firmly installed. This meant no physical movement each time the seacock was opened or closed.

...a vacuum gauge for visual filter indication, prompting filter maintenance...

The seacock is closed after each use, purely for reason of safety, due to the time we spend away from the vessel.

Additionally, our yacht could beach at low tide exposing the inlet point and a slow drain of piped water will occur.

If the seacock were not closed each time, this would require bleeding of air each time we used the unit,

Perko Marine Seacock

making the process very cumbersome and even more complicated.

A simple safe solution - we see it as easy 'Insurance'.

This continual opening and closing, will take its toll on the seacock unless correctly installed on a very solid base.

----- : -----

Filtration(1 of 4)
Raw Water Strainer

We found that options here are limited and expensive.

Given that the pressure in the lines prior to the Low Pressure Pump (LPP) are very low around 0.55 bar (8 psi), a standard plastic strainer from a reputable manufacturer (such as Shurflo) could be an alternative to the bronze types sold by Perko or Groco.

This flies against that recommended by some LPP manufacturers, so be cautious and do the homework. It needs to be capable of passing 100lts of water at a minimum.

The Filter insert should be of the stainless steel type and easily replaceable.

Diverging a little, while meandering through a scrap metal yard one afternoon, we stumbled across a container of discarded 60-micron fine mesh.

The off-cuts were remnants of material used to prevent termite and ant infestation, commonly called Termi-mesh.

It just happens that this is also stainless steel, so we now have a lifetime replacement supply of filter mesh.

Strainer units with a bowl at the base make it very easy for cleaning and the odd mudskipper or snail can be quickly removed before decomposition occurs.

This component should be installed in a position below waterline that is easily accessible and can get the odd splash of saltwater during filter cleans.

An upstream shut-off valve can be very helpful here too, to minimise fluid loss during filter cleaning or LPP repair.

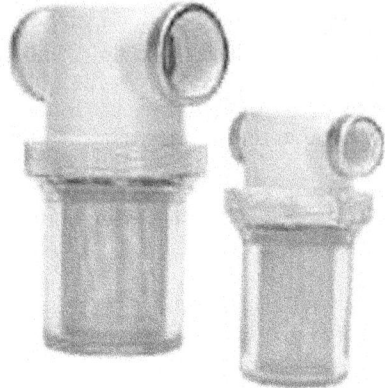

Raw Water Strainer

Pentek Canister Filters

----- : -----

Filtration (2, 3 & 4)
Carbon & Fine Micron

This is provided by way of three 10-inch canisters, two canisters for desalination filtration, and one for mains water filling.

Firstly mains water, this contains chlorine, which is very harmful to the membranes and must therefore be removed prior to being placed in the tanks.

This unit contains a good quality carbon filter.

One would think that this would normally not be a concern but remember that freshwater from the freshwater tanks is used to flush the components and purge the units for short-term storage.

This includes the membranes and its here the damage occurs. To counter this, we have inserted a filter housing with a good quality carbon filter.

Once filling is complete, the carbon filter is removed and then dried for at least a week before storage.

The other two canisters must be capable of corrosive fluid transfer and carry a safety valve.

These too must be in a very easily accessible position for maintenance, some saltwater will also be lost below the canisters during the filter changes.

The filter housings should be moulded from polypropylene and carry O-rings in the lid. These units will house 10 and 5-micron filters respectively.

To prolong the life of the membrane and system components, it is necessary to monitor the sediment collection of the filters.

One way is to maintain a log detailed further on in this section, or an alternative way is to install a vacuum gauge for visual filter indication, prompting filter maintenance.

The initial expense was worth every cent. As the filters soil, the Vacuum indication will increase.

With a little trial and error, a figure can be worked and logged as the prompt for filter changing.

We chose a stainless steel 70mm face

0 to -1Bar Vacuum Gauge that we located on Ebay.

Make sure that it is glycerin filled as the vibration of the HPP and motor can make it vibrate to the point of destruction.

It is far more advantageous to be proactive with maintenance, rather than re-active with breakdowns. This would be a 'Desalination Log' item.

----- : -----

Desalinator Log

Maintaining a system specification log is very critical if the unit is hands on. The log should include all the filter sizes as well component replacement numbers.

This is especially important at the start stage of the new desalinator as it provides the foundation for the life of the components and their maintenance.

A section should also be maintained to monitor water quality with the handheld TDS meter and the time it takes to reach this level (not required if the system has an automated TDS sensor and Solenoid/motorized valve).

This is another indication of adverse sediment build-up within the filters (or within the membranes) and is a key to the change intervals required.

----- : -----

Membrane Housing

Housings come in many various shapes and sizes, the most common lengths being 14, 21, and 40-inch. Then there are their diameters, which vary from 2" to 4".

Our studies have shown little differences between sizes and diameters against effective use.

Pointers we have include the space available for a particular size and surface area available in the membrane.

...the prefix 'SW' on the membrane item number...

At the time of writing we found that an initial higher expense in the more popular 2.5" x 40" housings, linked in series proved cheaper in the long run with replacement membranes and as a last resort, redundancy.

In the event one membrane failed with no replacement membrane - just removing the membrane and continuing with the desalination on the remaining membrane will still provide fresh water at a reduced rate.

We found that increasing the number of housings did not increase the amount of freshwater given our careful planning of the pump size.

The additional housing may allow longer use of the membranes, however twice the membrane replacement cost.

Housings for high-pressure membranes (that are used in desalinators) are normally found in Stainless Steel or fibreglass.

Rigid PVC is an option that with the correct pressure rating could be used. We chose 2 x (2.5" x 40") Fibreglass housings, commonly listed as FRP.

Our Pressure Vessels were purchased from American R.O. in the US and are Fibreglass PVF-2540 (x 2)

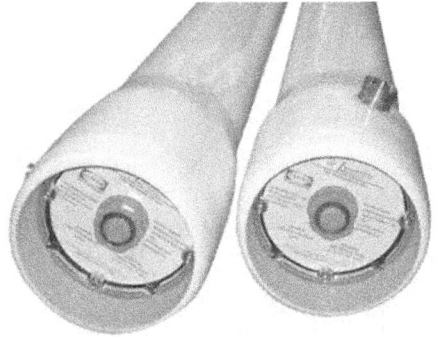

Membranes and Housings

Membrane choice

Here there is a choice between saltwater units, brack-water, and standard house-water membranes.

All are specific, especially the saltwater units and these can sometimes be picked by the prefix 'SW' on the membrane item number.

It is important to ensure that this is closely followed, as error here will cost dearly down the line with component failure.

Other digits on the membrane can indicate their unit size (as in our case, 2540 indicates a 2.5" diameter x 40" long), simple when you know how. Not all membranes are listed like this though.

Our Membranes were purchased from American R.O. in the US and are Filmtec SW30-2540 (x 2).

----- : -----

Pressure Regulator

The pressure that the system operates at is variable. With the slow blocking of filters by contaminants, temperature, variation of pumps RPM and to a lesser extent, aging of the components, the system needs to be manually controlled.

The regulator should be stainless steel and able to withstand very high-pressure loads, in excess of 100bar (1450psi).

We purchased a new Cat Pump Pressure Regulator - model 7066 for this purpose.

It should also have an easy usable strong knob, sounds silly - but not when ones hands are wet and fine

Cat Pump Pressure Regulator - 7066

Typical Pressure Gauge

adjustment is needed.

Pressure Gauge

We have inserted a pressure gauge in the brine line after the membranes to monitor and provide accurate system pressure indications.

The pressure gauge is stainless steel 70mm (0 - 100bar (1500psi)), which was again purchased off Ebay.

----- : -----

TDS Meter

A TDS meter measures the salinity of the water. We chose to automate our system and have included a TDS meter with controller power to activate a Solenoid N.O. selector valve.

Once a programmed value is met (i.e. 200ppm) the unit supplies power to activate an in-line valve allowing freshwater to be diverted to the tanks.

The unit we chose is made by Hanna and is a panel mounted TDS Controller BL 983319-0. Don't forget to order the TDS Probe HI 7634-00 at the same time.

TDS Controller BL 983319-0

Pointers:

1. Use only 'BSP threaded' or only 'NPT threaded' fittings.

2. Calculate your minimum water quantity per day.

3. Use the largest inlet size (1 1/2").

Traps:

1. Mixing thread types.

2. Making a too complicated unit, you can always add later.

Chapter Four: Watermaker Automation

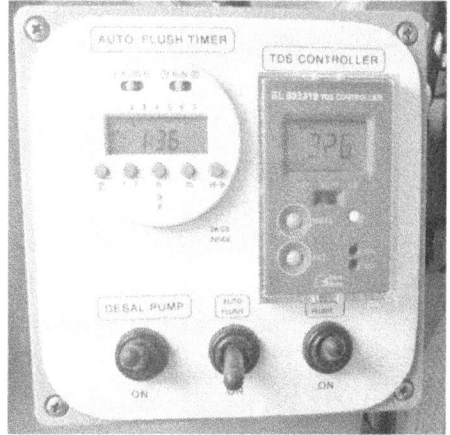

Auto Flush Computer

To be able to leave the yacht for periods exceeding four days between desalination making, we wanted the system automated.

A company called Quality Water Works makes a neat bit of gear that has a timer that can be set to flush the membranes.

All it needed was the ships normal freshwater pump system to operate. We purchased their Automatic Flush Module and have to say that they were very patient with our questioning.

Our Auto flush works by using the vessels own freshwater pump and existing tank water to flush the membranes at regular intervals. Once flushed, the water is vented overboard.

To accomplish this, the vessels freshwater pump needs to be wired 'hot'.

By 'hot' we mean that it remains on continually when other electrical mains power is removed, such as switching off the main batteries switch when one leaves the vessel.

For those who have purchased either of our books; 'A Sailing Catamaran Building Project' or 'A Sailing Catamaran Building Adventure', will find an electrical circuit drawing called the 'Hot Battery Bus'.

The other important item is 'freshwater water in the tanks'.

Sufficient water needs to be present to flush the entire desalinator unit at regular intervals while away from the vessel.

Sounds silly and obvious, but with lack of water (or pumps running on an empty tank), will cause the fresh water pump to burnout.

It is very important that the flushing be done with NON-CHLORINATED water. Chlorine damages the membranes.

This links back to the Filter section discussed a few chapters back where we mentioned three canister filters. Two for the desalinator and the third filter carries a carbon insert to remove any tap water chlorine, if you choose to fill the tanks this way.

...third filter carries a carbon insert to remove any tap water chlorine...

The amount of water to do each flush needs to be calculated. We used a bucket to measure the wastewater during a trial run, and at the same time, timed the flush duration. The timer can then be set and we recommend a 4-day cycle or a particular flush duration.

----- : -----

Flow Meters

These units are used to provide a visual cue to the operation of the whole system. There are normally two placed in the system and the preferred position is 'panel-mounted' somewhere.

Panel mounting does incur additional plumbing requirements, but allows effective use of the flow meters.

The meters show freshwater output per minute and brine water output per minute, the latter having much higher flow increments per min or hour than its freshwater counterpart.

Qualities that we required within the gauge included:
> Stainless Steel float, float guides and wetted parts (many have brass

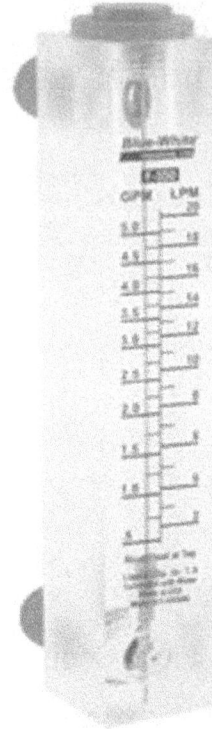

Blue White Rotameter - F550

or nickel coated brass),
> Acrylic frame,
> 125mm in length, and
> No valve
> Panel mounted

The most common gauging is in gallons per minute or gallons per hour (the US standard).

To remain within metric boundaries and based on the desalinator that we have built, we have chosen gauge ranges of:
> 1.5 - 18.0 Lpm (litres per minute), and
> 22 - 230 Lph (litres per hour)
> Alternative to Lph above:
> 0.4 - 4 Lpm (litres per minute)

There is also a Ccm range that can be used:

> 1500 - 19000 Ccm (cubic centimeters) and
> 23000 - 227000 Ccm (cubic centimeters)

The Flow Meters proved the hardest to track down. While there are a few quality manufacturers around many have agents throughout the world, some quick money-spinners and others better priced.

In all cases, it was cheaper to buy through the US with all shipping and insurance.

We chose the Blue-White F-550 (0.4 - 4 LPM) for the fresh waterside and the Blue-White F-550 (2 - 20 LPM) for the brine water.

The more common acrylic 'flow-meter' manufacturers include:
1. Dwyer - Visi float - VFB range .
2. Key Instruments - Flo-Rite series FR Flowmeters.
3. King Instruments - 7520-5C Series.
4. Omega Instruments - FL-2000 range.
5. Blue White Rotameter - F550 range.

----- : -----

Valves - Solenoid / Motorised

There are two main types of valves used with desalination units, those that are Motorised and those operated by a solenoid.

The main reason people choose one over the other is the speed of closing / opening of the valve.

The motorised units are a lot slower, anywhere from 4 - 12 seconds from one position to the other extreme. When compared to the solenoid speed of one second, there is a huge

Motorised Solenoid Valve

difference.

Motorised Valves

These units are well-built and normally costly to purchase and replace when component failure is at hand.

Occasionally, it has been known for these valves to not function correctly or remain partially open.

Normally not too much of an issue however, when talking salinity in fresh water, these small malfunctions could wipeout 200lts of fresh water in 30 seconds.

Not only that, but if one has components in the fresh system that is not compatible, then there follows component failure (remembering back to the Desalinator Cheese theory).

----- : -----

Solenoid Valves

A solenoid valve is an electrical valve that uses a magnetic force via a small yet strong coil to open and close the valve.

*...TDS unit will close the
valve once the correct
salinity is reached...*

These types of valves are said to fail
less and when they do, the parts are
easily interchangeable.

While we would have preferred a
stainless steel or bronze unit, they
were outside our price range, so we
settled for brass.

As the valve will be in the freshwater
line only, we are not expecting any
corrosion that is normally associated
with saltwater and brass compounds.

The unit is a 'Normally Open' type
(discussed below), which operates to
a closed valve position when 12vDC
power is applied.

Remove the power and the valve
automatically opens allowing water
to flow through. This is a fail-safe
feature in the event of power loss.

The valve will open allowing water to
be vented overboard instead of
contaminating the fresh water tank.

Installation Theory:
Fresh water is routed vertically down
700mm directly below the
membrane outlet and overboard.

A 'T' is placed on the inlet side of the
valve and the valve placed in the line
just before it vents overboard
(roughly 600mm).

From that 'T' we turn the line back
up 600mm then around and to the
freshwater tank.

Theory at work:
Gravity will force the water *to take*

the most direct route which is down
the pipe, past the open 'T', through
the solenoid valve and overboard.

The TDS unit (discussed later) will
close the valve once the correct
salinity is reached and water will be
forced up the piping and finally
through to the fresh water tank.

The solenoid type was our preferred
when it comes to the automation of
the TDS unit.

We managed to get four as a package
off Ebay and will closely watch their
wear with spares readily available.

----- : -----

Valve Terminology

Where one has an inlet and outlet
and shuts the fluid off, this is known
as a 2-way valve.

A 3-way valve has an additional
outlet, sometimes called the diverter
outlet. The other two ports being the
inlet port and exhaust port.

The reason we make this statement is
that an option exists whether these
ports are open (called Normally
Open or N.O.) or closed (called
Normally Closed or N.C.)

Sometimes the fluid is used to
operate (or assist in operating) the
valve and this is called a Differential
Operated valve.

Valves that operate on their own
power are called Direct Acting Valves
and are preferred in the build.

The shock here is the cost of these
units. They range anywhere from
AUD $300 - AUD $700 for the
stainless steel units.

This put a totally different tack on the build and the way that our unit was designed; we only needed one for the TDS unit.

In summary, one should source:
> A stainless steel 2-way solenoid valve,

> N.O. - which makes it fail-safe to the open position if power is lost saving good water

> Largest in size - the larger the better,

> 12Vdc power operated, and

> Teflon (PTFE), where Stainless is not used

> Depending on position in the system, the correct pressure rating (+ 20% as a safety measure) must be considered.

Swaglock SS-R4M8F8

----- : -----

Pressure Relief Valve

This component functions as a safety valve within the whole set-up monitoring:
> The 'Membrane Housing maximum pressure - rated to 68bar (1000psi),

> 'HPP Unit' maximum pressure - rated at 68bar (1000psi), and

> System pressure in the event of Pressure Regulator' failure.

It has been set to open at 66bar (960psi), venting brine water overboard, and closing at 55bar (800psi).

Here we have used the Swaglock SS-R4M8F8 with a purple spring. We located these on Ebay.

Mounting Frame

Our frame mounting has been cut from 10mm (5083 grade) Aluminum. While it sounds rather complicated, this was through choice.

We divided the desalinator into three units in an effort to minimize the space that the units occupy, they are:

> The Motor and HPP unit (double story to minimize space)

> Control Panel (has been separated to reduce vibration of the components), and

> Membrane unit.

If you are about to tackle this challenge, there are really no boundaries with the exception of the base, it needs to be extremely sturdy,

243

and components must be bolted down securely.

----- : -----

Hoses - Joining the three Assemblies

The use of high pressure flexible hosing is strongly encouraged. Our ratings from the HPP to the membranes and then the Pressure Relief Valve are in excess of 135bar (2000psi).

The fittings proved to be the hardest part with these connections.

Flexible hosing is required given the movement around the various parts and a word of caution, if you intend fixing the tubing to a surface, ensure that it is within rubber grommets to stem the vibration.

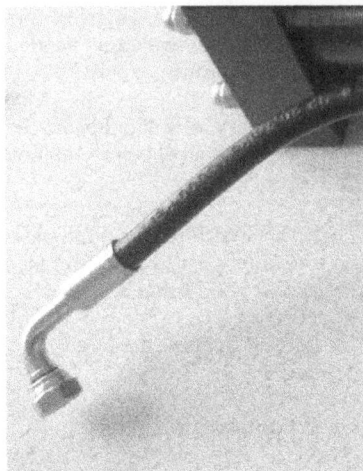

High Pressure piping and fittings

----- : -----

Chapter Five:
Electrical Ideas

The electrical system works off a 'Hot Battery', which then covers power availability when on board (under normal operation) and while away (for auto-flushing of the membrane).

The 'Hot Battery' is a battery with connections that stay 'live' while away from the vessel.

In our case the Hot Battery Bus carries live power to the Bilge Pumps, Freshwater Pump, Auto Flush Controller & Navigation Panel (certain units that require continual power to maintain pre-set settings.

To disconnect the Hot Battery Bus (or HBB), we have installed an HBB Switch specifically for this purpose.

Our books; 'A Sailing Catamaran Building Project' or 'A Sailing Catamaran Building Adventure', carry much more information on this topic.

With an HBB, the auto-flush controller can be programmed to flush periodically while away from the vessel with normal power off.

Auto flushing will require the vessels normal freshwater pump to run, which is why we have this connected to the HBB.

Please follow on the diagram on the next page.

----- : -----

The Hot Battery Bus is key to the whole electrical operation.

Freshwater Pump

The vessels normal water pump system is powered via a 10Amp circuit breaker.

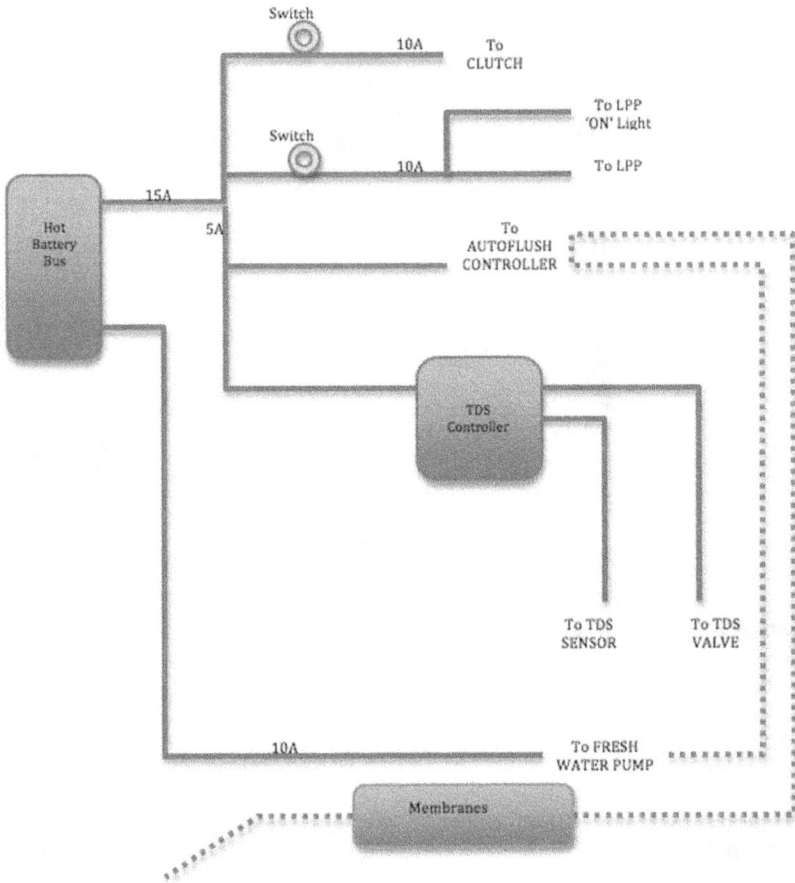

Switch

10A   To
CLUTCH

To LPP
'ON' Light

Switch

10A   To LPP

15A

5A   To
AUTOFLUSH
CONTROLLER

Hot
Battery
Bus

TDS
Controller

To TDS   To TDS
SENSOR   VALVE

10A   To FRESH
WATER PUMP

Membranes

Solid Line - Power to component
Dashed Line - Water flow on activation

Watermaker Electrical Diagram

This line remains pressurised at 6psi at all times. Any drop in line pressure will activate the *freshwater pump* to re-pressurise the line.

Under normal conditions, using any tap in the freshwater system inside the vessel will lower the water pressure, automatically activating the *freshwater pump* to ON to re-pressurise the line.

Alternatively, the same occurs when switching the *Auto-flush Controller*. Power opens the 12vDC auto-flush *water solenoid valve* (not shown) allowing water to flow to the membranes.

The *freshwater pump* senses the water pressure drop in the freshwater line and re-pressurises the line.

De-activating the *Auto-flush Controller*, closes the *water solenoid valve* (not shown). The *freshwater pump* will continue to run until line pressure reaches 6psi, then the *freshwater pump* automatically switches OFF.

----- : -----

Powered via a 15Amp circuit breaker are the vessels:
> Desalinator Clutch,
> LPP Pump and LPP Light,
> Auto-Flush Controller, and
> TDS Controller.

7-Day Timer
When *7-Day Timer* sends an open signal, power is supplied to OPEN the *water solenoid valve* (not shown). This allows water passage, dropping internal water pressure as a result.

The vessels *freshwater pump* senses this pressure drop and it starts to

automatically re-pressurise. The *freshwater pump* will then run until the *water solenoid valve* is closed (or de-powered in our case).

This 6psi pressure is enough to flush the membranes on a regular basis.

The freshwater used is then vented overboard.

The TDS controller

The TDS controller has a sensor to test water for purity (its primary function). This 'water purity level' can be manually set and we use 200ppm (parts per million), which is very safe for drinking.

Once this 200ppm value is reached, power is supplied to the *TDS Solenoid Valve*, it OPENs and water flows into the freshwater tank.

If > 200ppm is sensed by the probe, the TDS Controller cuts the power and the *TDS Solenoid Valve* – it then CLOSES, stopping water to the freshwater tank and instead vents overboard.

The TDS controller secondary function is to supply 12vDC power, switching once the 200ppm value is reached, very neat and handy.

We linked this secondary function to the *TDS Solenoid Valve*. This means that the *TDS Solenoid Valve* is controlled to power/depower by the TDS Probe in the controller.

Low Pressure Pump (LPP)
The LPP and its ON light are controlled from this electrical bus.

The Clutch
Power to activate the clutch is controlled from this electrical bus.

Basic Set-up

Basic Set-up	Part Number	(Actual) Manufacturer	Inlet Size	Outlet Size	Max Press
Membranes SW 2540 (2)	Filmtec SW30-2540	Americanro	-	-	-
Housings FRP (2)	PVF 2540 1000psi	Americanro	1/2" NPTF	1/2" NPTF	1000psi
Housings FRP		Freshwater oulet	-	1/2" NPTF	1000psi
Filter Housing (2x10") + SS bracket		Clarencewaterfilters	3/4" BSP	3/4" BSP	100psi
Filer - 5 micron		Clarencewaterfilters	-	-	-
Filer - 20 micron			-	-	-
Pressure Gauge	AS254RB1500	rodpierce@houston.rr.com	-	-	1500psi
HP Cat Pump	Cat 00241 Pump	EDI Distributors	1/2" NPTF	3/8" NPTF	1200psi
Cat Clutch	Cat 34961 Clutch	EDI Distributors	-	-	-
Cat Regulator	Cat 7070 1000psi	EDI Distributors	1/2" NPTF	3/4" NPTF	1000psi
Cat nut set	Cat 34090	EDI Distributors	-	-	-
Flow Meter	Blue-White F553375L 0.4 - 4 lpm	Rose Industrial Marketing, Inc.	3/8" NPTM	3/8" NPTM	200psi
Flow Meter	Blue-White F553375L 0 2 - 20 lpm	garycrose@msn.com	1/2" NPTM	1/2" NPTM	200psi
Low Pressure Pump	Jabsco Cyclone Model: 50830-2012 12v	Peter Snell - RW Basham	3/4" BSP	3/4" BSP	100psi
Raw Water Strainer	Shurflo 0 3/4" SS strainer	Peter Snell - RW Basham	3/4" BSP	3/4" BSP	100psi
Pressure Relief Valve	SS-R4M8FB	Ebay - pipedotor1207	1/2" NPTM	1/2" NPTF	1500psi
Pressure Relief Valve - Spring	177-13K-R4-C Purple Spring750-1500psi	Supplier BNE 07 3256 2327	-	-	950psi

Automatics

Automatics	Part Number	Manufacturer
Autoflush unit		qwwinc.com
TDS Meter	Hanna TDS Mini Controller BL-983319-0	Ebay cmcgehee01@comcast.net
Solenoid Valves		
		Subtotal

Other Filters and Componets

Other Filters and Componets	Part Number	Manufacturer
Spare O-rind for housing (2)		Clarencewaterfilters
Filter Housing Spanner		Clarencewaterfilters
Undersink Filter Housing - Testa Twin		Clarencewaterfilters
U'sink Filters - GTS1-10 silver carbon 2		Clarencewaterfilters
U'sink Filter - 0.5 micron poly spun 2		Clarencewaterfilters
Undersink Housing Spanner		Clarencewaterfilters
Spare 5 micron 2		Clarencewaterfilters
Spare 20 micron 2		Clarencewaterfilters
Filter Housing (1x10") + SS bracket		Clarencewaterfilters
Vacuum Gauge	302DFW-254A	rodpierce@houston.rr.com

System Operation & Maintenance

Chapter Six:
System Operation and Maintenance

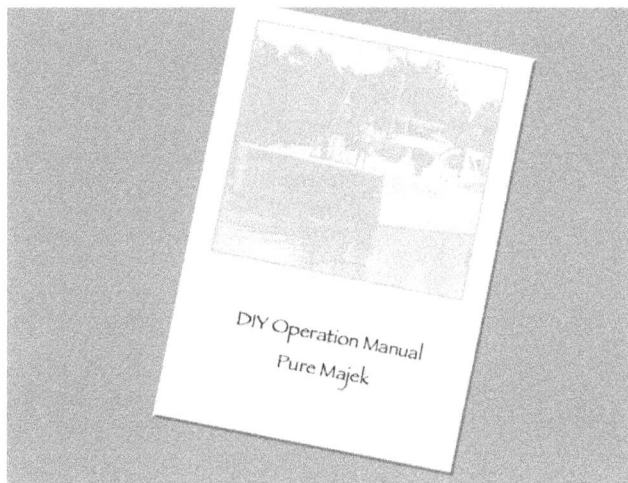

To prolong the life of all components, it is critical that clean water be used for the desalination process, even while testing the unit.

Chatting with Dow Corning (who make quality membranes), there preferred water quality is 'where you can see the bottom'.

While a very broad comment, you can get the gist. Clean ocean flow is the preference, away from shore margins with mangroves.

----- : -----

It is assumed that the oil and fuel quantities have been checked and that all manufacturer data has been complied with in regard to the operation of their equipment.

Additionally that all filters are free of debris and that filters have been cleaned.

<u>To Start:</u>
1. OPEN the seawater inlet valve. Ensure that water is available at the LPP.

2. Ensure the Pressure Regulator is FULLY OPEN.

3. Ensure the Clutch is switched to OFF.

4. Turn ON the LPP and;
   > Confirm that low-pressure salt water is flowing through the system, watching the Brine Flow Meter

   (Note: This Flow Meter value needs to be ascertained early, noted and used at each start sequence).

5. START the Motor and;
   > Allow Motor to warm to operating temperature, and

   > Set 2500RPM, ensuring that the throttle is secured

(Note: It will slow back to 2400RPM with the clutch engaged. This value must not be exceeded for this engine).

6. ENGAGE the Clutch switch, and
a. SLOWLY CLOSE the Pressure Regulator. Monitor;
   > The system pressure via the Pressure Gauge, 58 - 62bar (850 - 900psi) must be adhered too.

   (Note: 62bar (900psi) MUST NOT be exceeded).

   > Lock this setting with the 'Regulator Lock Nut'.

Continue to monitor this setting at regular intervals adjusting as required. (Note: a drop of more than 15% of a set value is an indication of soiled filters or a blockage. This can be confirmed against the Vacuum Gauge setting increasing).

7. Monitor the TDS Gauge, at;
   > 200ppm, the valve should open allowing fresh water to the tank.

To Stop:
1. DISENGAGE the clutch,
2. OPEN the pressure Regulator,
3. Switch OFF the LPP.
4. Switch OFF the Motor.

------ : -----

Pickling

The period that the membranes should be left unattended (being no flow) varies from manufacturer to manufacturer.

They are all clear though on one issue, that is that the membranes are temperamental and need all the pampering they can get.

Left unattended for just four days with no flow allows the fluids to settle, stagnate and provide active fertile grounds for bacterial growth.

To counter this, two things can be done. Either cycle the system for one minute with either fresh or saltwater, or 'Pickle' the system.

Pickling is normally left to periods of extended duration because of the effort required to set-up and then cleans out, and we have chosen periods of more than two months, as our benchmark.

If we intend having the desalinator inactive for this long, we would consider pickling.

The 'Pickle' is basically a liquid preservative. The liquid solution is then fed through the system from beginning to end and left to do its job.

It should also be noted that to restart the unit and have available fresh unpreserved water, it should be left running for 1 hour, even if the TDS indicates good water quality.

The pickling solution can and does cause headaches, diarrhoea and in some cases joint swelling.

The most common preservative is Sodium Metabisulphite. Chemists, local brewery houses, and some chain supermarkets sell this powder as it's used in the beer or wine markets.

Mix 1/2 cup of Sodium Metabisulphite with 15 litres of freshwater, and then put all the fluid except for the last 1/2 litre, through the system.

The fluid is pumped into the system via the pickling valve, with the freshwater valve closed and the'needle valve' turned to the full open position.

This ensures that all excess pickling fluid will vent overboard. As it nears the bottom of the pickle solution, stop and lock all systems.

Do not allow air to enter the piping system. This can then be left for extended periods.

----- : -----

Membrane storage

We have trialed a great way to store a membrane and have listed this on our diycatamaran.com website.

It really is a novel way of looking after a membrane other than running an automated system.

----- : -----

Chapter Seven:
ERS – Watermaker Rebuild

While conducting the monthly pilgrimage on Ebay, we spotted an auction for a well used Schenker Smart 30 desalinator.

Understanding that these quality Italian made watermakers retail from USD$4500 upwards, we tracked the progress of bidding with interest.

In the end we managed to win (sight unseen), the complete package for USD$700 (including postage). And its here that this document begins.

----- : -----

General

Schenker watermakers are manufactured in Italy with agents strategically positioned around the world.
They use an ERS assembly system (Energy Recovery System) which in short allows for 'low pressure water pumping' while utilising high-pressure membranes.

The internal dual-piston uses the intake low-pressure water (on one side of the piston) to build high-pressure water on the other side of the piston and presents this higher-pressure water to the membrane.

The spent (or brine water) from the membrane (still under pressure) is then returned and presented to the reciprocal ERS piston.

The two pistons work in unison delivering energy to further pressurise water membrane intake water.

The pressure increase is amazingly from 70psi - 800psi using this system.

It is a very clever, effective, and smart way of using hydraulics to your advantage while halving your energy consumption.

From the outset, it needs to be said that Schenker and its distributors in Britain and Australia were very helpful, a credit to Schenker.

For the world cruiser, this is a real asset in the event of malfunctions in difficult places. This unit can be worked on effectively with their help via written/email correspondence.

...surprisingly got a prompt reply from a very helpful Ricardo Verde...

This unit reminds me of two others on the market that use similar techniques - Katadyn and Spectra.

----- : -----

Many of the components and TDS units and automatics used here are the same as those discussed earlier in this book.

----- : ------

So what's all the fuss about?

Two keys things:
> The only high-pressure sections are the membrane and hoses connecting that membrane pressures around 800-900psi.

The remainder of the unit uses low pressure - around 60-80psi.

>The only pump needed is a 12vDC saltwater pump that draws a maximum of 9A to produce 25lts o water (we discuss this 25lt and not 30lt further in this document).

The watermaker package is made up of two key components, the 'Watermaker Group' and the 'Pump Group'.

Simple connections of saltwater inlet, brine overflow, and freshwater outlet are all that are needed.

Understanding that the unit we had purchased, no longer had a warranty attached (given its age), we chose to expand on the unit's installation and add a few creature comforts.

----- : -----

The Pump Group

The old pump group had to all be discarded, including the 12vDC pump and electrics, so it was back to the drawing board using the theory presented earlier in this document.

Our 'new' pump group purchases included:
> 12vDC high-pressure pump (up to 150psi),

> Overpressure relief valve (Swagelok),

> Water Filters - 1 x 60micron and 1 x 5micron, and

> Fittings - various high pressure PVC fittings

----- : -----

The Watermaker Group

The purchased unit was relatively well in one piece. However, there were a lot of rust and apparent areas of leakage.

Additionally, we found a crack on one of the upper blocks, which we later found, presented no problem.

New 12vDC pump with cooling fans and Over Pressure Relief Valve

ERS Unit in place , membrane at the back and filters below.

Appears that the unit may have been dropped somewhere along its journey.

The work here included:
> Replacing all O-rings,
> Resealing all fitting points,
> Replacing a cylinder sleeve,
> Regreasing all internal areas (with exception to the 4 valves), and
> Replacing the membrane.

----- : -----

Disassembly and clean

Finding a 'Service Manual' on the Internet proved to be very difficult, even on the Schenker website. We sent an email directly to Schenker and surprisingly got a prompt reply from a very helpful Ricardo Verde.

This reply and attached documents proved to be our saviour.

The ERS unit has a million O-rings, many of which are not available from our normal sources, but are available through the agents of Schenker.

We can only encourage those rebuilding their units to have the Service Document at hand, especially with the valve components.

This is critical in re-assembly.

The greasing compound we chose to use was INOX MX6 with PTFE. It is a no melt, high temperature, extreme pressure, food grade premium machinery grease, highly resistant to water, salt, drying and chemicals.

----- : -----

Rebuild/Assembly

ERS Unit:

We found much of the corrosion to be surface corrosion. With the only exception being scarring inside one of the carbon-fibre sleeves (replacement part from Schenker).

We carefully wrote down the disassembly process, found that the ERS had been worked on previously, and not correctly put back together.

Of major concern was sand/grit found within the sleeve chamber around one of the pistons. This indicated a lack of saltwater filtration.

It also meant that damage might exist within other components.

We incorrectly greased these pieces when assembling and it wasn't until the 15th frustrating disassembly that we realised this problem.

We kept the old membrane for testing of leaks and water flow.

----- : -----

Membrane

We made contact with Dow and found a Filmtec membrane to suit.

The high-pressure membrane was ordered from Freshwater Systems (model SW 30-2521) in the USA.

Their delivery was also fast and efficient. Of interest was some information from Mactrashop (in Britain) about looking after the membranes and servicing from the opposition membrane maker Hydranautics.

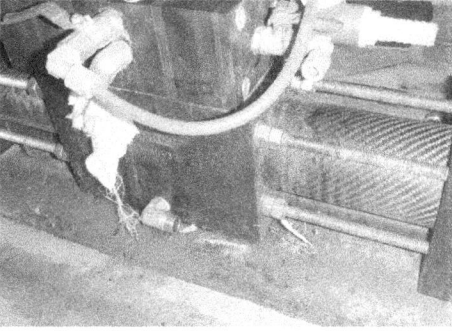

ERS Unit - Sad Disrepair

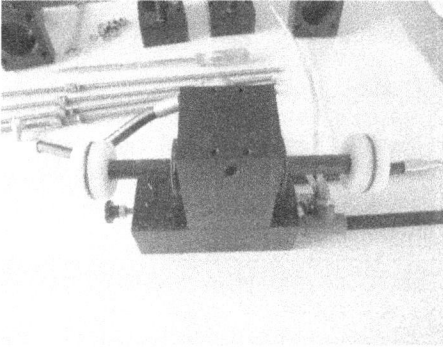

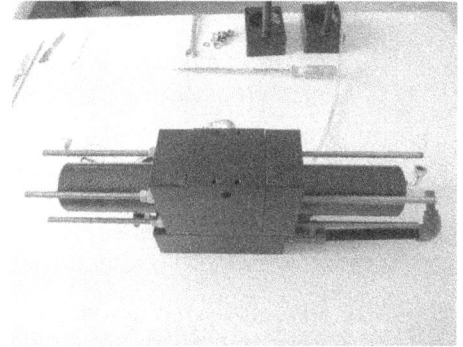

ERS Unit - Rebuilding from seals to stainless work

ERS Unit - Completing fore and aft connections

Together with that of Filmtec, we managed to get a good library for care and maintenance information.

----- : -----

Pump Group

We rebuilt the whole 'pump group' using our own components and consists of:
1. Filters (3),
2. Shurflo Pump
3. Shurflo Accumulator,
4. Control Box, and
5. Proportional Relief Valve.

...good thing about this motor is that it can run dry temporarily with no internal damage...

Filters:
The single Schenker filter was replaced with two new filters in very accessible positions away from the motor and electrical.

Plumbing was also large æ" PVC high-pressure piping, removing the possibility of cracking and leaks, while allowing high volume water flow to the pump.

1 x 10-inch - 60-micron washable filter to remove larger solids. The key is the high flow rate of the filter.

The unit we have unscrews at the ends allowing the screen to be removed and washed.

This also negates the 'normal' filter at inlet point allowing direct water flow to the highest point of the Watermaker before adding hurdles like a filter.

1 x 10-inch - 5 micron poly-spun polypropylene filter mainly to remove sand, rust and algae. It is

expected to replace these on a regular basis and the reason for a common brand and filter housing to contain the replacement cost.

The filter needs to have good debris holding capacity (which removes pleated filter types) and still allow high flow rates.

1 x 10" impregnated carbon filter to remove chlorine that may be in the tanks from town water top-ups.

While we have no concern with it in the tanks, it is the biggest no-no for the membranes of the desalinator in rinsing, in fact, it will 'kill' the membrane.

The Motor:
The only motor that suited our needs was the Shurflo 12vDC (Specifically - 8030-813-239), which we tracked down in the United States.

We eventually installed this unit upright to prevent any saltwater flow over the pump.

The installation inlet sits 1 meter from the seacock, almost at its upper lift point of 1.2 meters.

The other good thing about this motor is that it can run dry temporarily with no internal damage.

Rated at 9A, it is a high power consumer however; we later show this to be at its very upper limit.

Over-pressure relief Valve:
We found a Swagelok proportional relief valve (R series) on Ebay (got a mixed set of 6 for $20US used).

This is the same valve discussed in the 'Watermaker Component' parts area earlier in the volume.

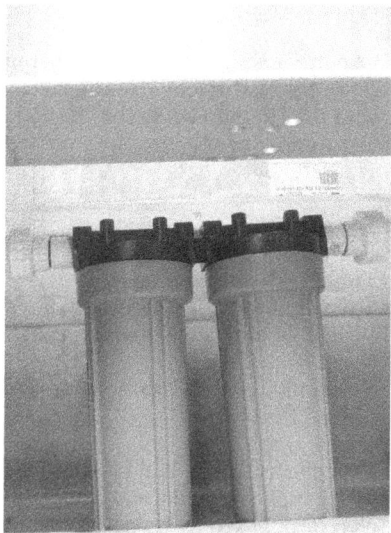

Filters (5 and 10 micron)

Carbon Filter, Shurflo Pump
(bottom), Accumulator (right)

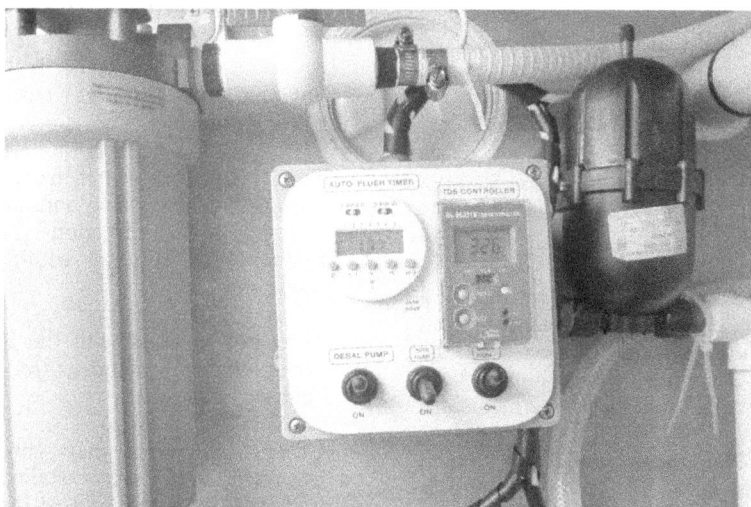

Auto-Flush Controller installed - 3-switches, TDS controller and
timer

The reason we went this way was for the quality brand and stainless steel build. While the pressure can be preset and lock-wired, we preferred the option of manual control.

This is available with this particular type by screwing the top and then locking with a nut.

This allowed us to easily vary the pressure release as the membrane and filters age.

----- : -----

The Electrical connection

Here we made some advanced changes by automating the flush system.

The control box has a timer, TDS meter, and three switches.

The timer is installed for controlling the 12vDC *water solenoid valve* to allow freshwater from the vessels freshwater system to clean and flush the ERS and membrane automatically.

It utilised the vessels pressure system, so did not require the Shurflo pump to operate during this cycle.

It was also necessary to install a carbon filter to remove chlorine from the flush system (discussed in the 'filter section'), prior to entering the ERS units. This is a critical inclusion.

The TDS meter was from Hanna Instruments (BL 983319-0) and is also 12vDC operated with a connection to a æ" valve that allows auto-switching from the overboard outlet to the freshwater tank inlet, when the desalinated water is suitable for drinking.

In our case we have set the value to 175ppm, but this can be higher (around 200ppm) without a salty taste.

One other thing to remember here is that the instrument does not come with the Hanna TDS Probe (HI 7634-00) and needs to be ordered separately.

The three switches control:
> Shurflo 12vDC pump (main switch to operate the desalinator),
> Flush Auto Timer (to switch the timer to 'auto' mode) with 2A CB, and
> Flush Manual Switch (to manually flush the unit).

This electrical box is then wired into our ships Hot Battery Bus (the electrical bus that is 'hot' when we leave the vessel) via a 9A CB.

----- : -----

Accumulator

An accumulator in essence is there to dampen pressure surges within the water system.

The ERS pistons switch from left to right around every 6 seconds and this change in direction causes momentary surges within the plumbing.

This is dampened with the Shurflo Accumulator (model 182) pre-charged to 40psi.

Given that water may enter the chamber, we have installed this higher than normal and with the air outlet toward the top for easy access.

In our photos, you may see a darkened discolouration on many of our components including the Shurflo pump.

This is deliberate as we are huge fans of Tectyl 506.

We use a lot of this on the yacht and cover anything that can come into contact with the elements (it dries brown and translucent in colour and lasts for many years).

Testing Home:

We tested the system at home using the old membrane and fresh tank water all screwed onto a basic frame. Using an Esky, we then introduced the saltwater - tuning the system to suit.

During the restart process, Jim from Mactrashop assisted us and pointed out that we needed to improve the fresh water with salt to provide more accurate pumping action pressure.

'With seawater you will get a greater pressure as it is denser than fresh water. If you mix fresh water with sea salt at 35g per litre, you can replicate this'.

This was key in balancing the operating pressure.

Even after this, we found the unit lacking consistent movement and again Mactrashop came to the rescue.

The accumulator was very low on pre-charge; this was pumped up using a bicycle pump to 40psi. It wasn't until these tweaks were accomplished that the unit performed, as it should.

Given that the unit appeared 'well used' and that components may have worn (due to neglect with the filters), we were expecting around 15lt/hour.

After running the ERS in for an hour,

we changed the membrane to a new membrane and the testing showed 18lt/hr.

----- : -----

On-board

The motor consistently draws 6.5A - 7.5A and delivers 15-20lts per hour.

The electric valves draw 0.2A and are the 'Normally Closed' type (i.e. they only draw power when they are activated to open and as a safety feature, will therefore close if power is lost.

The flush module delivers 14psi - 20psi consistently, well below the maximum of the pump operation limit of 30psi.

The flush cycle uses 7lt per 4-minute freshwater flush and we have this set on a Tuesday and Saturday flush cycle.

During operation, the unit produces 15 litres per hour, not bad for the old girl.

To date the support from Mactrashop and Schenker watermakers has been first class.

We expect to get use out of our watermaker but note that it does take some effort to keep everything in good order.

----- : -----

INDEX

www.ingramcontent.com/pod-product-compliance
Lightning Source LLC
Chambersburg PA
CBHW020607270326
41927CB00005B/209